REREADING *BEOWULF*

University of Pennsylvania Press
MIDDLE AGES SERIES
Edited by Edward Peters
Henry Charles Lea Professor
of Medieval History
University of Pennsylvania

A listing of the available books in this series
appears at the back of this volume

REREADING

BEOWULF

EDWARD B. IRVING, JR.

upp

University of Pennsylvania Press
Philadelphia

Library of Congress Cataloging-in-Publication Data

Irving, Edward Burroughs, 1923–
   Rereading Beowulf.

   (Middle Ages series)
   Bibliography: p.
   Includes index.
   1. Beowulf.   I. Title.   II. Series.
PR1585.173   1989   829'.3   88-33828
ISBN 0-8122-8155-1 (cloth)
ISBN 0-8122-1428-5 (pbk.)

Hæfde ða gefohten   foremærne blæd
Iudith æt guðe.

CONTENTS

PREFACE

It has been twenty years since I published *A Reading of Beowulf*. During that time I have accumulated more ideas in the natural course of teaching. Most particularly, however, my critical imagination was fired a few years ago by the "oral" theory of Old English literature, and as a result my whole point of view toward the poem shifted. What used to seem like troublesome flaws in a remarkable poem, cracks to be anxiously papered over, now seem merely structural features of this kind of early poetry, features that are now open not only to our understanding but also to our fresh appreciation.

The first chapter discusses other recent approaches to the poem before reviewing its many "oral" characteristics. Chapter 2 focuses on peculiarly oral modes of characterization, and on some of the problems they have caused critics, while Chapter 3 takes up typical methods of narrative construction. Chapter 4 examines the ubiquitous symbol of the hall as a unifying factor.

The book grows out of a faintly oral tradition itself, since most of it first saw day in the form of lectures and papers read at conferences. I am most grateful for the encouragement and helpful comments of audiences in many places over several years. In earlier guises, much of the chapter on the hall was presented at the Old English Colloquium at Berkeley and as a public lecture at King's College London. I discussed dragons and kindred matters at a session of the Southeastern Modern Language Association, at Manchester University, and at the Swiss universities of Geneva, Neuchâtel, Zürich, Basel, and Bern in 1986. Other sections were first given as talks at sessions of the Modern Language Association and at the Medieval Conference at Western Michigan University in Kalamazoo. A portion of Chapter 2, under the title, "What to Do with Old Kings," has appeared in *Comparative Research on Oral Tradition: A Memorial for Milman Parry*, ed. John Miles Foley (Columbus, OH: Slavica Publishers, 1987), 259–68.

In addition to the audiences I mention, the following individuals have commented on parts of the work; they should be credited with helpfulness and not blamed for the stubborn deficiencies that remain. Katherine O'Brien O'Keeffe, John Porter, Phyllis Rackin, Paul Beekman Taylor. The person to whom the book is dedicated does not need to be told how much I owe her, but the world does.

Philadelphia, June 1988.

The Approach to Heorot

Present-day readers of *Beowulf* have as yet reached no general agreement on the best critical approach to the poem, and they may not do so for some time, if ever. Two main critical approaches have dominated the field in the last thirty years. The first is the application to Old English verse of the oral-formulaic theory that Milman Parry and Albert Lord developed out of their study of contemporary South-Slavic oral poetry.[1] The second is the exegetical or neo-Augustinian form of interpretation associated particularly with the name of D. W. Robertson in the area of medieval English literature.[2] We should probably add an important third approach, though its beginning and subsequent course are less sharply defined, namely, the technique of close reading of poetry developed under the aegis of the New Criticism.[3] One might, however, argue that, since close reading of this kind has been used by critics of all denominations, it should not be seen as forming any very distinct class of its own.

A major reason for the popularity of the first two theories is that they seem to offer structured approaches to a poetry that for many modern readers lacks any clear and familiar structure. Imagine for a moment the naive first reactions to *Beowulf* of a reader hitherto accustomed only to modern literature (i.e., literature in Modern English, since Shakespeare). Such a reader will respond quickly and positively to some of the poem's descriptions of violent action; will find curiously attractive some of the exotic atmosphere of mead-hall and dragon-mound; and may experience familiar emotions when reading a few highly lyrical passages. But surely he or she will find large sections of the poem imaginatively inert—slow-moving, redundant, didactic, often simply opaque. Such a reader— I might as well confess that this devil's advocate I have in mind is myself at a very early stage—may wonder why in the world the poet has chosen to direct his attention where he does. *Why* does he keep tirelessly making the same points and telling the same kinds of illustrative stories over and over, yet spend so pitifully little time on the literary things we have been taught to think important? On characterization, for instance, with its problems of development, complexity, clear motivation; on richness of detail in the natural and physical background; on informal, natural, and "real" interactions between people; on a broad or "rounded" or ironic view of the world the poet presents. If we judge *Beowulf* by novelistic standards, it shows us a cast of ornately dressed and stuffed (or stuffy) mannequins, always ready to restate the obvious, acting out rituals as obscure as they are strenuous.

The point I wish to make is not mysterious. So long as we look in the poem for what is not to be found and ignore what is there, we continue to have trouble in understanding it. I am not merely scolding others, but speaking of myself. Only in recent years have I come, like many others, to believe that it is our invincibly "literate" way of engaging the poem that has been the chief obstacle to understanding it in a satisfactory way. In large part through the most severely practical kind of criticism, that slow and abrasive evolutionary process of readjusting my interpretation of the poem as I have gone on teaching it year by year, I have significantly shifted my viewpoint. I am ready to accept the poem as a most distinguished descendant of a long and skillful oral tradition.

Although my recognition of the validity and importance of the oral theory came quite late, for reasons I will make clearer in a moment, it has furnished me, as a theory generated elsewhere, as something from *outside* the poem, with a compelling and illuminating explanation of many things I had already noticed from *inside* it, without really understanding what I was seeing and without the support or sanction of any theory. From this experience I draw the conclusion that oral and written poetry overlap enough in their poetic techniques to allow us to use quite similar critical methods most of the time. The more ideological oralists who argue for the uniqueness of oral form might well, however, oppose this conclusion.

Go back now to our observant novice reader and with this reader look more closely at the strange text of *Beowulf*. On written pages, written (at least in this sole surviving manuscript) about the year 1000, though probably copied from earlier versions,[4] we find a text largely composed of formulas. For my purposes here, I describe these as simplified, generalized, and impersonal verbal patterns. They are impersonal in bearing no trace of any jagged originality or individual stamp; the patterns are almost always perfectly predictable and may be found in any Old English poem. They hang in clusters from a very limited number of hooks. It is the unmitigated severity of such limitations of style (and of subject as well) that our novice reader notices first and resents most. What is actually said often seems monotonous; what is not said is alarmingly much. But perhaps the resentful reader does not realize that many things—the kinds of things he or she misses most, indeed—cannot possibly be said in *Beowulf* because there is no language available to say them. This is the only expressive medium we have.

A concrete instance may serve to illustrate this idea of limitation. That highly conventional beast the dragon is a simple example. If a dragon, a *wyrm*, a *draca*, appears in a given passage, we can be sure that the terms applied to it and the actions it performs will all lie well within a small compass of convention. In what follows, the numbers in parentheses indicate my rough count of the "formulaic" epithets and phrases applied to various aspects of the dragon in *Beowulf*. The count can only be approximate, since there is much overlapping. It will be noted at once that some aspects are copiously, even redundantly, exemplified and restated.

The dragon is above all inveterately hostile toward all human beings (17 references).[5] He guards treasure habitually (18).[6] He lives in a barrow-grave or earth-house (14).[7] He is very ancient (6).[8] He flies (7).[9] He breathes out destructive fire (15).[10] Just as clearly delineated by their total absence are attributes the dragon lacks. Even though dragons are somewhat similar to kings in their power and treasure-guarding function, they do not rule anybody or sit on thrones; though they hoard artefacts, they never use them; they do not speak, cooperate, or even interact with other beings (except to incinerate them); they have no emotions other than avarice and fury; they are invariably solitary and do not reproduce or indeed have any kin-relationships at all, though their species as a whole may be vaguely referred to as *wyrmcynn*, 'the dragon-race or family'. The sly and chatty dragon Smaug of Tolkien's book *The Hobbit* has come a long distance from anything the poet of *Beowulf* could have imagined.

Though there is ample variation within each of these tight clusters of patterns, and though this variation indeed forms a striking feature of the style (admittedly one our novice reader will need some time to appreciate), the examples of variation never range far outside a drastically restricted number of fixed bases. We might call these bases normal expectations. Oral poetry as we see it in *Beowulf* is precisely, almost forbiddingly, the poetry of normal expectations. They appear in all its patterns. More specific terms for some of these patterns (though my use of terms will lack the rigorous clarity of definition the theorist demands) include the following: epithets habitually attached to characters or objects (*ece drihten* 'eternal lord' or *eald sweord* 'ancient sword', the attributes riveted tight to their nouns); type-characters (the gracious mead-pouring queen Wealhtheow); traditional narrative sequences (voyages, gift-giving, fights); gnomic assertions of permanent ethical values (*swa sceal man don* 'thus should a man [always] do'); certain heavily symbolic objects (weapons, ships, halls, barrows); stock settings and props (benches to sit on, cups to drink from); habitual use of contrast to highlight and define (the pairing for effect of good Sigemund and wicked Heremod); certain recognizable emotional tones or attitudes (boasting, the "elegiac" tone), with their own characteristic vocabularies. Such a catalogue is only an incomplete outline, and in any case is deficient because it cannot show the complicated interweaving of these separate constituents that is so fundamentally typical of the verse.

There is no explanation for these highly conspicuous features of the poetry other than their origin in the style of traditional oral narrative. This point will be developed and illustrated in some detail later in this chapter. Exactly how the oral style managed to persist well into the period of literacy, after writing was introduced in 597, is a crucial and possibly insoluble problem.[11] But we cannot wait for the answer to it before we accept what is on internal evidence a *fait accompli. Beowulf* is oral in style as we have it, however that phenomenon may have come about. Of course all students of Old English in some sense know this fact, but I think not all have taken into account the full critical implications of the poem's close relation to orality.

One important reason for the lag in accepting such implications is that the oral-formulaic approach to Old English poetry seemed anything but promising when it was first introduced into the local scholarly field by Magoun and his successors. Unfortunately they tended to echo the rather peremptory and messianic tone already adopted by Parry and especially by Lord, a tone that presented the new approach in aggressive and challenging terms. In true oral fashion, issues were polarized. One could be born again as an oralist or else smolder in outer literate darkness. Furthermore, rightly or wrongly as the theory first presented it, the process of oral composition seemed to many to be wholly mechanical in nature, a versecraft well adapted to our dawning computer age, with the alliterative cogs and wheels dolefully clanking into their fated *good & bad of formulaic patterns* (handwritten annotation)

metrical slots and the glassy-eyed programmer-poets deprived of all free and intelligent choices. Some remembered gloomily that critics have always been eager to aggrandize themselves by depriving poets of their creative freedom, as much recent literary theory of a reductionist sort has shown.

Thus the oral-formulaic theory disturbed traditional literary critics and scholars, who at first saw no clear way of discriminating between the "bad" conventions of the oral style, as they saw them— dull stereotyped effects, narrowness of interest, recycled language, and a frankly low level of expressive achievement—and its "good" conventions—swift, intense action-descriptions, a concentrated exuberance of tone and feeling, and the supporting strength of long tradition and deeply rooted myth. Important differences in the relative artistic skill of various poets seemed harder to isolate when all poets used the same language. The question of originality seemed particularly acute.[12]

Scholars also wondered (and still wonder) about the historical plausibility of assuming the orality of this poetry, since there are no surviving tapes. All we have to go on are written texts of unknown provenance. Many students were then (and still are) quite uncomfortable with constant talk of the "singer" of *Beowulf*, considering him merely a convenient phantom summoned up by oralist ideologues bent on asserting an absolute incompatibility between oral and literate poetry.

It should be realized that very similar debates between individualists (that is, believers in a single literate poet as author of a work) and oral traditionalists have been going on in other medieval fields as well. The *Cantar de Mio Cid*, Spain's only medieval epic, has been the focus of much scholarly controversy, conveniently and lucidly summarized by one of the partisans, Ruth H. Webber.[13] She argues cogently for the oral-traditional origin of the poem on the Cid, and assumes as well an oral origin for such early French poems as the *Song of Roland*.

Since those vexed early years in the Old English field, however, new developments have altered the picture and made the oral-formulaic approach seem more attractive. There has been a distinct slackening off, for instance, of the first strenuous and Procrustean attempts to make the patterns of Old English verse, especially its metrical patterns, correspond in any significant detail with patterns of Homeric hexameters or South-Slavic decasyllabics. In addition, a more sophisticated and realistic definition of the Anglo-Saxon verse formula as something more than a phrase periodically repeated verbatim has also begun to emerge.[14] Information gathered by anthropologists, folklorists, and other field investigators has greatly enlarged our understanding of other kinds of oral artforms.[15] Of special importance is the way such studies have illuminated the complex interfaces that exist in our century between the stage of pure orality and the gradual, often piecemeal, adoption of literacy, since most of the Anglo-Saxon period was such a transitional time. For example, Jeff Opland adds his knowledge of present-day Zulu and Xhosa oral poetry in Africa to what is basically a review of the external historical evidence for or against the existence of a similar oral tradition in Anglo-Saxon England.[16] Opland's new viewpoint is of real interest, though the book's chief weakness, significantly perhaps, is its neglect of the internal evidence, largely stylistic, that can be found in Old English verse and in early Germanic verse more generally.

Since *Beowulf* must have originated at some point during such a transitional period—or even at several points, if we prefer to think of several successive versions—it matters little, from the standpoint of this line of argument, where precisely we place the disputed date of its composition. It is 500 years from the introduction of writing to England until the end of the Anglo-Saxon period, and at the end most people were still quite illiterate, though certainly affected by literacy through the church. In *Beowulf* we do see many Christian references that are ultimately bookish in origin, though that fact does not necessarily imply that the poet himself acquired such knowledge directly by reading books. But such "literate" allusions coexist there with a much larger body of legendary material almost certainly transmitted orally. For most of it we have no other written record in any language.

It is admittedly painful to concede that this is all we are ever likely to know for certain about the poem's origin. Perhaps each reader needs to have some working hypothesis, a model in his or her head, in order to read the poem, however. Perhaps each critic ought to risk stating publicly his or her own private belief. The safest hypothesis is to see the poem as "transitional" or "oral-derived," which fudges a bit but leaves open a spectrum of possibilities, at some point along which each individual may want to locate a best guess as to the conditions of *Beowulf*'s origin. At one end of the line, one could see what we have in the manuscript as a verbatim transcript of a single actual performance by a singer, a version that is one of many once existing multiforms, similar but always varying oral performances. At the other end, one might imagine the poem as being an artful imitation or recreation of the oral tradition by a wholly literate poet of antiquarian bent, as interested in old language as he is in old feuds and old funerals. A very loose parallel to this in later English literature might be the synthetic medievalism of Spenser or Thomas Chatterton. In between the extremes, any hypothesis of successive revisions and modifications might have us traveling some distance along the line.

I boldly state here my own best guess, aware that the evidence for it is the merest gossamer. I think *Beowulf* is (or was originally) an eighth-century Mercian court poem, very close to oral tradition and carefully preserved thereafter, perhaps because of its excellence, by later transcribers. The poem shows no signs of having been influenced directly by writings in Latin, whether Virgil or the Fathers of the Church, or Roman rhetoricians. The awkwardly introduced Offa episode (lines 1931–62), if, as seems possible, it was intended to flatter the Mercian royal house by praising one of its eminent ancestors, would be squarely in the ancient oral tradition of eulogistic court poetry given so much prominence by Opland. Its presence in the poem gives faint but definite support to the Mercian origin of *Beowulf*.[17]

What remains entirely mysterious is the use that the poem may have been put to once written down. Was it ever read privately— signed out, so to speak, from some monastic library? Was it read aloud to audiences in imitation of performance, and were those audiences likely to be secular or monastic? Was it something like a script to be committed to memory for dramatic recitation? Might it have been one of the Saxon poems included in the book with the beautiful illuminated initial that his mother is said to have tempted young Alfred with—a poem first to hear read aloud, then to memorize, and finally to read for oneself?[18]

Though we may now remain groping in a fog of such questions, ongoing studies of modern analogues will probably provide a few tentative answers to them eventually. But speaking for myself, and perhaps also for my own generation of scholars, I believe we were born too soon to profess, or now acquire, much real understanding from the inside of how oral poetry is currently being produced and received. We will not carry out hands-on studies of the fascinating process or do investigation in the field. But our long acquaintance with Old English poetry from the inside in a different but important sense can be usefully modified and sharpened by such recent studies.

A literary critic's first job is to understand how rich and powerful meaning can be expressed in an oral-derived style subject to such narrow limitations of range, if we compare it in this respect to the more familiar styles of written literature. To do this we must move from seeing the oral-derived style as a crippling restriction to perceiving it as generating through its very conventions the unmistakably high quality of the verse.

Some who choose this path to follow may find that it is necessary to give up another one. They will no longer be able to profess the neo-Augustinian approach. They will have to declare themselves Cannibals rather than Missionaries.

Probably the great wave of exegetical criticism has by now passed over and spent its force, but it has left a great deposit of sea wrack on the shore. It has left in the minds of many students of *Beowulf* the odd conviction that the poem is a covert operation. Some painfully literate theologian-poet, an Anglo-Saxon Umberto Eco, has left instructive Christian messages hidden in hollow Germanic trees. One has to supply the concept of a body of original readers who found the decoding of this text stimulating relaxation from their usual daily labors in the monastic library. For such imagined readers and for their all too imaginable present-day descendants, the poem may cleverly pretend to be in a pagan/oral tradition, but that is only its cover. Behind the scenes the preacher-poet, like the later evangelizing friars, is writing new pious lyrics for the bawdy old tunes that draw the crowd.

But those who still remain converted to this approach cannot, alas, be preached to. Not very sensitive to poetry, they do not notice or care that their reductive *a priori* assumptions usually result in interpretations that stand the poem very awkwardly on its head. They are always serenely sure of finding what they have already decided they will find. Once established and in operation, the sacred circle cannot be broken into by mere inconvenient fact.[19]

It is more telling to illustrate this point from a good book rather than from any of a host of pedestrian allegorizations. The danger of this approach stands out all the more strikingly in a critical work distinguished by much acute and illuminating commentary, Alvin A. Lee's *The Guest-Hall of Eden*.[20]

Lee comes to discuss *Beowulf* after detailed study of what he calls the basic Christian myths found in Old English religious poetry. This order sets up a silent argument by analogy. The whole considerable weight of the foregoing elaboration of "Christian myths" seems calculated to persuade us that *Beowulf* too belongs in the same series. It is true that one can have no objection on historical grounds to this order of presentation, since, as the Cædmon story suggests, Christian poetry was probably being composed long before *Beowulf* found its way into written form. But it is clear that Lee believes that at its very core *Beowulf* is also a didactic Christian poem, and that is another matter.

Some examples will make clear Lee's way of thinking about the poem. He claims, for instance, that the Danish hall Heorot is doomed "in the mind of a Christian poet" to become polluted, *unclæne*.[21] It becomes polluted, he argues, because its sinful inhabitants resort to "the self-destruction of devil-worship, symbolized by the cannibalistic monsters,"[22] that is to say, the race of Cain to which Grendel belongs. We are in the midst of all sorts of serious distortion of meaning here, and it is not hard to detect its ultimate source. The phrase "in the mind of a Christian poet" suggests the *a priori* assumption that Christian poets would always apply strict theological views to any stories they tell. It is easily demonstrable that Anglo-Saxon Christian poets do reveal such views when they compose verse on religious subjects, but it is not evident that they consider such applications to be appropriate to secular stories.

We can look at the evidence in the poet's own words. We find that he never comes close to saying that the Danes have in any way "polluted" Heorot. I cannot see that this idea is anywhere even implicit in the poem; indeed it contradicts the central meaning of this part of the poem. It is Grendel, not the Danes, who has befouled the hall and put it out of service. Heorot must later be cleansed and exorcized for the Danes' future use by Beowulf, who is several times said to be acting as God's agent.[23] It is only Lee's initial assumption about the "Christian poet" that compels him, like other allegorists, to equate Heorot with Augustine's City of Man, or with wicked Babylon, and other irrelevant communities.

Lee seems mistaken in simple matters of fact. Grendel and his mother do not make their appearance *because* the Danes have taken up the worship of devils, though that seems clearly to be what he implies. Grendel attacks because he is angered that the Danes are making music in their newly-built hall. His mother later attacks to gain vengeance for her son's death. We do not have to search in hollow trees for the motives of the monsters. It is certainly absolutely plain that the devil-worship on the part of the Danes is a despairing response to Grendel's first attacks, not at all a cause of them. We have no evidence that they ever did this kind of thing before he appeared.

One telltale sentence betrays the nature of Lee's bias. He points out, quite correctly, that the poet connects Grendel with hell, but then concludes with: "which should make it easy to recognize the metaphorical structure barely concealed beneath the relatively slight surface realism of the poem."[24] How eager Lee seems in his desire to get to this concealed structure, and then to go on to equate Grendel with the standard devil of Christian theology. And how quickly he brushes aside the "slight surface realism"—by which he must after all simply mean the words of the story, all that we can know. His attempt to introduce the Christian system ("the metaphorical structure") makes dissonant nonsense of the structure of meaning that the "slight surface realism" of the poem has been creating in its own right. A poem cannot serve two masters. And, as I shall be insisting regularly and monotonously henceforth, *Beowulf* does *not* conceal its structures of meaning. Its serious statements are almost without exception entirely recognizable and explicit.

In this case, it is true that the mention of hell in connection with Grendel does bring in the "Christian element," but that is only one element in a rather complicated mixture that will be examined later in this study. What is stressed at all points in the poem is a narrative present where heroic behavior is displayed and praised. It is heroic behavior, not Christianity, that is the true subject of the poem.[25] Grendel is above all important in his relation to that. Fitting occasional Christian allusions into the frame of a heroic ethos has often been a problem for *us*, though apparently it was no special problem for the Anglo-Saxons.

Explicitness seems to be a constant feature of oral-derived poetry. When the poet wants us to give our attention to something, he talks about it, and usually at some length. When things are not on stage in this way, they do not exist. As has been pointed out by many, a listening audience (and even if one is convinced that *Beowulf* was only minimally or imitatively "oral" in its mode of composition, that must have been the kind of audience it usually had, even as a written work read aloud) cannot pause to reflect, interpret, or uncover hidden meanings no matter how "barely concealed." It cannot even carry explicit ideas for long unless they are constantly and redundantly repeated and overstressed.

For an example of this in *Beowulf*, we find that there are a few occasions in the poem when the poet tells us that Grendel belongs to the race of Cain. We are invited to think about that association then, but only then. Thus we should resist Lee's attempts to persuade us that "the feuding or Cain motif . . . lasts throughout the poem, becoming almost omnipresent in Part 2, even though the explicit naming of Cain and Abel has by then faded out."[26] The explicit naming of Cain and Abel has rather by then ceased entirely, not "faded out," it would be more correct to say. Since Cain is not mentioned in Part II, I would stoutly maintain that Cain does not exist in Part II. When Lee goes on to assert that the cowardly Geats who abandon Beowulf in the dragon-fight are "now members of the outlawed race of Cain," he makes a gratuitous theological statement that may please him but one which in terms of the poem is baseless and meaningless. Even if true believers wish to say that all wicked folk must belong to the Cain race, the Cain race is simply not there in Part II. If the poet is not thinking about it, there is surely no reason for us to do so.

Other arguments, many, could be advanced against this exegetical approach to *Beowulf*. I am here attacking it on one front only by emphasizing its incompatibility with what I must see as the habitual explicitness of the traditional oral style of this poem. Indeed a similar kind of explicitness is also quite characteristic of the Christian poems in Old English—as, for that matter, it is often enough typical of the Latin exegetical commentaries that may lie behind them— even though these poems may stand at some greater distance from the primary oral stage than *Beowulf* seems to. The important religious symbols of the highly typological poem *Advent (Christ I)*, for example, are never "barely concealed" but are presented directly. We are told with pedantic thoroughness the exact *significatio* of the Phoenix and the Whale. These meanings were thought too important to leave for cryptographers to solve. In fact it is a common medieval weakness to try to be consistently more explicit about meanings than it is possible to be, to search out and find meanings everywhere in the universe and to report them in full when they are discovered.

Today's critics in their own way search constantly for clear causal relationships that rationally ought to exist in the poetry, but often are not to be found there. It is easy to understand why they do this. Teachers of *Beowulf* can testify that they spend much time dissuading their students from trying to discover such causal sequences. They are looking for motivations and explanations of a kind they are already familiar with in literature. All of us arrive at *Beowulf* thinking in these terms because it is the way we have been trained to think in a literate society.

One question, for example, that students always want a definite answer for is why Grendel attacks Heorot. As we have just seen, Lee quickly finds a sufficient cause: the hall has already been polluted by the Danes' sinfulness, and Grendel is consequently made God's unwitting agent of punishment. Sinning and being punished are always good causal relationships. More secular readers may propose political reasons, rather than religious ones: the Danish empire (or is it only King Hrothgar?) is rotten with complacency, glutted with wealth, swollen with imperialistic ambitions (an explanation popular during the sixties), and so on.

But these suggested causes are trifling. They are merely logical and thus alien to the highly irrational context in which *Beowulf* seems to exist. Grendel is a hobgoblin who has long obsessed our little modern minds, but we need not be foolishly consistent about him. Could the poet, if we called him back, have been able to explain to us his own concept of Grendel's motivations? The entire sequence of behavior must certainly have been based on his audience's familiarity with certain traditional givens in their experience of life and of poetry: darkness, deformity, fenlands, deep black waters, all that is threatening, all that is the obverse of the hero's own bright clarity of act and purpose. Perhaps all he might have been able to say in explanation is something unsatisfactory: Grendel, as I gather and amass and assert these traits that go along with him, is something already familiar to you from other songs and stories, and so he does just the kind of thing you all know such creatures do. If the audience once feels the reality of Grendel in such vague but immediate terms as this, perhaps the poet sees no harm in draping his fen-dwelling outlaw-troll in some selected strands of enriching Christian meaning in order to place him in yet another context already familiar to his audience. Not only is Grendel what I said—he is a sort of devil, too; he lives in a terrible place that's really hell; he's descended from the famous brother-bane Cain; Hrothgar thinks God has sent Beowulf expressly to kill this evil creature, and that must be the truth. Quite obviously the process could have been nothing like this, since we have no way of knowing when the basic Germanic story line and the Christian thought-world encountered each other. But it should be said that the Christian references are in no way *necessary* concomitants of evil monsters. The poet does not need them to define the meaning of the other two monsters, Grendel's mother and the dragon, who are equally malevolent antagonists of the hero. Some exegetical critics have striven mightily to enlist these two as well in the Great War between God and his enemies. But a good critic can survive a poor theory. Lee scrupulously respects the facts of the poem and does no such theologizing in his excellent discussion of the poem's ending.

I have spent so much time on the exegetical approach because it has doubtless been the most widely practised application of "literate" standards to the poem. It is not, however, the only one. Earlier, a bumptious generation of very New Critics (I Ishmael was one of that crew) issued forth from graduate schools to grapple with *Beowulf*, having sharpened their critical tusks on ambiguity, irony, and paradox in Donne and James. Their abuses of the text were less flagrant and discouraging, but often nearly as misleading. They may not have had quite as fixed a preconception of what the poem was going to mean, but they were very sure they knew how it was going to mean it and what literary devices it would use. But of course the style they assumed the poet worked in was a literate style; the critical method they used was designed to handle such a style. Used to cross-indexing interlocking metaphors and ironies in metaphysical poems of enormous specific density—poems that could be read, reread, disassembled and put back together—they saw nothing amiss in pointing out the fine appropriateness of an ironic allusion in line 1752 to a word used earlier in line 8. No listening audience could ever have registered such a connection, and it is certain no performing poet used to the ways of oral poetry would have bothered to set one up, even granting that he could have remembered it himself when the right time came.

Where the New Critical approach is most clearly seen is in the treatment of the digressions and episodes in the poem. Such passages, roundly condemned earlier by the literal-minded scholar-critics of the older philological tradition as being simply irrelevant (at one time the theory of scribal interpolations and multiple authorship could account for such problems), were now found to be pregnantly apt and sweetly ironic in every imaginable detail, the massed relevancies and correspondences stretching out of the text far out of sight into some unstated or imagined background. The greatest thing in literature, organic unity, was always, *a priori*, assumed to exist, and a critic simply searched till he found it; or maybe he invented it, just a little. The obscure, opaque, and elliptical nature of some of the allusions in the *Beowulf* episodes has always invited commentators to exercise some critical fancy and we will have to go on doing our best guessing, but we should now realize that we cannot work out every detail of these puzzles in terms of perfect unity of meaning. The episodes are all *roughly* relevant, but not always a perfect fit by any means. The oral poet is simply not very tidy about trimming off all the loose ends that trail along after a chunk of allusion he needs to use. Wanting to praise Hygelac's virtuous young queen Hygd, the *Beowulf*-poet brings in for contrast a wicked young queen, but this particular chunk has a life of its own. The passage on the wicked queen ends with praise of King Offa, who is no part of the contrast.[27] Elsewhere in the poem, the story of Finn and Hengest (1068–1159a), since it tells us about a war-ravaged hall in a hall soon to be ravaged itself, is ironically apt (prophetic or ominous), but quite obviously the poet becomes involved in his good story for its own good sake. His audience would be expected to become similarly involved. John Niles's statement of the same principle is brief and useful: "In time-bound oral poetry, each passage stands alone."[28]

It is common knowledge that New Critics suffer from chronic irony-deficiency, but too often they search for what they crave in the wrong places. Irony can often be used to impose consistency or organic unity. Thus a critic who has decided (probably on shaky grounds, as I shall argue in the next chapter) that Unferth was an evil plotter and troublemaker will be obliged to regard the poet's application to him of the complimentary phrase *eafoþes cræftig* 'mighty in strength' in line 1466 as a deliberate bit of scathing irony rather than as praise. But I think it is just what it sounds like, a compliment. It may be, however, that we have here something like the fixed and not especially meaningful epithet so frequent in Homeric verse. One recalls those heroes in the *Iliad* routinely called "brilliant" or "godlike" at the moment they were fleeing in terror from battle. The adjectives refer to their permanent condition as certified heroes, rather than to their temporary situation. If Unferth then is said to be mighty in strength, it is because he is a warrior and that is what warriors are, generically. Even though Unferth's lack of courage in confronting monsters is being described at this point, the epithet contains a form of permanent truth.

Although such language may have grown out of the incessant demands for fillers in metrical situations, even though such fillers might be inexact and not finely tuned to context, it serves in the event to preserve stability and decorum. Everything tends to become binary or polarized in the heroic world. A warrior you meet must become either your friend or your foe. Neutrality, ambivalence, or indifference seem not to be possible. Thus here, if Beowulf

Possible functions of formulaic phrases.

does not go on actually to fight Unferth (he has already fought him verbally in the formal and ludic flyting), he must—and does—befriend him. The phrase in question then makes a little more understandable Beowulf's generous and comradely attitude toward the Danish warrior.

Obviously irony does exist in *Beowulf*, but it is not hidden or subtle where it occurs. We find it as dramatic irony in a tragic situation, as, for example, in Wealhtheow's anguished and apparently vain pleading with Hrothulf to look after her sons (if, as is generally assumed, he will have something to do with robbing them of their future) (1169–87), or as a gloat over an enemy's foreknowledge of what he is about to encounter, as, for example, the way the poet dwells on Grendel's anticipation of feasting when he makes his way toward Heorot for the last time (728–34a), or simply as a sarcastic taunt, such as Beowulf's stinging reply to Unferth in the flyting (583b–89). And of course loftier "cosmic" ironies about the ultimate meaning of life and death cluster thick about the close of the poem. But I would agree strongly with T. A. Shippey's statement that the poet "never presents as right things known to be wrong."[29] *Þæt wæs god cyning*, for instance, can never be taken to mean "he was a bad king," though it might very well mean just that if it were to be used in the mode of irony familiar to us from Swift or Fielding or Joyce. Niles also makes this point, citing as an example of the later kind of irony the remark Chaucer makes about the unscrupulous Shipman: "he was a good felawe."[30]

Finally, before going on to look more closely at some of the features of oral-derived poetry that are to be found in *Beowulf*, I should state here my absolute conviction that an acceptance of the oral basis of *Beowulf* rules out of court altogether any conclusions about the poem's meaning that are based exclusively on the text in its present *written* state. The meticulous counting of lines in order to reveal ingenious and significant numerical patterns of structure ("tectonics") is based on a wholly unwarranted faith in the stability and integrity of the single manuscript we have, and assumes that Anglo-Saxons unprovided with Klaeber's third edition could have had the faintest concept of such line-counts.[31] Open to similar objections would be Huppé's recent analysis of the poem's meaning structure in terms of the scribal division of the text into marked and numbered sections or fitts.[32] He gives special attention to the opening lines of such fitts. But I see no way a listener could grasp the importance of any of these divisions, nor how someone reciting the poem could bring it out for the audience. We may learn more about them some day, but at this point the fitt divisions seem to me arbitrary and without structural meaning.[33]

In discussing these various approaches, we have touched now and again on the chief differences between oral and literate ways of formulating experience; it is time now to examine them systematically. In order to do this, for the rest of this chapter I will take time to go over the excellent summary of characteristic features of oral compositions compiled by Walter J. Ong in his book *Orality and Literacy*,[34] finding illustrations for most of them specifically from the text of *Beowulf*.

In Chapter 3 of his book, Ong first describes in general terms the necessity of the "mnemonic base" that underlies all oral art-forms. Various ways of becoming supremely *memorable* include the "heavy patterning" of story-plots, the repetition of formulaic phrases and themes, and frequent didactic maxims that restate the ethos of the work. He then lists the following nine "oral" characteristics, in most cases defining them in terms of sharp contrast with the more familiar features of literate works:

(i)   Additive rather than subordinative
(ii)   Aggregative rather than analytic
(iii)   Redundant or "copious"
(iv)   Conservative or traditionalist
(v)   Close to the human lifeworld
(vi)   Agonistically toned
(vii)   Empathetic and participatory rather than objectively distanced
(viii) Homeostatic
(ix)   Situational rather than abstract

Some of these may need explaining. We will take them up one by one and explore their relevance to *Beowulf*.

(i) *Additive rather than subordinative*

We can readily connect this characteristic to a well-known and much-discussed feature of Old English verse style that has usually been known by the syntactic term "parataxis," though the term is often extended in usage beyond the area of syntax proper to the area of rhetoric generally. Ong uses as an example of "additive" style the first chapter of Genesis, presumed to be originally an oral narrative by most recent biblical scholars, where we find a series of discrete narrative statements linked only by the conjunction "and." Old English poetry typically proceeds in a similar way, adding statements or narrative units in a linear string one after another, while at the same time, as we have already noticed, omitting much of the subordinating framework that could have served to explain cause and effect and to introduce qualifications of the discrete statements. We could restate the example we used earlier when dealing with the question of why Grendel attacks Heorot. The poet makes essentially two discrete and paratactic statements: (1) Grendel lives in gloomy fens, silence, darkness, and so forth *and* (2) he suddenly attacks Heorot. Some modern readers have found this a disturbingly blank and uninformative "and," although most of us are quick to supply causality by seeing Grendel's lonely isolation as an adequate reason for him to hate the happiness in the hall. But the connection here, as often elsewhere, must be supplied by us.

Closely linked to this kind of additive narration, I would suggest, is the ubiquitous and incessant Old English habit of variation, where a series of statements (they may be only descriptive adjectives, nouns, or phrases) is made about whatever is at the center of description, paralleling on a micro-scale the larger sequences of narrative. An example from Hrothgar's lament for Æschere:

> Dead is Æschere,
> Yrmenlafes   yldra broþor,
> min runwita   ond min rædbora,
> eaxlgestealla. . . .   (1323b–26a)[35]

(Dead is Æschere, Yrmenlaf's older brother, my secret adviser and my counsellor, [my] shoulder-comrade. . . .)

This little series could be put in paratactic statement form: Æschere is dead, and Æschere is Yrmenlaf's brother, and Æschere is my secret adviser, and so on. Neither this kind of variation nor the larger linear narrative series is usually subordinative. This series creates no special hierarchy of precedence or necessary sequence among its constituent variational parts—at least formally and ostensibly, though we can see (if we fine-tune) that in the quoted series there is a little movement toward greater emotional intensity as Hrothgar moves back in memory to the days of fighting beside Æschere when they were both young warriors. But this movement toward intensity is given no grammatical or syntactical signals.

To use Grendel as an example once again, we see that he is

referred to at different times as a devil (*feond on helle* 101, *feond mancynnes* 164); a destitute man (*feasceaft guma* 973); a hall-thane (*healðegnes* 142); a sorcerer (*helrunan* 163, *he sigewæpnum forsworen hæfde* 'he had put a spell on weapons' 804); a giant (*eoten* 761). His mother is said to be a sea-wolf (*brimwylf* 1506). So what is Grendel really, since these descriptions are hardly consistent with each other? This series of epithets again seems much like the successive steps in additive narration or aggregative description in that no clear distinctions or discriminations are provided. Hence scholars are left to wonder, as they have, whether Grendel is actually human, or has somehow changed over time, or is a fiend taking human form, or really has any genuine magical powers. The poem never answers these questions in a way that logically tidies up all loose ends and contradictions.[36]

(ii) *Aggregative rather than analytic*

This characteristic is clearly closely connected with (i), and can usefully be applied to the important and controversial area of characterization. The conventional loose clusters of associations that accumulate or "aggregate" around traditional figures like a hero, an evil monster, or a good king cannot usually be analyzed. That is to say, they are not subject to disintegration or unmasking by irony or any other means a literacy critic might use to pierce the bright blank surface of explicit statement. As we will see in the next chapter, where Hrothgar is examined in detail, there are ways of providing a fairly complex picture of character, but it is done within the terms of the oral system rather than through "literate" forms of irony.

To accept Beowulf himself as a wholly ideal hero, for example, that is, as one viewed entirely without irony, goes very much against the grain for many modern readers, as teachers of the poem can testify. Readers often feel that they are expected to search out the hidden flaws in this radiant portrait. Yet we must accept Beowulf's perfection as an ineluctable fact, something not only consistently stated and restated in the poet's descriptive words of encomium but borne out in full by the hero's actions.

Unwilling to credit such an impossible ideal, some exegetical critics (I have in mind especially Margaret Goldsmith) have tried to cut incisively through the marshalled phalanx of laudatory language that surrounds Beowulf in order to identify some heart of darkness within. Goldsmith arraigns the old king for the secret sin of coveting the dragon's hoard.[37] In a more plausible and sophisticated way, other critics have seen the very perfection of Beowulf's beneficent strength as itself a fault in the poet's eyes. They argue that, by his kindly over-protectiveness as king, Beowulf left his people weak and untrained to face the reality of violence in the world outside Geatland after his death.[38] Both hypotheses analyze and split the single aggregative picture the poet offers us, in the interest once again of finding a hidden message or some ironic subtext. They do not exist.

(iii) Redundant or "copious"

This characteristic needs a little explaining and probably some defense. Unlike written discourse, where a reader can go back to retrieve a train of thought or check a reference if necessary, the oral utterance vanishes completely as soon as uttered. "Hence," Ong points out, "the mind must move ahead more slowly, keeping close to the focus of attention much of what it has already dealt with. Redundancy, repetition of the just-said, keeps both speaker and hearer surely on the track."[39] We find this kind of abundance or *copia*, on the small scale of individual verse and line, everywhere in *Beowulf*, with its tireless restatement and variation of statement. Literate readers, as we saw, often find this style not only tedious but singularly inefficient in advancing the story. There is however more than one kind of efficiency. Perhaps we should modify our usual expectations.

The "copious" style can be illustrated by a decidedly redundant yet in its way certainly efficient passage that immediately follows Beowulf's death and describes the reactions of the survivor Wiglaf.

Ða wæs gegongen   guman unfrodum
earfoðlice,   þæt he on eorðan geseah
þone leofestan   lifes æt ende
bleate gebæran.   Bona swylce læg,
egeslic eorðdraca   ealdre bereafod,
bealwe gebæded.   Beahhordum leng
wyrm wohbogen   wealdan ne moste,
ac hine irenna   ecga fornamon,
hearde, heaðoscearde   homera lafe,
þæt se widfloga   wundum stille
hreas on hrusan   hordærne neah.
Nalles æfter lyfte   lacende hwearf

middelnihtum,   maðmæhta wlonc
ansyn ywde,   ac he eorðan gefeoll
for ðæs hildfruman   hondgeweorce.   (2821–35)

(Then the young man had this pain happen to him—that he
saw on the earth that dearest man faring wretchedly at the end
of life. The killer lay there also, fearful earth-dragon bereft of
life, pushed down by evil. The curving reptile was not left to
rule ring-hoards any longer,—no, the edges of iron swords,
hard, battle-shards, the hammer-leavings, had taken him off, so
that the far-flyer motionless in wounds fell onto earth near the
hoard-house. In no way whatever did he surge up in play at
midnight to show his face, proud with his treasures,—no, he
crashed down to earth through the hand's work of the battle-
prince.)

The factual or prose meaning of this passage is meager. It does
not even offer any new information. It tells us Wiglaf feels sad
when he sees Beowulf dead. It tells us the dragon is now dead. I
deliberately state these two "actions" in a way that brings out their
paratactic form. As is always the case with such poetic use of parataxis, the imaginative energy of poet and audience must pour into
the interstices between statements to form and expand relationships between ostensibly unconnected statements. In this passage
the redundancy plays an important role as well. It keeps nudging
and nagging our attention back to this sad scene, keeping us from
looking away from it, making us brood over it, making us explore
its implications. This process is what is being forced on Wiglaf in
the story-world and we share his feelings—very much the "participatory" mode mentioned by Ong as his seventh characteristic of
oral poetry.

The poet thus encourages us to imagine what seeing a dead
dragon might feel like. To describe a dead dragon (or a dead person) memorably, it is effective to picture a living one as vividly as
you can and to reflect on the difference. The dragon's lifetime activities are stressed. The difficulty of accepting death is dramatized
here. The dragon redundantly lies dead (læg, hreas, gefeoll), but it
takes long and heavy sword-play (two lines of it, 2828–29) to make
him lie there, to keep him dead there. Though we may be consoled
a little in our grief about Beowulf's death by the vengeful thought
that the dragon can no longer fly with the old exultant joy, that
same exultant joy is what the beloved king as well has now lost. The

scene generates blurred and complicated "circling" feelings of simultaneous loss and triumph, feelings that blend into the dominant emotional tone of the poem's closing.

(iv) *Conservative or traditionalist*

This category is of course entirely applicable to a poem that pleads so eloquently and unflaggingly for the heroic values of old Germania. Illustrations can be found in every part of the poem. Yet here we must immediately add an important qualification, for complications arise when, as in *Beowulf,* the tradition celebrated is neither single nor unalloyed. In the poem a story of pre-Christian times and heroes is being told to a Christian audience, and clearly being adapted for it. The potential at least exists for a truly serious clash of incompatible traditions. Under such circumstances, the *Beowulf*-poet appears to avoid such a clash by tingeing his Germanic values with just the right amount of "Christian coloring" so that his audience can view the old values as venerable, and universal, and at the same time acceptable to modern Anglo-Saxon Christians.

But such modification must have somehow affected the nature of the transmitted tradition. We may at least surmise that such a Christian tincture put the pagan ethic off at some distance, made it seem a little outmoded, and created, in short, what we might call the Malory effect, in reference to a common way of defining the emotional atmosphere, reverent and nostalgic but always distanced, of the post-chivalric *Morte D'Arthur.* But these are in the end mere guesses, so long as we know so little about the very mixed culture in which *Beowulf* must have originated.

(v) *Close to the human life-world*

In describing this category, Ong mainly focuses on the absence from oral poetry of such alienating literate abstractions as documents or lists. The point is not easy to illustrate, but perhaps one could compare the text of the poem with the text of its editors' commentaries, in cases where the editors are essentially rewriting the poem in more familiar terms.

During Part II of the poem, from line 2200 to the end, the narrator recounts a number of incidents of Geatish and Swedish history, using them as flashbacks to fill in the fifty years or so that have elapsed between Beowulf's return from Denmark to his kingdom and his death in the dragon-fight. These historical incidents are consistently presented in typical "oral" form. They appear as discrete and self-contained narrative units or anecdotes, but never as lists of events or progressive chronologies. Each incident is invariably coupled with vivid action and is strongly personalized. We cannot separate the name Ongentheow from the story of his grim and valorous death-struggle, or think of young Heardred without recalling the generous and misguided hospitality toward Swedish exiles that led to his early death. These stories of the past are memorable for the strong emotions they evoke. They are firmly embedded in the "human lifeworld" in this special sense. No attempt is made to put them in any rational chronological order or to see them as historical background, in our present way of thinking. The story of Hygelac's death in the continental raid and Beowulf's revenge and later escape—obviously an important one—is indeed told again and again, reshaped each time to fit a different context.[40]

Page xxxviii of Klaeber's introduction to his classic edition of the poem shows us visually how the literate mind tends to see this same material: precisely in the form of "documents and lists." We find there a large chart or diagram laid out for our patient study, with the incidents in question organized by time-sequence and genealogy. The historical material is now actually quantified and measured by the addition of some entirely imaginary numbers, hypothetical dates suggested by Klaeber to help us keep events in the correct order. The chart precedes several densely detailed pages retelling the events methodically, but now in their proper historical sequence.

It is unfair to sound sarcastic at Klaeber's expense. What scholar has not found this kind of help badly needed in his or her attempt to make sense of the poem? After all, we must painfully puzzle out obscure and confusing allusions to material that the original audience must have been far more familiar with than we can ever be, and they would have been perfectly used to the poet's way of presenting these events. But I think Klaeber's systematic rearrangement implies his silent criticism of the poet's untidy and illogical habits. Klaeber is not so silent elsewhere on such matters, most notably in the often-quoted unfavorable comment he makes on the poet's technique in the account of the fight with Grendel:

> Partly excellent, vigorous narrative—yet the story is very much interrupted by interspersed general reflections on the situa-

tion and by remarks on the persons' thoughts and emotions, which greatly lengthen it and detract from its effectiveness.[41]

Most would now take these remarks as evidence that he judges the poem by inapplicable standards.

Yet neither Klaeber nor anyone else at the time he wrote his comments had any standard available to apply that measured the poet's achievement more nearly in its own terms. We can see now that in Part II the poet knew exactly what he wanted to do. He presents a vivid narrative in the present foreground, alive with the tension of the dragon-fight and totally focused on the final glory and death of his hero, but he mingles this present with many abrupt flashbacks to the past, inserted at just those points where they are most directly relevant to the narrative taking place in the fictional present. This is psychologically and emotionally realistic. In times of stress and crisis we may remember a series of key scenes from our own pasts in the order of their emotional importance to us and their relation to our feelings of the moment, certainly not in the temporal sequence in which they originally happened. How the *Beowulf*-poet interweaves past and present will be examined in more detail in later chapters.

(vi) *Agonistically toned*

In addition to offering a general definition of this term, under this heading Ong refers specifically to the flyting or wit-combat between Beowulf and Unferth, an extension of violence into the area of language. He also includes here, as generally typical of oral poetry, the "enthusiastic description of physical violence" and the pervading tendency to polarize attitudes, qualities, and relationships into exaggeratedly binary patterns: good/evil, light/dark, adulation/invective. Such polarization has long been noted in *Beowulf*.[42] Large-scale polarities such as Virtuous Hero/Destructive Monster make up the poem's very plot, and on the small scale the binary or adversative style is habitual and ingrained.[43]

There is a problem here for us. Modern readers resist the reduction of issues and relationships into simple conflicts and melodramatic contrasts. One area where we may especially resist such reduction is the conversion of complex problems of war and peace into agonistic form. Many of us criticize our current political leaders for just such simplification. Their appeals to patriotism and belligerence may seem a deplorable regression to an earlier stage of delight in carnage and barbaric violence. Thus we may find it hard not to over-respond enthusiastically to the *Beowulf*-poet's detached and tragic emphasis on the wanton destructiveness of warfare and feud, because such a view corresponds so closely with our own feelings. But *Beowulf* is obviously the product of a violent and barbaric age. We must refrain from the temptation to use words like pacifism to describe the poet's guarded and compassionate attitude toward killing, lest we indulge in polarizing on our own account.

It is however true that barbarism is somewhat modified in the poem. At least we may be persuaded, as I remarked earlier, that the Christian intermixture has led to some detectable softening of the older starkly heroic values and virtues. Some may feel that they detect an implied criticism of traditional pagan savagery.[44] But, whatever the effect of the intermixture, the poet shows no sign of repressing his natural and bloodthirsty joy at the often brutal action during the hero's fights with the monsters, and it is clear that he expects his audiences to share that joy. But, as has often been noticed, he has held descriptions of ordinary human warfare to a remarkable minimum; has not involved his hero deeply in such warfare at any point (though one can easily imagine opportunities for him to do so); and has tended to shift the focus toward the losers and the victims in such conflicts rather than toward the exultant victors. Some of the older *Germanisten* voiced impatience at his tameness in avoiding accounts of violent action.[45]

Whether Christianity in fact brought a softening of the attitude toward violence could indeed be argued either way. One could invoke the analogy of the Icelandic *Njal's Saga,* where the conversion of Iceland to Christianity at the story's midpoint seems to cast a new and unflattering light on the turbulent and murderous heroics of the endless vendettas. But it is possible that we read this shift of tone into the saga because we want to see it. The example of *The Song of Roland* should remind us that Christianity does not invariably bring a lessening of the lust for violence. On the other hand, Christianity has nothing to do with the balanced and often intensely tragic view of war that we find in the *Iliad.*[46] Indeed what Homer appears to show us is that such a view can make itself evident in the poetry of any warrior society, whenever a thoughtful poet lifts his eyes above the mindless butchery admired by a patron class of aristocrats.

In *Beowulf* there is at least one place where a modern attitude may noticeably distort the meaning of the story, and that is the Finn

Episode. By lucky chance another version of this story has come down to us, the fragmentary *Fight at Finnsburg*.[47] Its survival provides us with a rare and hence valuable control that lets us define more sensitively the tone the poet of *Beowulf* adopts. Because this is so, the contrast in tones between the two works has sometimes been exaggerated. Readers have found, or perhaps have fabricated, a significant difference between the unthinking and headlong battle-fury so marvellously evoked in the *Fragment* and the apparent suppression in *Beowulf* of any explicit representation of such exciting action in favor of a more reflective and multi-dimensional version of the story.

Two scenes in *Beowulf*, for example, describe the passive sufferer Queen Hildeburh, who has close kin-ties on both sides of the feud between Frisians and Danes, and hence has no obvious stake in anyone's victory. She is seen first lamenting the deaths of her brother on one side and her son on the other, and then seen later placing their bodies on a joint funeral-pyre during the truce, watching the greedy flames devour the dead of both warring parties. The poet undoubtedly is using her as a device to give expression to the catastrophic effect of feud-violence on bystanders and non-combatants. A woman, the *geatisc meowle* (3150), is used for the same purpose in the lament in anticipation of future suffering that forms part of Beowulf's funeral at the end of the poem. Certainly it would be inappropriate, perhaps even impossible within the constraints of traditional social and sexual patterning, to show a man registering such emotions, unless under very special conditions where, for instance, similar feelings are voiced by the essentially helpless and thus "feminized" old man Hrothgar (473–88) or the totally incapacitated and moribund Last Survivor in Part II (2236b–70a).

While Hildeburh makes a strong impression as tragic sufferer, the more problematic character in the Episode is Hengest, who is forced by unusual circumstances to accept an agreement whereby he swears allegiance to Finn, the man who killed Hengest's own king. We have in him a man who is temporarily prevented from taking the revenge he wants and his society requires. The first modern reader to draw an analogy between Hengest and Hamlet in this situation is probably already lost back in the mists of time, but in the oral tradition of talking about *Beowulf* I have encountered others. Perhaps we make this analogy because we want very much to see a conflict in Hengest. We want him to be the sort of divided character we are used to and can best understand and admire. We want to see him as a loyal but nonetheless compassionate

and thoughtful man who has watched Hildeburh grieving at the
pyre and who wishes for no more killing—yet is inexorably forced
to kill by the urgings of others. At last Hengest, this rogue and
peasant slave, does kill, whether reluctantly or not, breaking his sol-
emn treaty-oath and leading the Danes in the extermination of
Finn and his Frisians and the looting of their hall.

Is there in fact anything in this story that can really justify our
reading it in terms of an internal conflict in Hengest's soul? Can we
reconstruct the way the original audience, and the fictional audience in the poem for that matter, regarded this tale? Within the
story-world of Denmark, certainly the tale of Finnsburg forms an
integral part of the friendship and fellowship, the glee and games,
at the banquet held to celebrate Beowulf's victory over Grendel.
Such a happy context of entertainment and enjoyment is suggested
by words like *gomenwudu* (1065), *healgamen* (1066), *gamen* (1160),
gleomannes gyd (1160), and *beorhtode bencsweg* 'the bench-sound
brightened' (1161). What game and glee did the fictional audience
find in this story? Probably they enjoyed hearing of treacherous behavior, dilemmas of shared rule and delayed vengeance, pleasantly
mournful sentiments of bereavement rather condescendingly rele-
gated to a woman—but above all they must have enjoyed the glorious outbreak of releasing *action* after all these things were over. So
too possibly, if there is any truth to the scholars' fantasies about audiences in the Globe Theater, it was not only the ignorant groundlings
who especially enjoyed the last act of *Hamlet,* not for its cosmic
meanings but relishing the bloody achievement of long-deferred
revenge. In both stories, it is treachery that fully justifies the hero's
violent reprisal. In the Finn tale, it was probably treachery (a night
attack?) that first killed Hengest's king Hnæf, and, if so, it would
then seem fair enough that more treachery would be required in
order to gain revenge. Hengest would not be blamed for breaking
his oath. He is not suffering serious internal conflict, but pretends
to abide by his oath until he has collected strength or else found the
right moment for a sudden assault (the exact details of the action
are notoriously unclear in the Finn Episode). We might say that
Hamlet behaved much the same way if we could for once see him in
his original guise as hero of a Germanic revenge-saga, rather than
through the mists of romantic interpretation (much of it added by
Shakespeare, more by his interpreters).

In the Finn story, Hildeburh's deep and tragic grief and Hengest's
enthusiastic though delayed revenge are both real, but their feelings seem to exist in separate worlds without making contact.

Perhaps our error is to try to combine them into one world of sensibility. Their feelings are paratactic narrative units, happening "meanwhile" in two different emotional locales, each unit perfectly appropriate in itself and for itself. We not only want to unify the Episode, we are also moved by the urge to extract from it as a whole a didactic lesson congenial to what we think the poet ought to mean, which is to say a lesson congenial to our own time.

Feeling such urges myself, in *Introduction of Beowulf* I once suggested a bitter irony in the Episode's ending, where the gloating Danes escort Hildeburh back to "her people" after they have completed the elimination of her family by killing her husband Finn.[48] I implied that the Episode carried a pacifist lesson for the Anglo-Saxon audience, though it was one foolishly ignored by the Danish audience inside the poem, since they seemed to have hurrahed noisily over the great Danish victory. But that was to overstep the bounds of permissible interpretation. Probably the original audience was conscious of no such irony and no such message.

But I think they were quite aware of another kind of irony, one inherent in the similarities in situation between Hildeburh in the past and Queen Wealhtheow in the narrative present, when she is seen immediately after the telling of the Finn story pleading for future peace and harmony in the Danish royal family. It is likely that Wealhtheow will have no more reason than Hildeburh to put faith in men's promises to maintain peace and harmony. Yet in the end all such guesses about how an early audience responded to so complex and densely-styled a tale as that of Finnsburh should remain clearly ticketed as guesses. What we can do is try to correct our own most biased responses when, in a glass darkly, we are able to glimpse them.

One final instance will support this point. It is not easy for us to recognize and imitate in our response the strange combination of cool objectivity and heady passion with which the battle of Ravenswood is described by the Messenger in one of the poem's great moments. Probably we have trouble here with the same kind of parataxis we have been observing. Full credit is given to the old Swedish king Ongentheow for his courage and ferocity in avenging his wrongs and defending his life. Full credit is given to the young Geats Eofor and Wulf who overcome him in a difficult fight. If the fight seems unfair, that fact only enhances the old man's glory without diminishing the young men's. But, almost obsessively, modern readers try to moralize the song in ways probably unthought-of by the poet. There are many things we ought not to be concerned

with: whether such fighting is generically condemned as evil violence; whether the Geats brought it all upon themselves in reckless
fashion; whether it is "wicked" of the Swedes to want to avenge
their gallant old king in later years; whether it is "wrong" of the
Geats to want to resist the anticipated attack with all their powers.

The battle happens. Ravenswood is a fiery emblem of past and
future feud-violence, seen as a given reality, and not subjected to
moral judgments or political analysis or to those feelings of despair
or pride or loss that may occur elsewhere, and not too far away, in
this poem. But there is no elsewhere while the battle goes on, in its
time-bound space. We are immersed in an experience that transcends time, just as Hengest was immersed in the urgencies of a
dilemma conceived as separable from the strongly felt misery of
Hildeburh, even though we see both characters as parts of the same
story. But this is not to say that we are not deeply moved by the
juxtaposing of the two characters, and perhaps in complicated
ways. Life itself is paratactic.

(vii) *Empathetic rather than objectively distanced*

This criterion of oral poetry, already touched on under other
headings, has much to do with the question we have just been ex-
amining in connection with Ravenswood. Some degree of objective
distancing does seem to occur in *Beowulf*, though it is not likely to
be explicitly stated or defined. It is rather simply the result, as we
have been saying, of the paratactic style. We are drawn into close
identification with Hengest and Hildeburh separately; we share the
feelings of both combatants, Swedes and Geats, at Ravenswood.
Such objectivity is achieved silently; it happens within the minds of
members of the audience. Simple and strong forms of empathy are
used together to build a more complex combination of meaning.

Since Ong's discussion limits itself to the simpler aspects of oral
poetry, he makes no attempt to add to our understanding of the
more sophisticated and evocative judgment on human experience
that *Beowulf* provides. Much of the remainder of this book will be
concerned with exploring the expanded poetic capacities of an unusually gifted creator working in the oral tradition.

(viii) *Homeostatic*

Ong uses this term to describe how oral works exist in a con-
tinually updated present, with a stabilized style, and to show how

they are adjustable to taking into account, among other new factors, such demands as the varying wishes of patrons and audiences. Here we are of course quite at a loss to make any connections with *Beowulf*, because we know so little about its background. We have no earlier or later variant versions of the text that might enable us to gauge the extent of updating. We know nothing for certain about the poem's audiences, although Dorothy Whitelock has done some well-informed guessing on that subject.[49] If the poem ever had patrons, we know nothing of them.

(ix) *Situational rather than abstract*

This phrase (perhaps referring indirectly to "situation ethics") is certainly applicable to *Beowulf*, as we have already seen. No poem showing so many features of orality is likely to be hospitable to the imposing on it of abstract theological principles, nor is it likely to obey intellectual rules of logic or causality. Ong points out that oral folk "cannot organize elaborate concatenations of causes in the analytic kind of linear sequences that can only be set up with the help of texts."[50]

In the conclusion of his chapter entitled "Some psychodynamics of orality," from which the nine characteristics discussed above were taken, Ong describes the ways in which sound creates in us a sense of immersion and harmony.

The centering action of sound (the field of sound is not spread out before me but is all around me) affects man's sense of the cosmos. For oral cultures, the cosmos is an ongoing event with man at its center. Man is the *umbilicus mundi*, the navel of the world.[51]

In an oral world without maps or other kinds of visualization, we *hear* about other more remote lands, times, nations, or individuals, all in oral reports brought in to this center. This exactly describes the atmosphere of *Beowulf*, an atmosphere established by the *we gefrunon* 'we have heard about' of its opening lines. In such a culture, the single goal of the hero is to ensure that he is heard about and spoken of, during life and after death. The immortality such a society grants him is to be widely known (*widcuþ*) and to acquire *kudos, fama, dom*. The quality of this reputation is essential. Like

Roland, he must always be concerned that no *malvaise cancun* be sung about him, after his departure into the world of eternal silence, out of this intensely oral world.

NOTES

1. A compendious chronological survey of research in this field is John Miles Foley's introduction to his edition of *Oral Traditional Literature: A Festschrift for Albert Bates Lord* (Columbus, OH: Slavica Publishers, 1981); see also his more recent publication, *Oral-Formulaic Theory and Research: An Introduction and Annotated Bibliography* (New York: Garland Publishing, 1985). A bibliography specifically for Old English is Alexandra Hennessey Olsen, "Oral-Formulaic Research in Old English Studies: I," *Oral Tradition* I (1986), 548–606. I cite here only a few landmark works in this field. Milman Parry's chief essays of the twenties and thirties are assembled in *The Making of Homeric Verse: the Collected Papers of Milman Parry*, ed. Adam Parry (New York: Oxford University Press, 1971). Francis P. Magoun, Jr., first applied the theory to Old English verse specifically in "The Oral-Formulaic Character of Anglo-Saxon Narrative Poetry," *Speculum* 28 (1953), 446–67. The general thesis is stated in Albert B. Lord, *The Singer of Tales* (Cambridge, MA: Harvard University Press, 1960). See also John D. Niles, *Beowulf: The Poem and its Tradition* (Cambridge, MA: Harvard University Press, 1983), especially Chapter 2, "The Art of the Germanic Scop." The medieval transition from orality to literacy, together with some of its social and intellectual consequences (though he deals with a later period), is thoroughly discussed by Brian Stock, *The Implications of Literacy: Written Language and Models of Interpretation in the Eleventh and Twelfth Centuries* (Princeton, NJ: Princeton University Press, 1983).

2. Robertson's first important publication dealing with Old English is "The Doctrine of Charity in Medieval Literary Gardens: A Topical Approach through Symbolism and Allegory," *Speculum* 26 (1951), 24–49. His general approach is most fully exemplified in *A Preface to Chaucer* (Princeton, NJ: Princeton University Press, 1963). Four books emphasizing a similar allegorical approach to Old English poetry are Margaret E. Goldsmith, *The Mode and Meaning of Beowulf* (London: Athlone Press, 1970); Alvin A. Lee, *The Guest-Hall of Eden: Four Essays on the Design of Old English Poetry* (New Haven, CT: Yale University Press, 1972); W. F. Bolton, *Alcuin and Beowulf* (New Brunswick, NJ: Rutgers University Press, 1978); Bernard F. Huppé, *The Hero in the Earthly City: A Reading of Beowulf* (Medieval and Renaissance Texts and Studies, vol. 33, State University of New York at Binghamton, 1984).

3. One important shift in the direction of applying purely esthetic criteria to the poem was J. R. R. Tolkien's British Academy lecture of 1936, "Beowulf: The Monsters and the Critics," often reprinted, most recently in *The Monsters and the Critics and Other Essays*, ed. Christopher Tolkien

(Boston: Houghton Mifflin, 1983). Organic unity, invariably a key phrase of the New Criticism, is assiduously stressed in Adrien Bonjour, *The Digressions in 'Beowulf'*, Medium Ævum Monographs, 5 (Oxford: Oxford University Press, 1950); see also his *Twelve 'Beowulf' Papers: 1940–1960*, with Additional Comments (Neuchâtel, 1962). My own study, *A Reading of Beowulf* (New Haven, CT: Yale University Press, 1968), reflects this approach. A great body of criticism of this kind has appeared in the form of essays and articles.

4. A very late date, perhaps near the time of the surviving manuscript (c. 1000), has been argued for by Kevin S. Kiernan in *Beowulf and the Beowulf Manuscript* (New Brunswick, NJ: Rutgers University Press, 1981); see also the essays favoring a late date included in *The Dating of Beowulf*, ed. Colin Chase (Toronto: University of Toronto Press, 1981). Such arguments seem interesting speculative hypotheses rather than proofs in themselves. If the older scholarly assumption of an eighth-century date has been shown to be rather insecurely based (there was always a good deal of wishful thinking in that assumption), the late date has as yet been no more firmly established.

5. Lines 2220, 2227(?), 2271, 2273, 2278, 2296, 2304, 2305, 2314, 2315, 2318, 2414, 2560, 2670, 2688, 2691, 2699. Examples of hostile behavior not found in epithets are not included, however.

6. 2221, 2293, 2302, 2304, 2344, 2413, 2524, 2554, 2580, 2593, 2746, 2779, 2826, 2833, 2841, 3066, 3081, 3133.

7. 2212, 2213, 2232, 2241, 2276, 2279, 2322, 2410, 2411, 2415, 2553, 2712, 2825, 3046.

8. 2271, 2277, 2278, 2415, 2760, 2778.

9. 2315, 2346, 2528, 2760, 2830, 2832, 3043.

10. 2272, 2274, 2296, 2305, 2308, 2321, 2333, 2549, 2557, 2569, 2671, 2672, 2689, 2691, 3040.

11. See Brian Stock, *The Implications of Literacy*, for a penetrating study of this general question at a later period of the Middle Ages.

12. See Arthur G. Brodeur, *The Art of 'Beowulf'* (Berkeley and Los Angeles: University of California Press, 1959), for an instance of a literary critic struggling with some of the implications of the oral-formulaic theory as it was first presented to Old English scholars. Brodeur's chief aim is to demonstrate the originality (equivalent to creativity, in his judgment) of the *Beowulf*-poet's style and phrasing. A recent essay by a literary critic reflecting some of the same struggle is Peter Clemoes, "'Symbolic' Language in Old English Poetry," *Modes of Interpretation in Old English Literature: Essays in Honour of Stanley B. Greenfield*, ed. Phyllis Rugg Brown et al. (Toronto: University of Toronto Press, 1986), 3–14.

13. "The *Cantar de Mio Cid*: Problems of Interpretation," in *Oral Tradition in Literature: Interpretations in Context*, ed. John Miles Foley (Columbia: University of Missouri Press, 1986), 65–88. For the often cited reminder that, while Old English poetry is formulaic in appearance, some of it is certainly

by literate and even bookish poets, see Larry D. Benson, "The Literary Character of Anglo-Saxon Formulaic Poetry," *PMLA* 81 (1966), 334–41.

14. See, for example, Ann Chalmers Watts, *The Lyre and the Harp: A Comparative Reconsideration of Oral Tradition in Homer and Old English Epic Poetry*, Yale Studies in English, 169 (New Haven, CT: Yale University Press, 1969), a patient and detailed argument against making hasty analogies between Homeric and Old English meter and verse-form. A series of articles by Donald K. Fry, the first being "Old English Formulas and Systems," *English Studies* 48 (1967), 193–204, proposes concepts of formulas as "syntactic frames" that seem better adapted to the peculiarities of Old English. The newer concept of a "formulaic system" would, for instance, include as members of the same system (and I think correctly) verses like *hwæt we Gar-Dena, hu hit Hring-Dene*, and *to West-Denum;* an example of another set would be *in geardagum, samod ærdæge*, and *ne his lifdagas.* See also Chapter 5 of John D. Niles, *Beowulf: the Poem and its Tradition* (cited above).

15. See, for example, Ruth H. Finnegan, *Oral Poetry: Its Nature, Significance and Social Context* (Cambridge: Cambridge University Press, 1977); Dan Ben-Amos, "Folklore in African Society," *Review of African Literature* 6 (1975), 165–98; Isidore Okpewho, *The Epic in Africa: Toward a Poetics of the Oral Performance* (New York: Columbia University Press, 1979).

16. *Anglo-Saxon Oral Poetry: A Study of the Traditions* (New Haven, CT: Yale University Press, 1980). In the spring of 1988 on several occasions I was fortunate to have the chance to hear demonstrations of improvised poetry by David Manisi, a Xhosa poet, as well as lectures on his performances by Professor Opland.

17. A carved stone found in 1979 at Repton (in old Mercia) shows a rider brandishing a sword and wearing a short sword or *seax.* The broad *seax* (used by both Grendel's mother and Beowulf in the poem) seems to have been a weapon popular in eighth- and ninth-century England. The archeologists who supervised the Repton excavations remark: "As combat on horseback with sword and lance became less intimate, so the role of the *seax* declined. If one prefers the view that *Beowulf* is an eighth-century (perhaps Mercian?) work, the correspondence of Beowulf's weapon-set to the arms of the Repton rider is of more than passing interest" (Martin Biddle and Birthe Kjølbye-Biddle, "The Repton Stone," *Anglo-Saxon England* 14 [1985], 282). They speculate that the rider pictured might be Æthelbald, king of Mercia and Offa's predecessor.

18. Asser's Life of Alfred, chs. 22–23. Most easily accessible in the recent translation by Simon Keynes and Michael Lapidge, *Alfred the Great* (Harmondsworth, UK: Penguin, 1983).

19. The circularity of this approach was well described long ago in an essay by R. S. Crane, "On Hypotheses in "Historical Criticism": Apropos of Certain Contemporary Medievalists," *The Idea of the Humanities and Other Essays Critical and Historical*, 2 vols., (Chicago and London: University of Chicago Press, 1976), II, 236–60. Although exegetical criticism continues

to appear up to the present writing, most recent works show little interest in it. Examples are to be found in the following works of the last decade: the full commentary in Howell D. Chickering's dual-language edition of the poem (Garden City, NY: Anchor, 1977); T.A. Shippey, *Beowulf*, Studies in English Literature No. 70, general ed. David Daiches (London: Edward Arnold Ltd., 1978); John D. Niles, *Beowulf: The Poem and its Tradition* (cited above); Fred C. Robinson, *Beowulf and the Appositive Style* (Knoxville: University of Tennessee Press, 1985); Stanley B. Greenfield and Daniel G. Calder, *A New Critical History of Old English Literature* (New York and London: New York University Press, 1986).

20. Alvin A. Lee, *The Guest Hall of Eden: Four Essays on the Design of Old English Poetry* (cited above).

21. Lee, 181.

22. Lee, 192.

23. See such passages as 381b–84a; 625–28a; 696b–700a; 928–31; 939b–46a; 1270–74a; 1841–43.

24. Lee, 182.

25. See my discussion in "The Nature of Christianity in *Beowulf*," *Anglo-Saxon England* 13 (1984), 7–21.

26. Lee, 187.

27. For what now seems somewhat too strained an effort to fit this passage into a larger context, see my "Beowulf Comes Home," in *Acts of Interpretation: Essays . . . in Honor of E. Talbot Donaldson*, ed. Mary J. Carruthers and Elizabeth D. Kirk (Norman, OK: Pilgrim Books, 1982), 129–43.

28. Niles, *Beowulf: the Poem and its Tradition*, 169.

29. T. A. Shippey, *Beowulf*, 35. His discussion of irony in the poem is thoughtful and balanced.

30. Niles, 201.

31. Thomas E. Hart has written several articles on this topic, including "Tectonic Design, Formulaic Craft, and Literary Execution: The Episodes of Finn and Ingeld in *Beowulf*," *Amsterdamer Beiträge zur älteren Germanistik* 2 (1972), 1–61, and "Tectonic Methodology and an Application to *Beowulf*," in *Essays in the Numerical Criticism of Medieval Literature*, ed. Caroline D. Eckhardt (London and Lewisburg, PA: Bucknell University Press, 1980), 185–210.

32. Bernard F. Huppé, *The Hero in the Earthly City: A Reading of Beowulf*, 61–96.

33. See the discussion by Fr. Klaeber, *Beowulf and the Fight at Finnsburg* (3d ed., Boston: D. C. Heath, 1950). Klaeber concedes the inappropriateness of some of the divisions, but finally concludes: "Altogether there is too much method in the arrangement of 'fits' to regard it as merely a matter of chance or caprice" (p. ci). I can see neither method nor chance, only mystery, in the division of *Beowulf* into sections.

34. *Orality and Literacy: The Technologizing of the Word* (London and New York: Methuen, 1982).

35. The quotations from *Beowulf* here and throughout are taken from *Beowulf and Judith*, ed. E. V. K. Dobbie, vol. IV of the Anglo-Saxon Poetic Records (New York: Columbia University Press, 1953). Fred C. Robinson in *Beowulf and the Appositive Style* (Knoxville: University of Tennessee Press, 1985) discusses many of these variations and appositions, though consistently from a somewhat different viewpoint.

36. For a study from a different point of view of the various epithets applied to Grendel, see Katherine O'Brien O'Keeffe, "Beowulf, Lines 702b–836: Transformations and the Limits of the Human," *Texas Studies in Literature and Language* 23 (1981), 484–94.

37. Margaret E. Goldsmith, *The Mode and Meaning of Beowulf* (London: Athlone Press, 1970).

38. Harry Berger, Jr., and H. Marshall Leicester, Jr., "Social Structure as Doom: The Limits of Heroism in *Beowulf*," in *Old English Studies in Honour of John C. Pope*, ed. Robert B. Burlin and Edward B. Irving, Jr. (Toronto: University of Toronto Press, 1974), 37–79. Barbara C. Raw, *The Art and Background of Old English Poetry* (London: Edward Arnold, Ltd., 1978) also sees Beowulf's death as demonstrating "the failure of the principle enunciated at the beginning of the poem: that the result of courage and generosity is loyalty" (96). She sees the hero as a figure of the ideal never to be encountered in reality. Colin Chase finds serious contradiction in the confusion of a heroic military ethic with a more constructive ethic of sovereignty (*"Beowulf*, Bede, and St. Oswine: The Hero's Pride in Old English Hagiography," in *The Anglo-Saxons: Synthesis and Achievement,* ed. J. Douglas Woods and David A. E. Pelteret [Waterloo, Canada: Wilfred Laurier University Press, 1985], 37–48). See also Norma Kroll, *"Beowulf:* The Hero as Keeper of Human Polity," *Modern Philology* 84 (1986), 117–29, who applies a complex hypothesis of double selves to Beowulf in his relation to the monsters.

39. Ong, *Orality and Literacy*, 39–40.

40. The raid is described in 1202–14a; 2354b–66; 2501–08a; 2913b–21.

41. Klaeber, 154 (note to line 710). See also the discussion of the poem's "lack of steady advance" by E. G. Stanley, "The Narrative Art of *Beowulf*," *Medieval Narrative: A Symposium*, ed. Hans Bekker-Nielsen et al. (Odense, Denmark: Odense University Press, 1979), 58–81.

42. For example, by Herbert G. Wright, "Good and Evil: Light and Darkness: Joy and Sorrow in *Beowulf*," *Review of English Studies* n.s. 8 (1857), 1–11, reprinted in *An Anthology of Beowulf Criticism*, ed. Lewis E. Nicholson (Notre Dame, IN: University of Notre Dame Press, 1969). See also Betty S. Cox's chapter entitled "The Principle of Contrast," in *Cruces of Beowulf* (The Hague: Mouton, 1971), 33–55.

43. See Chapter I of my *A Reading of Beowulf* for a survey of many such strongly polarized adversative constructions.

44. For discussion of some of these issues, see Stanley J. Kahrl, "Feuds in *Beowulf*: A Tragic Necessity?," *Modern Philology* 69 (1972), 189–98; James

E. Cross, "The Ethic of War in Old English," in *England Before the Conquest: Studies in Primary Sources Presented to Dorothy Whitelock*, ed. Peter Clemoes and Kathleen Hughes (Cambridge: Cambridge University Press, 1971), 269–82; Eugene J. Crook, "Pagan Gold in *Beowulf*," *American Benedictine Review* 25 (1974), 218–34.

45. Scattered remarks by Klaeber reveal such disappointment. "The absence of battle challenge and defiance (see *Finnsb.* 24 ff.) is an obvious inherent defect of our poem" (lvi); "In the use of genuine heroic motives the main story of *Beowulf* is indeed inferior to the Finnsburg legend" (liiii); "We have every reason to be thankful for those episodes which . . . disclose a wealth of authentic heroic song and legend, a magnificent historic background. Still we may well regret that those subjects of intensely absorbing interest play only a minor part in our epic" (lv).

46. For a memorable analysis and interpretation of this tragic view, see Simone Weil, "L' *Iliade* ou le poème de la force," in *La source grecque* (Paris: Gallimard, 1953). This essay, first written in 1939–40, is now a classic pacifist tract published by the Quakers (*The Iliad or the Poem of Force*, tr. Mary McCarthy, Pendle Hill Pamphlets 91, Wallingford, PA, 1956).

47. Accessible in Klaeber's edition of *Beowulf*, and separately edited by Donald K. Fry, *Finnsburh: Fragment and Episode* (London: Methuen, 1974).

48. *Introduction of Beowulf* (Englewood Cliffs, NJ: Prentice-Hall, 1969), 54; see also *A Reading of Beowulf*, 134–37.

49. *The Audience of Beowulf* (Oxford: The Clarendon Press, 1951).

50. Ong, *Orality and Literacy*, 57.

51. Ong, 73.

T W O

Characters and Kings

In this chapter I will examine some forms of characterization in oral-derived poetry. Although medievalists are perfectly familiar with flat type-characters of the kind we find in *Beowulf*, such characters may present some problem to readers more accustomed to the subtleties of characterization in later literature. Traditional types—the venerable and wise old king, the intensely suffering woman, the hero oddly and remotely wrapped in his sacred violence, the ravening monster from hell, the "twisted" young king unceremoniously pitched headlong off Fortune's Wheel—these types can seem childishly simple. Exactly: they are indeed the archetypal folk characters of our fairy-tales. Yet very often, as I suggested in the previous chapter, present-day readers try to mitigate their disappointment at such primitive stuff by searching for more interesting ironic wrinkles behind those age-polished smooth facades.

The oral-derived language of *Beowulf* is in fact capable of making characters interestingly complex in something of that sense, but it may manage to do this in unfamiliar and oblique ways. Even if it could not do this we should nonetheless reject the assumption—if anyone still holds it—that "rounded" characters are essential for good literature. We need only note that *Everyman* and *King Lear* are two successful and powerful plays where more complex characterization would only diminish the impact of the universalized and mythic story. In this respect they may illustrate the special closeness of such drama to "story-oriented" literature in the oral tradition.

Let us first consider the case of Unferth, a character who has constantly been made more interesting than he really is, obsessively rounded by the critics into more complex and pleasing shapes. In large part critics do this as a way of solving the major problem with Unferth. We have serious trouble discovering a way to make the different aspects of his behavior consistent with each other. So far there does not seem to be much agreement on a common solution.[1] At the time when I wrote *A Reading of Beowulf*, I was unable to make up my mind about him and could only point vaguely at some then current views.[2]

In so puzzling a case, the temptation to seek useful analogues outside the poem is especially strong, and perfectly legitimate. If Unferth really is a traditional type-character in medieval literature, then variants of the basic type should help us find the proper category for him. Some classifications that have been suggested would label Unferth as Evil Counsellor, or All-Licensed Fool, or Official Court Guest-Tester, or Tolerated Coward (like Sir Kay in some Arthurian tales), or Raw Youth (like the rustic Perceval), perhaps in need of the guidance of a seasoned warrior-mentor who will polish his manners and heighten his courage.[3] Yet Unferth seems to wander across the boundaries between these categories in a confusing way. He may be some new type unrecorded elsewhere, a combination of several types, or even no type at all but a new invention of the poet, though this last is unlikely.

It may well turn out that we cannot fully understand Unferth on the basis of the details provided inside the poem, but we ought to be sure first of all that we have made the most of what the poem itself offers, fitting the odd-shaped pieces together as gently and thoughtfully as possible, before subjecting them to often distorting pressures of other stories and other characters.

I shall try to center my argument by proceeding cautiously from stating what I feel the greatest confidence about toward testing those interpretations that seem increasingly unlikely as we move toward the periphery. The major stumbling block to critics, of course, has been the disparity between the fact, on the one hand, that Unferth is shown not only as failing the explicit test of heroism at the mere's edge (1465–71a) but as being sharply condemned by Beowulf (in the heat of the flyting, 581b–94) not only for cowardice but for having killed his own brothers, and the fact, on the other hand, that he evidently retains a place of honor at Hrothgar's court and generously lends Beowulf his sword, an act for which the hero warmly thanks him. In terms of the dominant heroic values of the poem, how can Unferth thus show himself to be both bad and good?

The inconsistency in the presentation of Unferth certainly exists, but I tend to think that it is not a separate problem but a part of the way the poet views the Danes, and especially the way he sees their king Hrothgar, a nation and a king both impotent and honorable, incompetent and magnificent. This point of view will be explored later in this chapter. I will say here only that I find it an easy first tentative step to see Unferth as not deserving any particular attention for his personal history but rather as being merely a typical Dane, indeed Everydane.

This is not a new approach to Unferth. I followed others when, in *A Reading of Beowulf*, I stressed Unferth's important role as a spokesman for the community of Danes.[4] Specifically I was interested in the way he seemed to vent the hitherto unexpressed resentment many Danish warriors must have been feeling at the intrusion of this brash young foreigner who claimed he could do what they could not. Beowulf's notable tact in his successive parleys with the Danes he met as he made his way to Heorot seemed to be evidence for his own awareness of this potential tension. The Danes must determine whether the Geat is nothing but a wandering showoff and braggart, coming *for dolgilpe* and *for wlenco*, out of foolish boastfulness and pride. If he is, it would be truly humiliating for them to betray their own desperate need for help by treating such a heroic charlatan with respect. Thus, even if Beowulf's very well-chosen words had placated some of the Danes, it is likely that not all were ready to embrace the visitor. Unferth's sharp challenge of Beowulf may thus dramatically fill a psychological need for the Danes as a whole. At the least, taking Unferth as the spokesman for many Danes obviates any necessity to explain why they show no disapproval of his challenge to Beowulf.

In fact, it seems most natural and a fair use of Occam's invaluable razor simply to see Unferth as one of those unsuccessful Danish warriors Hrothgar has just described.

Ful oft gebeotedon   beore druncne
ofer ealowæge   oretmecgas
þæt hie in beorsele   bidan woldon
Grendles guþe   mid gryrum ecga.
Ðonne wæs þeos medoheal   on morgentid,
drihtsele dreorfah,   þonne dæg lixte,
eal bencþelu   blode bestymed,
heall heorudreore;   ahte ic holdra þy læs,
deorre duguðe,   þe þa deað fornam.   (480–88)

(Very often warriors drunken with beer boasted over the ale-cup that in the beer-hàll they intended to wait for Grendel's attack with the terror of their swords. Then in the morning this mead-hall, home of fellowship, was stained red when day shone

on it, the whole bench-floor soaked in blood, the hall with
sword-gore; I had the fewer loyal men, beloved followers, when
death took them off.)

There is of course the quite important difference that, unlike these
unfortunates, Unferth does not stay around in the hall long enough
to be killed by Grendel. But seeing him as one of these boasters
over the ale-cup would explain later references to Unferth as a
braggart. We should remember that we do not ever hear Unferth
bragging, though the poet tells us (499–505) that Unferth dislikes
hearing any warrior praised as being any better than he is, an attitude consistent with being a braggart. But his only speech, the challenge to Beowulf, is no brag. There Unferth makes the charge that
it is Beowulf who is an empty braggart with a low heroic credit
rating, whereas Breca, Beowulf's competitor in the swimming-race,
is not. Later, when Unferth gives the sword Hrunting to Beowulf
to use in the mere-fight, the poet tells us that the Dane does not
remember what he had said when he was drunk (1465–68a). What
must be referred to here is not the occasion of his attack on Beowulf
which we witnessed but some boast we never actually heard (but
can infer from Hrothgar's description just quoted), since the poet's
remark is immediately followed by the statement that Unferth himself did not dare to risk his own life in the mere. This is not a very
distinctive failure. Neither did any other Dane. In this, Unferth
once again seems merely representative. But only if he had been a
conspicuous braggart in the past would his behavior now be considered reprehensible or even noteworthy.

Though I have assumed that Unferth in the flyting may voice
some communal ill-temper quite unconsciously, it is conceivable
that the Danes have deliberately assigned Unferth to play this role
for them. They may at least have permitted him to play it, knowing
by experience that he was by nature the quickest to resentment of
them all and thus an ideal "delegate," to introduce a useful word
employed by Carol Clover in her study of similar challenge scenes
in Scandinavian literature.[5] This interpretation would also explain
why no one reproves him for his rudeness to a guest. But I hear
alarm bells ringing at this point, signalling that we have crossed
the border into the unprovable if not the untenable. We had better retreat to firmer ground, and not assume an official role for
Unferth here.

That the poet sees Unferth as representative Dane may, however, find some additional support elsewhere. It should be noted

that Beowulf himself takes Unferth's attack on him to be a Danish attack, one that requires a counterattack as much against the whole nation as against Unferth individually. In his reply (starting at 581b) he begins by addressing Unferth quite personally indeed, pointing out that, while he knows evidence that Unferth has killed his own brothers (a serious charge of fratricide later validated by the poet, 1167–68), and perhaps by treachery, if the phrase *þeah þin wit duge* 'though your wit is keen' (589) implies some clever plotting, there is even more sensational evidence, twelve whole years of it, that Unferth has not been giving Grendel any trouble whatsoever. But Beowulf then moves on at once to broaden the charge to include all Danes. *Eower leode* (596) is a plural really addressed over Unferth's head to the listening Danes, and it is followed by the plural terms *Sigescyldinga, leode Deniga, Gardenum*. None of these people, though they may not be brother-slayers, have ever given Grendel any trouble either. It will take a Geat to do that. Unferth is then a symbol of national rather than merely private inadequacy. The closing lines of Beowulf's reply modulate out of mockery and into reassurance. Here Unferth may well stand for the Everydane who, the hero promises, will be able to go happy and safe to his morning mead in Heorot next day, after Grendel has been taken out of the way.

Indeed, one more trait that Unferth may share with other Danes is a tendency to drunkenness.[6] As in *Hamlet*, heavy drinking in Denmark is not only endemic but symbolic. In the passage quoted above from Hrothgar's speech, note the heavy stress on drinking: *beore druncne, ofer ealowæge, in beorsele, þeos medoheal*. Probably also underlying the description is the ironic idea that blood rather than the usual spilled mead and beer now soaks the hall-floor. A poet working in the oral tradition, by amassing and focusing a particular selection of his interchangeable parts, can suggest a physical and moral atmosphere almost without our being conscious of it. The Danes here are associated directly with Unferth, called *beore druncen* by Beowulf (531). Even more striking are the massed references to drinking in the later scene dominated by Wealhtheow: see lines 1015, 1025, 1161, 1169, 1192, 1231, 1233, and 1240.

Sober, Unferth might not have bearded Beowulf at all, as the hero gently suggests. Sober, Danish warriors might not have dared to face Grendel on suicide missions. Perhaps, cold sober, they might not have gone to sleep so peacefully in their hall the very night after Grendel's defeat, but the *druncne dryhtguman* (1231) so vehemently harangued by their cup-plying queen seem oblivious to any threats from within (she has been reminding them of those) or from without. Even the doomed Æschere is oddly described as *beorscealca sum* (1240) 'an important beer-warrior'. Only the general atmosphere of drinking seems to account for this compound.

If the Danes seem to drink heavily, that may reflect not so much deterioration of character as the same desperate state of mind that led them to resort to worship at pagan shrines. They are unable to cope with the attacks of Grendel. Is it fair to blame them for that? In lines 980–990, we see Unferth staring intently at Grendel's arm and claw hung up in the hall, at those fingernails like steel, impervious to swords. Unferth is then "a more silent man," but the other Danes too must fully share his conviction that none of their swords could ever have harmed that ghastly limb. They are right, of course. Common prudence should have kept them from risking their lives against Grendel, as it kept Unferth from doing so. The trouble is that common prudence is not a heroic virtue. It is a quality that belongs to Oliver, not to Roland. By behaving prudently, Unferth and the Danes have passed up the chance to star as heroes of their own epic tale. Yet, to be fair again, we should recall that Oliver was always accepted as the finest of comrades by the heroic Roland. We cannot all be imprudent.

But before we speak further of comradeship, we must deal with Beowulf's devastating assertion that Unferth will be damned for killing his brothers. The remark is made in the context of a Germanic flyting or word-battle. Unferth's challenge follows close on a long boasting speech by Beowulf (407–55) and Hrothgar's description of the failure of the Danish hall-boasters to survive their encounters with Grendel. This combination of speeches sets up a testing situation. If the Danes' many boasts about defeating Grendel could never be carried out, and if Beowulf's boast about beating Breca in the swimming-contest could never be carried out, why then should anyone expect that the hero's present boast offers any promise of fulfillment? Such is the gist of Unferth's speech, but its tone is even more important. It is full of the taunting terms of hot heroic competitiveness: *wunne* 'struggled'; *ymb sund flite* 'competed in swimming'; *he þe æt sunde oferflat* 'he beat you at swimming'; *hæfde mare mægen* 'he had greater strength'. All this language is couched to stir the quick anger of any proud and touchy rival.

It does stir Beowulf's anger, quite naturally. Even though his reply starts off mildly enough with an alternative version of the swim with Breca that greatly plays down its importance as real competition and tries to present it as boyish exuberance, it concludes

flamboyantly in the true spirit of flyting aggressiveness with the jar-
ring charge of fratricide landed squarely on target (*there's one for
you!*), and the charge is given special moral emphasis by the prediction of damnation for the crime.[7] So extraordinary a Christian reference may seem inappropriate for one pagan addressing another,
but I think the poet merely wants Beowulf's counterpunch to be as
crushing as possible and thus chooses to echo the terms of savage
anathema his Christian audience would know best. Similar language is later used (and modern readers may bring a similar charge
of inappropriateness to it) in the description of the old pagan curse
on the dragon's treasure (3069–73).

Yet fratricide seems to mean something much less heinous in a
different context in the poem. When Unferth's kin-killing past is
later mentioned by the poet himself, it is apparently in a tone of
tolerant acceptance.

> Swylce þær Unferð þyle
> æt fotum sæt frean Scyldinga;   gehwylc hiora his ferhþe treowde,
> þæt he hæfde mod micel,   þeah þe he his magum nære
> arfæst æt ecga gelacum.   (1165b–68a)

(Also Unferth the *thyle* sat there at the feet of the lord of the
Scyldings; each of them [I take this to mean each of the Danes
present, not just Hrothgar and his nephew Hrothulf] had faith
in his [Unferth's] mind, that he had great courage, though he
was not honorable to his kinsmen in the sword-play.)

Even though brother-slaying can be viewed as a terrible crime, as
it certainly is by Beowulf when he wants to be accusatory, it can also
be mentioned rather neutrally and casually, as I think is done here.
Unferth's virtue of great courage or spirit is in the main clause, and
he is granted amnesty for fratricide in the subordinate clause. Critics have not generally accepted this particular subordination of
importance, but I see no reason not to take this passage as straightforward and without any bitter irony, even though the poet himself
may be more critical of Unferth's murderous past than the Danes
seem to be. But this does not mean that the text here contains a
patronizing allusion to the Danes' lamentable and inexplicable
blindness to Unferth's real and rotten nature; it merely shows that
they are not presently engaged in a flyting with him. A flyting
would be the appropriate occasion to dredge up and bring forth
such bits of past scandal, but the duration of a flyting is limited and
time-bound. In a famous scene in *Njal's Saga*, eminent and respect-

able Icelanders at the Althing are reminded of similar scandals and crimes in their pasts by the acid-tongued Skarp-Hethinn, but they seem to reassume their old dignity and respectability after he has passed by, and the cupboard doors are shut once again on such skeletons.[8]

Nor does this passage offer safe grounds for the conjecture so often made that Unferth is involved in future treachery connected with the usurping nephew Hrothulf, in which presumed treachery Unferth will play the type-role of evil counsellor. The only faint evidence the poem itself offers is that Unferth is mentioned after Hrothgar and Hrothulf. In the scene that follows, Wealhtheow is certainly anxious about some threat involving her sons and Hrothulf. She pleads with Hrothulf to protect her children. But if she were also suspicious of Unferth she would probably say so, since that is the normal way in which things are brought to the audience's attention in the oral tradition. Is it not possible here to distinguish baby from bathwater? The real live baby is the threat of some plot by Hrothulf, but let us allow Unferth-Wormtongue, the fictional evil counsellor, to go safely down the drain into oblivion.

vs. idea that Unferth is treacherous

The flyting ends after a brief aftermath. We first hear hearty applause from Hrothgar who is pleased at Beowulf's display of "resolute thought," as is his grateful wife a moment later when she brings Beowulf the cup. Later, after Grendel has been defeated and his hand hung up in Heorot for inspection, we have the brief scene where Unferth looks at it and becomes a "more silent man." His silence here is nothing less than a statement that brings the flyting to a definite end. Together with the evidence of Grendel's hand—in its way an even more powerful statement—the silence acknowledges the inescapable truth: Beowulf achieved what he promised he would try to do. The verdict is plain: the charge Unferth brought has been shown to be untrue.

Yet, though Unferth is thoroughly beaten in the flyting and proved to be inferior to Beowulf in heroic achievement, he does not seem to be especially humiliated in this scene, partly because the poet's eye is, as always, on Beowulf's greatness and partly because Unferth as a Dane must accept the evidence that only a near-supernatural hero could have made any mark on Grendel. The Danes would much rather have saved their own great hall themselves but plainly they could not. So now they cheerfully set to work restoring Heorot to order (991 ff.), and, though nothing is said about it, one would not be entirely surprised to hear that Unferth was turning to and joining in the task.

If then we see the argument between Unferth and Beowulf as coming to a full stop here, it seems most unlikely that Unferth's later loan of a sword to Beowulf for the fight with Grendel's mother is to be construed as a reopening of hostilities, or as a malicious act reflecting ill-feeling and resentment. It has been surmised that Unferth might know Hrunting to be a defective weapon.[9] But the context argues most powerfully against any such assumption.

First of all, there is clearly a political situation to consider. The Danes are by now even more deeply involved in the operation against the Grendel-race than they were earlier. Grendel's mother has killed the Danish leader Æschere, Hrothgar's special friend from childhood; those previously killed were never given such particular identity. Hrothgar has adopted or coopted Beowulf into the new pseudo-Danish role of son and hall-guardian. The Danes, who had abandoned the hall to Beowulf before the first fight, have now themselves traveled across dangerous terrain and come up to the mere's edge in their most aggressive movement of the poem. Pursuing the monster has become an active Danish operation, rather than a passive enduring of assaults. Why may not all this be the reason that Unferth, as always playing some semi-official role as Danish representative, offers the new "Danish" champion Beowulf a venerable Danish sword, almost certainly the best one they have, to use in this fight?

Furthermore, what immediately precedes Unferth's offer of the sword is the account (1441b–54) of how Beowulf elaborately arms himself with a well-made mailshirt and helmet preparatory to diving into the mere. What Unferth then lends him is called "not the least of mighty helps" (1455) and forms one additional item in the same series of armaments. I find it quite impossible to believe that this kind of poet would secretly slip a defective weapon into a sequence describing excellent weapons. We would have our attention called to Unferth's base treachery if the sword Hrunting was its symbol. Silently inserting it in the series would be "analytic" rather than "aggregative," to use Ong's terms. Surely the main point here is that Beowulf is being systematically fitted out with the best available weaponry and armor, and Hrunting has had a long and honorable record of previous achievement. After all, the poet lavishes praise on it for an impressive ten lines (1455–64). We need no further indication of where our attention is to be directed, and there is no reason to search the fringes for secret ironies.

Even though it may be wise to eliminate some unnecessary complications that have been imposed on this scene, this is not to say that the scene does not convey some complexity of feelings. At the same time that the great sword Hrunting is being praised for what one might well call its record of courageous behavior, Unferth is being explicitly condemned for his cowardice. Thus the passage makes an interesting way of expressing the poet's consistently double view of the Danes. If all were going as it should properly go in the heroic world, a Danish hero would take this historic Danish sword and gain revenge for many Danish deaths in the past and for one in particular, for they have just found Æschere's severed head on the mere-bank. But the very act of presenting the sword to Beowulf shows the Danes giving up such an opportunity. The scene underlines all the more Unferth's near-tragic abnegation of the golden chance for heroic stature. He simply did not dare, and there he lost glory—þær he dome forleas (1470).

But of course we are falsifying the poem by making an artificial concentration on Unferth here. He is merely used as a dull foil, much like Heremod elsewhere, to set off Beowulf's dazzling superiority. If we did allow ourselves to give Unferth more than a passing glance, however, we might feel more sadness than anything else. The pathos lies in how far Unferth falls short of what he would wish to be—and not only how inferior he is to Beowulf, but how inferior he is to the glorious past of his own sword. Because of his past boasting he deserves the disgrace he suffers here, but it must be said yet one more time that he is something of a scapegoat for all the other Danes who have not volunteered to arm and plunge into the haunted mere. As Unferth earlier seemed to give expression to Danish resentment, so here he silently expresses the complexities of Danish failure. He is again representative: the Dane as loser, but not without dignity.

Is it imaginable that Beowulf senses any of this pathos? We must not say so, for we cannot know. We can only note that, in a generous reciprocal gesture, Beowulf asks Hrothgar to give his own sword to Unferth as a replacement for Hrunting in the event the hero fails to return (1488–91). If we are searching for some sign of reconciliation, we can find it here. In any event, there is surely no reason to take Beowulf's reference to Unferth as well known (widcuðne man 1489) as sarcastic. The remark is courteous and complimentary, a perfect match to the gracious gesture. We saw in Chapter 1 that there is no need to delete or distort the poet's own complimentary reference to Unferth as "skilled in strength" (eafoþes cræftig 1466).

There remains the question of whether we are to make anything significant out of the fact that the great sword does fail utterly in the fight, and Beowulf throws it away in impatient anger. Its failure ought probably to be understood as the failure of the normal in such an extraordinary battle: the failure of normal warriors, normal nations, normal swords. Beowulf's own sword later fails utterly against the mighty dragon. That a transcendentally magic weapon, one pointed out to the hero by God himself, is what is needed in the mere-fight is made clear in Beowulf's later report to Hrothgar. There is no reason not to accept this as the plain truth.

> Ne meahte ic æt hilde   mid Hruntinge
> wiht gewyrcan,   þeah þæt wæpen duge;
> ac me geuðe   ylda waldend
> þæt ic on wage geseah   wlitig hangian
> eald sweord eacen . . .   (1659–63a)

(I could not achieve anything at all with Hrunting—though that is a fine weapon!—but the Ruler of men gave me power to see hanging lovely on the wall a supernatural ancient sword.)

Beowulf does not blame Hrunting (or by extension its owner) either here or later when, about to leave Denmark, he returns the sword to Unferth with thanks.

>   Sægde him þæs leanes þanc,
> cwæð, he þone guðwine   godne tealde,
> wigcræftigne,   nales wordum log
> meces ecge.   (1809b–12a)

(He thanked him for that loan, said he considered that war-friend a good one, strong in war, not at all did he blame the edge of the sword with his words.)

It is certainly worth noting that the poet points to the possibility that such critical remarks might well be made! But perhaps for that reason the poet then remarks enthusiastically of Beowulf þæt wæs modig secg, approving, one supposes, of the hero's courteous magnanimity under the circumstances. It is probably taking things too far to go on to speak of the way Beowulf rehabilitates Unferth or brings about a great improvement in him.[10] We can only say that Beowulf gives Unferth what positive reinforcement he can; or perhaps we need only say that he is trying to cheer Unferth up, being tactfully aware of his discouragement. Yet it is quite apparent that the manner of this final compliment is not at all "personal," as we would understand the word in our century. Rather it displays

Beowulf in that new role as master politician and general peace-weaver that so impresses Hrothgar at the time of the hero's departure. He is the roaming Geatish ambassador carrying out the important diplomatic task of mending all fences before he returns home, and here we see Unferth for the last time in his customary garb as the Delegate from Denmark.

In this review of Unferth's career in the poem, I have tried not to explain difficulties or inconsistencies by resorting to hidden or implicit meanings. In addition to his conjectured complicity in future conjectured plots, some have emphasized the supposed etymology of his name to explain his nature.[11] I have not mentioned the much-discussed and still somewhat mysterious office of *thyle* that Unferth holds.[12] Certain things about him might well be a little clearer if we understood fully what that title means to the *Beowulf*-poet. In the meantime we have to be satisfied with the general consensus that it means something like "spokesman" or "public orator." Such a definition serves me well, for I have consistently claimed here that Unferth is always a symbolic spokesman for the Danes, whether we hear his actual words or watch his behavior and observe how Beowulf treats him. He speaks for their anger, their pride, their frustrations, their xenophobia, and their honestly grateful generosity of spirit. Above all, the poet makes use of him to point to negative and hidden dimensions of a people otherwise always officially honored in the poem's explicit language.

On a much more elaborate scale, a similar device to show the same double point of view is evident in the depiction of Hrothgar. He belongs to a more familiar and more clearly defined literary type than Unferth. The old man, specifically the old king, is a type-character obviously evolving out of long oral tradition. Nestor, Priam, and Charlemagne are three that come most readily to mind in our Western tradition.[13]

This type is interesting because of the built-in ambivalence that always hovers over it. On the one hand, in any tradition-directed oral society, old people must be accorded the highest respect. Age in such a society is an absolute value. Since the past is wholly dependent on living memories, the memories of the old carry its members as far back into the past as they are able to go. Age is power. Power may lie in the stored dynamic of proverbial wisdom which the tribal elders can use in articulating all-important codes of ethical conduct for the daily use of all the people. Power may reside in the indisputable excellence of old things like ancient and time-tested swords and heirlooms. We may see reflections of power in the submissive deference shown to "old law" (*ealde riht* 2330); or in the deadly longevity of vindictive recollection as in the Ingeld episode; or in the veneration of eponymous ancestral models like Scyld. Even the dragon may be more dangerous and harder to kill because he is an *old* dawn-flier (2760), and God himself receives the honorific title of *Ealdmetod* (945), an appellation that seems to stress his permanence and power.

Yet it is equally true, though much less frequently mentioned, that we find contempt as well as respect lurking in the attitudes of poets toward old men in a warrior society. For all their experience and wisdom, the old are fatally handicapped in the heroic world of incessant and violent physical action. Even when they try to enter it, their participation is necessarily limited. In the *Iliad,* Nestor struggles into his armor and hobbles out to make eloquent battlefield speeches in which he invokes the appropriate exempla from days long past in the days of everyone's grandfather, but he can never do much real fighting. In scenes of combat, he is screened and protected by others. Surely we admire him for tottering out to the fray, but he is not remotely in the same category as warriors like Ajax and Diomedes, let alone Hector and Achilles. Ancient Priam's heroism in going to beg Achilles for his son Hector's body is impressive because we know the tigerish Achilles could exterminate him with one offhand blow, but it is all the same a submissive and pathetic kind of heroism, totally unlike the kind that Achilles himself possesses, something lurid, terrifying and tragic. Charlemagne, though over two hundred years old and deserving a quiet retirement, does rouse himself from his earlier catatonia and show himself capable of undeniably heroic battle-action after Roland's death, but he must be helped out in his exertions by a large measure of direct aid from heaven that Roland and the twelve peers do not need.

Apart from Charlemagne, old men who fight with the recklessness and skill of the young are rare. The surviving Old English poetry, however, offers two striking examples: Beowulf as the octogenarian king of the Geats and Earl Byrhtnoth of Essex, a historical figure actually in his sixties in 991 when he was killed leading the English army against Viking invaders at Maldon. So fiercely energetic is Byrhtnoth in action that (at least in *The Battle of Maldon* as we have it, with its beginning lost) it is not until line 140, at the moment when the earl is first seriously wounded, that the poet even mentions his age (*frod wæs se fyrdrinc* 'old was that fighting-man'), and there *frod* may refer primarily not to his age so much as to his experience, for we see the practised way he uses his weapon to kill two Vikings.[14] Only when he is dying is his age mentioned a second time (*har hilderinc* 168 'white-haired battle-warrior'). Perhaps the poet continues the theme of the heroic old man after Byrhtnoth's death in his mention of the figure of Byrhtwold, the *eald geneat* (310) who later declares his resolve to die beside his lord in battle.

One could add as a third example of an old fighter a minor character in *Beowulf*, the Swedish king Ongentheow, who is presented as strenuously active. In one brief passage (2928–88) there are at least nine references to Ongentheow's advanced age, at the same time that we see him rescuing his aged wife from her Geatish captors, harassing the cornered Geatish army, and finally dying in grim unflinching combat with two bloodthirsty young warriors.

Hrothgar of course shows no such heroic ferocity in battle. But neither is he presented as a pitiable figure. Even the strongly agonistic or polarizing tendency of oral-derived literature does not succeed in drawing him entirely to one side or the other. At one time in my own experience of the poem, I chose a side and was strongly inclined to regard Hrothgar as wholly admirable, as Beowulf himself is, or as virtually perfect in his kind and in his role. As loyal critical thane I had to fight off the constant scornful attacks of students who saw another side clearly, the king's great weakness. We were both partly right.

What the students may have been too impatient to see clearly enough, however, is that Hrothgar must be granted the very maximum of formal dignity and respect as the great king of the famous Danish nation. But one must then instantly add: it must somehow be a dignity fully consonant with his real impotence. He must stand for and express, in full seriousness and in all aspects of his words and bearing, the highest social and moral values, and yet he must at the same time serve without ceasing as a humble and disposable foil to Beowulf, Beowulf both as energetic young hero and (more importantly) later as energetic old king. This is indeed a most peculiar and difficult balance to preserve. But, although the devices of oral-derived poetry may be quite simple in their basic structure, in combination they can be used by a master-poet to develop a strong illusion of realistic depth and complexity of emotion. The conventions are not subtle, but they work together like the combination of the crudely painted drops and flats of a stage-set to present a powerful three-dimensional illusion of an odd kind. We do have something resembling an impression of a "rounded" character in Hrothgar. We certainly cannot see him exclusively as a perfect paradigm of kingship, or as a senile and half-comic Polonius, or as the embodiment of some calamitous deterioration in Danish moral fibre, or of some sinfulness that may have elicited Grendel's attacks in some way, perhaps even as a cause of divine punishment for the sins of king and people. Not all these interpretations are equally supportable, but they all have occurred to readers.[15]

Prominent among the devices that keep Hrothgar's dignity distinct and vivid before us is the steady rain of honorific phrases and epithets that never slackens—for what that steady rain is worth. Here is an area of oral-derived language where we really cannot be sure how much such formulas are to be weighted, as we saw in glancing at Homeric epithets in Chapter 1. Conventional phrases like "helmet of the Scyldings" and "prince of the Bright-Danes," or "protector of warriors" and "shepherd of the people," are lavished on Hrothgar at all points. Perhaps such phrases have the deepest roots in the oral tradition of any that we encounter, coming as they do from the encomiastic lexicon of the court scop. It seems best to take them as words that are like his splendid robes of office. They are not at all ironic. They have a solid reality, even if they do not completely replace our own judgments about what the character does or fails to do.

Similarly, no one can deny that Hrothgar inherits enormous prestige from the mythic Danish past so vividly suggested in the story of the providential arrival of Scyld that opens the poem. Hrothgar is sixteen times called ruler of the Scyldings, and twice *the* Scylding himself. To be closely associated with such a resonant past is important. The quickest and surest way for the Danish scop, one of the veteran *ealdgesiðas* who ride back from the mere after Grendel's defeat, to praise Beowulf is to link him at once with the heroes of old half-mythical stories (853 ff.).

But of course Hrothgar not only inherits glory; he has earned an impressive amount of it himself. Heorot is built to accommodate the large new following of young warriors he has attracted by his early reputation for success in warfare. He is thus quite legitimately the founder and namer of this new hall, the new extension of the tribal domain. In his court at Heorot his reputation is jealously guarded by all, by his wife, his subjects, his visitors, even by the poet himself, who, it will be recalled, at one point must break off the flow of his narrative to insert a careful aside to the audience. The grateful Danes have been praising Beowulf with possibly too much enthusiasm, and have even been speculating on his absolutely predictable success as a king in the future.

Ne hie huru winedrihten   wiht ne logon,
glædne Hroðgar,   ac þæt wæs god cyning.   (862–63)

(But you should know they were not in the slightest way criticizing their own friendly lord, gracious Hrothgar; oh no, he was a good king!)

The temptation is to say that truly secure reputations need no such obtrusive defenses, but it is more to the point in the present context merely to note that the poet is quite sensitive to the potential tension inherent in any open comparison of Hrothgar and Beowulf.

Beowulf himself, as we would expect, is always especially careful to maintain intact and to foster the image of Hrothgar as mighty and venerable king. In the earlier passages of the poem, this solicitude can be seen as part of Beowulf's courteous and tactful strategy that moves him steadily past successive challenges into Denmark, until he gains at last access to the throne and to the coveted role of designated champion. This process culminates, as we have seen, in the flyting with Unferth.

Only in the context of the flyting do we see the hero being less than courteous about his royal host. At the end of his blistering reply to Unferth's charges, Beowulf departs from his practice of steadily feeding the Danish king's self-esteem by making blunt remarks about the Danes' total powerlessness against Grendel, capping these with the claim that only a Geat can help them. Since heroic convention imposes the tightest of identifications between king and people, one might expect that such caustic statements would offend Hrothgar, but in fact they delight him. He obviously cannot regard himself as included in any way in Beowulf's scornful condemnation of his people. Unferth has served well as lightning-rod. We might even view Unferth as a projection into a safe area of Hrothgar's real incompetence and failure, drawing Beowulf's justifiable charge while at the same time enabling Hrothgar to preserve his fine facade of effective kingship.

On two occasions (611–41 and 1162b–87), Hrothgar's queen Wealhtheow treats her husband with ceremonious deference, after we have been assured by the poet that she is a paragon of proper courtly behavior, being *cynna gemyndig* (613). By carrying out the rite of communal drinking and by applying the correct formulas to the correct formulas, she acts to "fix" the king firmly in his position as beloved guardian of his country and as king famous for his victories. There is no reason to think that she does not speak for the other silent Danes in voicing these respectful attitudes, and certainly she speaks without irony, even though we can plainly see for ourselves that Hrothgar is neither a capable guardian nor achieving any victories. But these scenes will require discussion at greater length later in the chapter.

Yet Hrothgar is not wholly powerless; he does possess some real powers other than hollow ceremonial ones. He can certainly refuse Beowulf and his band of adventuring Geats admission to his hall, both literally and in the sense of rejecting the hero's request for permission to serve as Danish champion in fighting Grendel. The herald Wulfgar begs Hrothgar not to exercise this power by refusing an interview to Beowulf (366b–67). His request once rejected, Beowulf could only sail back home. That is why he must work to win the king's consent by impeccable tact, flattery, and courtesy. When he makes his free choice to accept Beowulf's offer of help (and it is a choice a Dane like Unferth for one would not make), Hrothgar is not giving up this modicum of power, however, so much as showing the admirable courage to admit that his people cannot handle the crisis. Or at least so it is clearly made to seem. For the good of his people, he carries out the almost sacrificial act of deeding his hall over to a stranger to defend.

> Næfre ic ænegum men   ær alyfde,
> siþðan ic hond ond rond   hebban mihte,
> ðryþærn Dena   buton þe nu ða.   (655–57)

(Never before have I turned over to any man, since the first time I could lift hand and shield, the mighty hall of the Danes except now, to you.)

Furthermore, and this is a point of some importance, Hrothgar does have his one moment of genuine action in the poem. Ordinarily we see Hrothgar in passive, if not indeed in feeble, attitudes and poses: sitting on his throne, sometimes preaching, and sometimes presiding in dummy-like silence; weeping; going wearily off to lie down in his bed. Probably these are merely the conventionalized poses and gestures of old men in oral-derived poetry. At the beginning of *The Song of Roland*, for example, we see Charlemagne frozen in similar sitting positions, obdurately silent in the midst of the noisy and violent confrontations that surround him, tugging in grief or rage at his hair and beard. But on one occasion Hrothgar leaps to his feet and moves with speed and energy. It is when, after his bitter lament over the loss of his friend Æschere and his overwrought description of the horrible mere where Grendel's mother lives—both possibly to be taken as examples of excessive "feminine" emotionalism—he is firmly taken in hand by Beowulf. The hero urges him concisely to convert all that grief and fear into the active outlet of healthy vengeance, as any *warrior* should do, in the harsh terms of the all-embracing code of the poem. Offered this hope at the low point of his manic-depressive cycle, Hrothgar at once launches into what is the closest he comes in the poem to heroic male display, a Homeric aristeia worthy at least of Nestor. He leaves the hall, mounts his horse, and leads both Danes and Geats through the terrifying landscape of testing ordeal to the shore of the evil mere he has just described in nearly hysterical terms. The climax of this sudden surge of power is the horn-blast that penetrates the mere and enrages the sea-monsters (1422–32a), just as Beowulf's own heroic shout penetrates the barrow to call out the dragon to fight.

This bold action shows he has mastered both his intense reluctance to approach this unnatural and hellish place and his anguished paralysis at his friend's death, the latter state perhaps merely a symbolic intensification of his twelve years of immobilized suffering under Grendel's attacks. It shows, surely to the joy of all, that he still has some vigorous heroic energies. But Hrothgar's action here, though vigorous, is sharply limited; in this it seems to conform to the Nestor pattern. The action stops dead at the mere's edge, and there, in the usual fashion in this early narrative poetry, Hrothgar abruptly disappears. That is to say, he is no longer described. Even when Beowulf addresses a farewell speech to him before he dives into the mere, Hrothgar is not shown as responding to it. We hardly see him again until he is back in his hall again much later (1646). If Beowulf had followed this same pattern later in the story when faced with his own emergency as an old king, he would have led his band of men resolutely up to the dragon's barrow and pointed helpfully toward it, before vanishing from the scene.

In other less obvious ways, Hrothgar's fragile image is carefully guarded, through the poet's use of the narrowly limited focal range characteristic of oral narrative. On two occasions, the king is shielded from moral blame by the device of having the quite shadowy group of Danish elders take responsibility for reprehensible or unwise actions. The elders seem indeed to have been created for this purpose, since they have no other function. It is the counsellors, or at least some undefined "they," not King Hrothgar, who make the decision to practise or revive the worship of pagan idols, an action most strenuously condemned by the Christian poet (178b–

88). If we ever permitted ourselves to think realistically about this episode, we would be bound to conclude that Hrothgar must surely have known what was going on in his own kingdom. But the poet can erase him from our field of attention simply by never mentioning him in connection with the incident of idol-worship. And when the focus is switched away from the king, he does not exist for us to inquire about. Thus Hrothgar can and does maintain, whenever he comes into view at other times, his sacerdotal air of pseudo-Christian sententiousness. This kind of disjunctive treatment of the idolatry incident holds us tightly inside the poet's control. We cannot ask realistic questions or examine probabilities. It is no accident that students of this kind of oral-derived narrative poetry keep finding so useful the analogy of film technique, for film is a medium where we can see only what the camera is rigged to show us, and where out of sight is very nearly out of mind.

Similarly, it is later the same counsellors who decide, after some debate, to go away and leave Beowulf at the mere's bottom after they observe the evidence of blood in the water (1591–1602a). Presumably Hrothgar goes along with their decision, since he does not stay there but returns to Heorot with the other Danes. By not showing him taking any decisive part in the debate, the poet really directs us not to think of his having made any decision at all. He would have gained no credit for making it. That Beowulf's own men (young men in contrast to the old Danish counsellors, *gomele* 1595) stay on the mere-bank even though they have little hope of their lord's return alive shows us by significant tacit contrast that the Danes' departure is at its best no noble act, though certainly not a definitely ignoble one like the flight of Beowulf's retainers in the dragon-fight. But Hrothgar can be made simply not to exist in any relation to this act by the device of maintaining silence about him.

If this mode of non-existence inside the world of decision and practical action is one way to represent a chronic passivity, we can recognize another way in Hrothgar's very eloquence in articulating his feelings. It should first be freely and emphatically granted that his copious expressiveness and the intensity of his feelings are often signs of strength of character rather than of weakness, and they add a welcome warmth to the story. Hrothgar has the essential royal virtue of loving generosity and he displays it in abundance. Heorot was first built as a hall to be generous in (71–3), and the king's sumptuous and grateful gifts to Beowulf are praised by all.[16] In a less material sense than is suggested by the lavish awarding of presents—though no Anglo-Saxon would have seen *that* modern distinction as having any meaning—he loves Beowulf profoundly. His love reaches a culmination in his impulsive wish to adopt Beowulf as his own son (946b–50). Vivid in our minds is the farewell scene (1870–80a), with the old man weeping and kissing Beowulf for what he knows will be the last time. For his own men too he suffers deep *þegnsorg* (131), sorrow at losing them to Grendel, and he expresses intense grief in his elegiac lament for his friend Æschere (1322–29).

Yet expressing emotions like these—or, possibly, even having them—risks being called weakness in the harshly exigent heroic context that dominates the poem. The loser Hector in Homer is more touchingly eloquent in this way than the winner Achilles is, or than Achilles ever has to be. Pathetic expression comes with Hector's territory as a world-famed victim of fate. Hrothgar's love for Beowulf is admirable, but it can be seen as betraying a disturbing dependence on the young man. When he cannot stop Grendel from murdering his men, Hrothgar suffers that especially strong emotion the Anglo-Saxons called *torn* (147), not always an easy word to translate. His form of *torn* seems much like what present-day psychiatrists would call "impotent rage." It is the same kind of *torn* the despairing Wanderer in the Old English poem of that name is said to suffer from; he is explicitly warned not to express it, unless he first knows the remedy for it.[17] In *The Wanderer*, the remedy is faith in the security only God can furnish. No such remedy and no possible action are available for Hrothgar, however. His great wisdom, traditional compensation for age's debility, is of no more use to him than his illustrious ancestry. Every night for twelve years the brute Grendel rudely displaces him and deposes him as Heorot's ruler.

In this state of torment, and in the poetic lament he sings for the loss of youth and strength (a lament reported later by Beowulf when he returns home, 2105–14), Hrothgar indeed seems to approach in his wretchedness the condition of the passive sufferers of such Old English elegies as *The Wife's Lament*. Eloquent and moving as these poems are, they are fundamentally lyrical and not narrative, passive and not active, cast in the language of sufferer and victim. They thereby uncover a repressed and strongly negative underside of the heroic life, a "feminine" side, if that use of the word conveys any meaning. I think it does within the context of epic. The tragic story of Dido in Book IV of the *Aeneid*, though obviously it belongs to a more literate and sophisticated stage of epic development, is one of these swirling eddies of sheer pain left behind by the strong surging of "masculine" conquest, cruelty, and ambition.

It is quite true that Beowulf himself uses such strongly emotional "elegiac" language in his account of old Hrethel and of the father whose son has been hanged (2441–71), but that part of his long speech is no personal lament for his own troubles. Thematically, things are perfectly clear. The poet uses the opportunity to darken the emotional tones of that part of the poem. The passage may tell us as well that Beowulf, along with his other virtues, has deep sympathy for such helpless pain in others; perhaps it tells us too that the hero who speaks is an old man. But the speech does not end on such a sad note. Far from it: its outcome is a fierce rededication to the active valor of his youth, and the promise is at once validated by witnessed deeds.

Another important way of stressing Hrothgar's passivity has already been touched on. Probably entirely subliminal in its effect on an audience, this is what one might term "zero grade narration," to adapt a useful concept from the grammarians. The lack of one element is itself an element in a structure of meaning. By the term here I mean Hrothgar's total *absence* from the poem during a long sequence of particularly exhilarating action, a sequence that takes in both Beowulf's fight with Grendel and its aftermath. This is really an even more striking instance of erasure than the scenes mentioned earlier, though almost too obvious to be noticed at all. *Only if we think about it.* The poet might easily have included the king among those Danes who watch and listen on the outer wall in horror while the noisy fight between hero and monster crashes to its conclusion in Heorot, but he chooses not to. We may assume that the tired old man is sound asleep through all that din, and that he sleeps very late too, for he does not join or even send off the morning expedition that follows Grendel's bloody track to the mere and returns rejoicing and praising Beowulf's achievement. In this return we see the Danes, old and young, reassembling and acting together once again as we have not seen them do before, ending their long period of demoralization—and they manage to do this in the absence of their king. Only when all have finally come back to Heorot does Hrothgar emerge from his bower to peer at the great ripped-off claw hung up over Heorot's entrance. What this sequence *says* (exactly by what it does not say) is that action and Hrothgar exclude each other. He is fated to be the inveterate spectator and tourist, in a class with old Priam on Troy wall asking Helen to point out the more interesting Greek heroes to him. And furthermore here Hrothgar is a spectator who arrives only during the last act of the play.

In one more respect, a somewhat more controversial one, Hrothgar is in a certain sense a spectator. He is religious. To be specific, he is much given to voicing emphatic religious sentiments.[18] In his first speech, he expresses the hope or expectation that God, as an act of grace, has sent Beowulf to fight Grendel (381b–84a). After Grendel's defeat, he makes an elaborate speech of thanksgiving in which he directs special attention to God's miraculous powers (*a mæg God wyrcan / wunder æfter wundre* 930b–31a) and admits that he and the other Danes had lost faith in any fortunate outcome before the divinely-assisted Beowulf arrived. God has obviously given special grace to the hero's mother in this happy birth (942b–46a). The king's later sermon (1700 ff.) stresses the ways God grants everything to men, and how men like Heremod forget their obligation to him. It will be noted that these statements consistently attribute all power to God.

While we must make a reverent gesture toward the undeniable sincerity and religious validity of such remarks, we must also see that they are primarily negative and passive, within the heroic context of *Beowulf*. Hrothgar's view of the situation seems to be as follows. God has, for unknown reasons, permitted evil things to afflict the Danes, and such afflictions will continue until God decides to stop permitting them, at which time he will intervene by sending some special agent of his own to do what ordinary human beings cannot be expected to do. With more or less patience, Hrothgar waits for God to make his decision. The king never for a moment sees himself or his people as conceivably responsible for incurring Grendel's attacks. His careful defining of Beowulf's arrival as a miraculous instance of God's intervention is no doubt quite true in its way, but it is also face-saving, because it justifies the king's previous and habitual attitude of passive resignation.

The important contrast is between this passive behavior and what we see in old Beowulf's behavior when the dragon attacks. Beowulf first has a moment of puzzled guilt that he might have done something wrong, broken some law, after which he is completely ready to meet a personal attack with all the strength at his command. Hrothgar merely grumbles that God could easily have stopped Grendel long before if only he had really wanted to (478b–79).

If such religious attitudes in the poem tend to be linked with weakness and flaccidity, there is something like a converse to the proposition. Action passages and action speeches have fewer religious references. (This would not be true at all in *The Song of Roland*, for instance.) Even in the case of Hrothgar himself it is noticeable. The long speech he makes just before he does take his one action, the dangerous ride to the mere, contains no religious language at all. All Beowulf's speeches at the time of the dragon-fight contain only two brief religious references.[19]

It may properly be objected that I am not taking into account Beowulf's own ready acknowledgements in Part I that he benefits from God's help. There is not the slightest doubt that he sees himself, and the poet sees him, as being in active collaboration with God during the fighting. He reports that he seized Grendel intending to kill him there in Heorot, but he could not do so since God did not wish him to do it—and then too Grendel was also very strong in pulling away (963–70a). Beowulf must accept some disappointment here, but he cheerfully points out that, even when he had to let go, *sar*, pain, still kept its grip on the monster and would go on holding him (possibly in hell?) until the last great judgment (974–79). Perhaps the hero is here suggesting something like teamwork or shared labor between himself and deity. By maiming Grendel Beowulf has put a mark on him, just as God once marked the ancestor Cain. Both dark figures must now face the bright Lord. But the key to this close relationship is that it is *active* collaboration. Beowulf's constant input of vast energy into his dynamic cooperation with God is entirely different from Hrothgar's sedentary piety.

Another virtually zero-grade element contributing to our sense of Hrothgar's weakness is the remarkable *thinness* of his past. I have in mind our attenuated sense of his total life history as it is presented in the poem. He has had some vague and barely mentioned victories in youth (64–67a), but they lack the detail needed to fix them vividly in our memories. (Of course it is necessary to say that we can work only with what we have. It is quite possible that the original audiences knew a great deal more about Hrothgar's past exploits than we do, and the poet merely needed to allude to them.) We are told that he once settled the feud Beowulf's father was involved in, apparently quite capably (459–72). The saddle he once bestrode in battle is one of the gifts he presents to Beowulf, and the old relic bears with it some dim memories of his fighting days (1035–42). But that is really the whole sum of his past. Again we have the very strongest contrast with Beowulf, whom we see in spectacular and glorious action in youth as well as in old age. Indeed two-thirds of the poem is given over to describing his youthful deeds in detail. Thus, by the time he reaches old age, he has acquired a sheer depth of rich past experience that Hrothgar lacks, and it is a depth important to a hero in this genre. In fact, an epic hero is likely to be presented to us as an accumulated mass of past achievements, the slayer of X, the conqueror of all Y. Just this depth serves old Beowulf well in his final need, when he can renew his strength for the dragon-fight by running back over his past of dedication and victory. Lacking such a vivid youth of achievement, Hrothgar seems without any real third dimension in time. He is not only old now but was always old.

Finally, one more important zero-grade element contributes to our sense of Hrothgar's weakness, or our sense of his relatively diminished reality. It is his lack of close human contacts. Only one relationship is fully developed: his warm fatherly love for Beowulf. He speaks of Beowulf even before the young hero arrives, speaks to him often, praises him, rewards him, preaches earnestly to him, embraces him, and weeps on his shoulder when he leaves. This affection is so memorably and movingly rendered that it satisfies us completely. And, as a major part of the poem's tremendous concentration on its hero, it seems wholly appropriate. Only on second thought do we notice that Hrothgar scarcely ever even speaks to anyone else, even to his intimates. He once addresses the herald Wulfgar, telling him to let Beowulf come into the hall. But he never speaks at all to his wife Wealhtheow; never to his children; never to Unferth, Hrothulf, or any other Dane.

Direct address counts for much in this kind of highly dramatic poetry, with so high a proportion of the story cast into the form of dialogue and confrontational scenes. Since he or she encounters the audience directly, a character who speaks has a greatly enhanced reality. Although those Geats who follow Beowulf to Denmark are often mentioned, they remain shadowy because none ever speaks; they merely make up a decorative frieze, a dancing chorus upstage. The absence of direct address darkens large areas in the character of Hrothgar as well. The poet declines to develop clear potentialities. We could psychologize about it. Perhaps we might connect Hrothgar's lack of communication with those around him to other signs of distance from people: his fondness for abstract generalities, and for the hypothetical instance rather than the concrete one, a preference we see in his sermon (1700 ff.).

But it is again a comparison with someone else that makes very much clearer what is wrong with Hrothgar in this regard. The usual binary mode of oral-derived literature makes contrast always of crucial defining importance. Doubtless Hrothgar's isolation from others would seem of little consequence, perhaps only an instance of the way kings are, if we did not see Beowulf constantly communicating directly with others. He not only addresses Hrothgar at length on several occasions but speaks directly to the queen and to Unferth, as well as to other Danes. In these scenes in Denmark we see him in vivid and immediate contrast to Hrothgar, but the contrast also continues, though less sharply visualized, after Beowulf has returned home. The long scene where he makes his report to his uncle Hygelac is highly developed and warmly emotional.

But the essential part of the contrast involves comparing the two characters as old kings. When he has become king at an advanced age, Beowulf still maintains a close and direct relationship with those around him. He speaks to his subjects, greets them, gives them instructions, explains to them what he is doing and why, tells them stories of his youth. A new and intimate relationship with his young kinsman Wiglaf begins to develop even as he lies dying. Wiglaf is literally, physically, close to his dying master like Kent to Lear; he talks to him, weeps over him, holds him in his arms during his last moments.

At a somewhat farther remove, at second hand, the mead-hall scenes that Wiglaf recalls for the benefit of Beowulf's cowardly retainers (2633–60 and 2864–72) show us the same picture of intimate contact between lord and men. It is more than the conventional scene of a king doling out rings and weapons to his fighters because it is suffused with the intense and urgent emotion of Wiglaf, reminding his comrades of Beowulf's love for them and the obligation incurred by that love. And the same warmth persists even beyond death. Geatish sailors will look up in awe and sadness at Beowulf's barrow high on the sea-cliff (2802–08). Wiglaf explicitly passes on to the Geats the greetings Beowulf sends to his people (3093b–3100). The final description of Beowulf's funeral reaches its greatest power when the circling and mourning riders begin to speak of the beloved man they served.

The contrast is cruel, but nonetheless real. By comparison Hrothgar seems a stuffed king, a thing of empty formulas and patches, his inadequacy revealed most starkly in the slightness of the bonds that attach him to those around him. One telling instance of his lightness of heft, his strange invisibility, is the scene (1162b–1231) where his wife Wealhtheow takes over political functions the king should properly be carrying out for himself. Both his passivity and his lack of contact with his social environment were never better illustrated. She first reproves him sharply for his impulsive decision to adopt Beowulf as son; in her mind, this shows he has forgotten the interests of their own sons. Then, as if she really sees no hope there, she moves instinctively away from him toward where the real power lies, first pleading with her nephew Hrothulf to behave himself honorably in the future and then turning to Beowulf for help in protecting her sons' heritage. In visual or theatrical terms, we are made conscious of Wealhtheow's sweeping and urgent movements through the hall and at the same time of the contrast of Hrothgar's silent immobility. Once again he is there but not there, effectively erased as a vital participant in the affairs of his own family and kingdom. He is not even shown to us as listening to any of this highly significant conversation. Perhaps he has dozed off. Later we hear of an equally disastrous lapse of political wisdom and possibly of attention, when Beowulf tells Hygelac that Hrothgar cannot foresee the certain failure of the political marriage of his daughter Freawaru to Ingeld of the Heathobards (2026–31).

Furthermore, at the largely unconscious level of that mosaic of massed tiny details through which formulaic poetry does its important small-scale work, it is not surprising that the poet also stresses this contrast between Hrothgar and Beowulf as old kings through the compounds he applies to them. To mention only a few examples, one notes the following pairs. Hrothgar is called a *guþcyning* 'war-king' only once, Beowulf (in far less space) four times. Hrothgar is once called *þeodcyning* 'people-king', a term suggesting the responsibilities of rule, while Beowulf is called that four times. Hrothgar is twice termed *mandryhten* 'man-lord', implying close bonds between king and retainer; the same compound is used five times of Beowulf.

The tone adopted by the narrator's own voice also makes a significant difference. The poet makes almost no direct comments on Hrothgar, whose personality is established by the remarks of other characters and by his own long speeches. In strong contrast, in Part II, after Beowulf has become the old king, the poet positively hovers over him. He uses his licensed omniscience regularly to move into both past and future, in a sequence of comments that show his foreknowledge of the hero's death and his concern and grief about it, as he both summarizes a splendid career and bitterly laments the end of it. This passage will serve as one example out of many of this tone:

> Ne wæs þæt eðe sið,
> þæt se mæra   maga Ecgðeowes
> grundwong þone   ofgyfan wolde;
> sceolde [ofer] willan   wic eardian
> elles hwergen,   swa sceal æghwylc mon
> alætan lændagas.   (2586b–91a)

(That was not an easy venture, that the famous son of Ecgtheow [might] wish to give up this plain of earth; [rather], against his will he had to take up a dwelling elsewhere, just as every man must abandon his transitory days of life.)

Such a contrast in attitudes says this, and bluntly: Beowulf is cared about in a way that Hrothgar is not. I see the poet's own relationship to Beowulf as very similar to the other characters' relation to him: close, personal, involved, emotional. His attitude invites and urges the audience to feel such an intimacy with the hero, that kind of unrestrained identification Ong describes in the terms "empathetic and participatory."[20]

Such identification invites us to feel deep grief at Beowulf's passing, but it is a grief that fits into a supportive emotional structure already well established elsewhere in the poem. Conventional phrases keep suggesting to us that old age and death are to be calmly accepted as the majestic culminations of a natural cycle. Kings typically rule long (*lange ahte* 31) and die only after many years (*longe þrage* 54). After Beow of the Scyldings has died and gone elsewhere, his son Healfdene rules until he too is *gamol ond guðreouw* (58), 'old and ferocious'. The genealogical series sets up a heavy and compelling rhythm, enumerating a stately order of kings ruling all through the majestic length of their lives until their peaceful death, but all of them warlike and fierce till the end. Beowulf's own father Ecgtheow lives many years (*wintra worn*), before he departs *gamol of geardum*, (262–66) 'old from the courts'. Such is the natural course. So too Wiglaf's father moves outward in old age on his path toward death (*frod on forðweg* 2625). The familiar journey metaphor implies not only that death is part of the unceasing movement of life itself but that the traveller moves voluntarily along the road to his final fate. A necessary time comes for this last journey to be made, and the journeyer arrives at a terminus that has always been his goal. Although Beowulf dies violently in combat with the dragon, he has always reached this set departing time in his number of life-days. He is a *frod cyning,* an old king who has *lange heold* his life and kingship. We know he is now fated to die, and ready to die.

Yet, in some strange way, Hrothgar seems very old without being near death, as if he were even excluded from the dark dignity of this final wayfaring. His old age is not defined as part of a rounded-off and esthetically pleasing pattern or process of completed achievement, something earned and amassed over the long years, but it is defined rather in terms of the negative elements of old age: feebleness, helpless suffering, and painful nostalgia for lost youth and strength. Even his touching but dependent attachment to Beowulf brings out this loss of strength: he clings, he does not keep moving on. We need only compare old Beowulf's far less one-sided relationship with his young kinsman Wiglaf. Even though the Geatish king lies actually dying, he is not seen by us as helpless or dependent in this intimacy but as an equal partner in it, chiefly because the two of them have just fought side by side, sharing the same shield as they share responsibility for the nation's future.

Perhaps the last words the poet utters about Hrothgar—one of his few comments on the character—tell the story:

> Þæt wæs an cyning
> æghwæs orleahtre, oþþæt hine yldo benam
> mægenes wynnum, se þe oft manegum
> scod. (1885b–87)

(That was one king faultless in everything—until old age, which has often ruined many, took away from him the joys of his strength.)

We are never told that Healfdene and Weohstan lost their physical powers or became depressed as old men, or that Beowulf grew feeble and full of nostalgia at the end of his life. It is the old king who never loses the joys of his strength who is the poem's hero. Beowulf's old age, displaying the fullest heroic energies to the very end, is made to seem all the more right, all the more a part of the universal journey, by a complex set of contrasts with the merely pathetic old age of Hrothgar. It is not unlike the distinction drawn by Shakespeare between King Lear and Gloucester, the more passive and pathetic old man he adds to his play to strengthen by contrast the indomitable figure of Lear.

In his sermon, it is Hrothgar himself who holds out to the young Beowulf the prospect of disease and senility in "atrocious old age," *atol yldo* (1766), and the sermon is bleakly dominated by the simple fear of death. The ugliness and terror of aging and death exist in human experience and surely Beowulf knows that they do, but he does not talk about them. Hrothgar talks about them, and that is the finally appropriate part of his characterization.

Contrast with another individual is one important means of characterization in *Beowulf*. But a character is also involved in a relationship with the entire society that surrounds him; his role is all important. In a hero's case we can even speak of a conflict, at least a potential one, between his assertive selfhood, a selfhood necessarily far more imposing and demanding than other men's, and the equally powerful limiting forces of the social context. That context can be awesome. When we say that characters in *Beowulf* and other early narratives exist as types, we mean that they exist as a part of some rigid and generally accepted stereotype of social role and function. Whenever in prehistory it may have begun, this conventional mode of literary presentation lasts a long time. It is famously apparent, to choose a familiar instance, in the case of Chaucer's Canterbury pilgrims, who are in most cases occupations rather than individuals, and it goes on well into the nineteenth century, when at last social rank and function cease to be the chief determinants of character. In 1712, for example, we see a traditional stereotype, Rich Young Female, in the Belinda of Pope's *Rape of the Lock*. A hundred years later, we see a totally different kind of character in Jane Austen's *Emma*, even though Emma is also a rich young female.

A term I find useful in thinking of this aspect of characterizing is "embedding." The socially embedded character is all matrix, a locked together package, at the appropriate points wired into essential relationships and identifying connections. The figure of Beowulf is embedded firmly in such a social matrix when he is first introduced:

> þæt fram ham gefrægn   Higelaces þegn,
> god mid Geatum,   Grendles dæda;
> se wæs moncynnes   mægenes strengest
> on þæm dæge   þysses lifes, . . .   (194–97)

(From his home (1) *Higelac's thane* heard that, (2) *brave among the Geats,* about Grendel's deeds; he was (3) *strongest in might of mankind,* (4) *at that day of this life.*)

He is not named here or for quite a while afterward in the poem, but is instead identified as existing within a web of coordinates: (1) subject *of* King Higelac,[21] (2) a brave man *among* the tribe of Geats, (3) superlatively strong *in respect to* mankind generally, (4) existing at that specific moment *along the line of* historical time. Such placement in a context, or contexts, seems obligatory. Even the monster Grendel is carefully defined by his address (fen, moor, exile, giant-country), family background (descent from Cain and suspicious association with water-monsters), and social status (a fugitive from mankind, never invited to hall-feasts or rewarded at the gift-throne, and hated by God).

It is hardly necessary to say that what the characters are embedded in in this literary narrative is as much the preformed style of oral-derived poetry as it is the patterns of society. Using "style" to describe both the verse and the world it describes may run terminological risks but it is convenient. Perhaps we need not argue over which comes first, the chicken or the alliteration. The reasons characters never have any startling individuality about them is that they are predictable and conventional, and this is because, as we saw in Chapter 1, the style provides no alternative way to talk about them. It cuts them to size. It relentlessly typifies, stereotypes, polarizes, reduces, embeds. The character's social role forms his or her exoskeleton, something that gives shape and solidity, just as inner motivation or cognitive process constructs an internal spine for characters in more recent literature and perhaps in more recent life as well.

But of course if convention holds full sway we have dull poetry. *Beowulf* is not conventional in that pejorative sense. The embedded character may indeed often remain static and passive, always appearing to be an inert chunk of relationships; or else he can signal some vital reality by movement, by testing and proving what he is, by subjecting the stereotypes to pressure and strain. Because he takes no action, Hrothgar remains largely a static figure, lurking behind or composed of a dense cloud of formulaic language praising his royal perfections. What always matters more than anything else in narrative poetry is doing something. That is what brings the whole system, with all its built-in potential for significance already there in the formulaic style, to sudden life.[22]

*char. of
Beowulf*

The embedded chunk of relationships we are introduced to as "Beowulf" is not static even for a moment. It is a chunk that at once begins to move, though in the form of a cohesive social unit rather than as a distinct individual at first. It signals its vitality in a series of vigorous and decisive actions that culminate in the sweeping and awesome passage of ship and martial ship's crew across the sea to Denmark. On the Danish shore it is just this moving social mass that the coastguard challenges: he addresses them first as a group in the collective plural. Then, as he analyzes the group, he singles out of the matrix of men, ship, weapons, the one heroic individual:

No her cuðlicor   cuman ongunnon
lindhæbbende;   ne ge leafnesword
guðfremmendra   gearwe ne wisson,
maga gemedu.   Næfre ic maran geseah
eorla ofer eorþan   ðonne is eower sum,
secg on searwum.   (244–49a)

(Never have any shield-bearing strangers come here more familiarly, and you do not instantly know the warriors' word of permission nor the consent of kinsmen! I have never seen a larger warrior than one of you, that man in his armor.)

In his reply Beowulf seems quite content to let others pick him out of the crowd in this way. He largely eschews the first person singular, speaking as representative of his people and remaining placidly embedded in that social context. He merely fills in the necessary blanks in the defining coordinates: as to race, we are Geats, as for our king, he is Hygelac; as to my father, his name was Ecgtheow. The only other "I" in his speech comes when he remarks (277b–85) that he individually, rather than the group as a whole, has a suggestion to make to Hrothgar about how to solve the Grendel problem.

In the ensuing passage (301–31a), the Geats are also described as marching en masse, with no one singled out, up to the great hall of Heorot, although at several key points the poet reminds us that Beowulf is always the group's guide and leader, whether he leads them to the ship (208), to Denmark (370), or to Heorot (402). When the doorkeeper Wulfgar addresses the strangers (again in the plural), Beowulf must at last give his name in order to gain admission, but he continues to keep his personal presence as much under wraps as it can be. But, like the coastguard, Wulfgar intuitively picks the hero out of the group surrounding him. Consequently his report to the king moves interestingly back and forth between group and individual (plural 361–62, singular 363–64a, plural 364b–69a, singular 369b–70), but his last words come squarely to rest on Beowulf as outstanding leader and guide.

Beowulf begins to take a clearer shape in our imagination when we hear Hrothgar's enthusiastic speech. The king adds his own contribution to the process of embedding and identifying, mentioning both Beowulf's father and his mother, and reporting previous Geatish sailors' accounts of him as well as leaping to the conclusion that God has sent the Geat here on a mission. Out of these added details and this stronger focus, a remarkable personality is beginning to loom. Yet this is still once again kept restrained by the formality of the plural with which Wulfgar invites the band of Geats to enter the hall.

Beowulf's modest subordination of his individuality to a group—whether ship's crew, family, or nation—is in fact quite characteristic of the cooperative team-play he favors and exemplifies through the poem; however, as it appears here it is used by the poet chiefly as a preparation for an absolutely incandescent outburst of pure ego in his first "credentials" speech to Hrothgar. The important heroic credentials he presents to the Danish court include, in a speech of only forty-eight lines, no fewer than twenty-eight first-person singular forms, as well as a large number of forceful action verbs with their first-person subject unexpressed but nevertheless overwhelmingly there. It gives us a staggering impression of a self that annihilates constraints, and subordination, and limiting coordinates. And the poet here emphasizes not only Beowulf's powerful singleness of self but his abrupt and intimate closeness, not at all a formal one, almost a heavy-breathing one, to King Hrothgar, in the seven lines in which both *ic* and *þu* (or their by-forms) appear together (407, 417, 426, 429, 445, 450, 452, the last with subject of imperative understood). Such collocations increase our awareness of his confronting, crowding presence as a figure of power. The first-person pronouns begin in the nominative and end in the accusative when, at the end of his speech, Beowulf contemplates the possibility of his death when he will become only the direct object of verbs, acted upon by others, with his body dragged and hurled about by Grendel. This is the inert accusative we all end in.

We can see this explosion of ego within the bounds of a single sentence. First Beowulf describes in relatively quiet tones how his people (the surrounding social matrix) urged him to come to Denmark after they had observed his victories over sea-monsters. Then

we see him abruptly leave his contingent role as Hygelac's modest
and respectful thane and launch out boldly into his own career, his
own course of action, his own voice:

> Selfe ofersawon, ða ic of searwum cwom,
> fah from feondum; þær ic fife geband,
> yðde eotena cyn ond on yðum slog
> niceras nihtes, nearoþearfe dreah,
> wræc Wedera nið (wean ahsodon),
> forgrand gramum, ond nu wið Grendel sceal,
> wið þam aglæcan, ana gehegan
> ðing wið þyrse. (419–26a)

(They themselves were witnesses, when I came back from am-
bushes, all bloody from enemies, that time I bound five,
devastated the race of giants, struck sea-monsters by night,
went through agonizing necessity, avenged the attack on the
Weders (those monsters asked for their woes!), destroyed the
enemy—and now will, alone, hold meeting with the demon
Grendel.)

The many verbs reveal the powerful thrust and ranging dimensions of those energies the Geatish witnesses saw, and as the verbs
do so they pull the hero out of the matrix, out of the Geats' field of
vision, they hammer him momentarily free of the old social contexts. Violent action can do this. But even heroes in this kind
of society cannot stand truly alone for more than an instant. No
sooner is he cut loose from Geatland than Beowulf is pleading to be
incorporated into a new context and a new formulaic pattern: to
become Hrothgar's new man and Denmark's chosen champion. If
Hrothgar accepts this contract and takes him on in this role, the
king will then have to take responsibility for Beowulf's funeral and
the disposition of his effects, should he die in the fight. Beowulf by
now can safely assume that Hrothgar will do so, and the new agreement is as good as ratified.

During his fights with the monsters, Beowulf remains (to use the
military phrase) temporarily attached to Denmark, but immediately
thereafter he must disengage himself from that relationship. Indeed, it has been persuasively argued that Beowulf extricates himself from Danish dynastic politics with some difficulty, if we believe
that Hrothgar has actually offered him the succession to the Danish
throne (though opposed in this offer by Wealhtheow).[23] In any
event, he hands the borrowed hall back to Hrothgar.

Ic hit þe þonne gehate,   þæt þu on Heorote most
sorhleas swefan   mid þinra secga gedryht
ond þegna gehwylc   þinra leoda,
duguðe ond iogoþe,   þæt þu him ondrædan ne þearft,
þeoden Scyldinga,   on þa healfe,
aldorbealu eorlum,   swa þu ær dydest.   (1671–6)

(I then promise you this, that you will be allowed to sleep without anxiety in Heorot with your band of men and every thane
of your people, old and young, and that you have no need to
dread the evil deaths of men from that direction, lord of the
Scyldings, as you had to before.)

The detail of this sentence pictures a hall once again filled entirely
with Danes and one without the presence of Beowulf. The picture
in itself advances the narrative and foreshadows Beowulf's disen-
gagement from Denmark, in transit back to his own national context. Seen from this viewpoint, in its tone of valedictory advice
Hrothgar's ensuing sermon also acknowledges the young warrior's
imminent departure; Beowulf matches the same tone in his final
speech the next morning when he offers his help if Hrothgar
should ever need it again. Denmark has become future, indeed con-
ditional. Beowulf is already seeing himself as once again Hygelac's
thane when he assures Hrothgar that he can get royal permission
to bring any necessary expeditionary force to the rescue of the
Danes (1830b–35).

Though Beowulf himself scarcely needs readjustment when
he returns home, the Geats need a little time to adapt themselves to
his novel glory, and that fact justifies the space given to Beowulf's
long report of his Danish adventures to Hygelac. I have already
discussed this episode elsewhere, where I stated my belief that
Hygelac's inquiry and Beowulf's reply contain elements of the same
challenge-and-response pattern—a familiar type of episode in oral
poetry—that we saw in the scene between Unferth and Beowulf.[24]
Beowulf must clear himself of all possible suspicion of previous
laziness, incompetence, recklessness, or lack of proper concern for
his own nation's interests. His brilliant reply can be seen as a way of
re-embedding himself elaborately and memorably into the very
heart of Geatish society. The act is largely accomplished by ritual
exchange, he offering all his hard-won treasures to his beloved
kinsman and being rewarded in return with enormous gifts of land
and power that symbolize and validate the fervor of their new relationship. Though it will take a little time for it to happen, no Geat

will now ever hesitate to offer Beowulf the throne; he has now in Geatland much the same heir apparent role he was offered in Denmark. Later we will have occasion to look at some tensions that will develop between King Beowulf and his people, when he must once again assert himself as an independent individual, but there is no doubt that Part I ends and Part II begins with Beowulf solidly embedded in the hearts and minds of family and nation.

Achieving rewards of this kind for your strenuous activities is much easier if you are a human being and not a monster—and if you are male. The concept of embedding is of interest from a quite different point of view when applied to a character almost the exact opposite of Beowulf, the monster Grendel's mother, a warrior who also shows much heroic energy, but it profiteth her not at all. That she is extraordinarily deeply embedded in her natural (or unnatural) surroundings in the evil mere was clear to me when I wrote *A Reading of Beowulf*[25] But it now seems remarkable that my own unconscious biases then prevented me from perceiving an even more significant way of embedding someone in a stereotype. She is, once you notice it, systematically reduced, ignored, discredited, and deprived of the ordinary dignity any ravening monster is entitled to—because of her sex. It is important to acknowledge that the feminist movement has given us the power to open our eyes to this kind of embedding, in a degraded social role and status.[26]

Grendel's mother is first of all just that, of course, and merely that. She has no name. She has no identifiable mate or spouse, and no past history or ancestry, other than what is implied in the vaguest of references to the long time she has ruled the mere-depths and some possible kinship, entirely unspecified, to the sea-dragons that live with her in the mere-waters and help her attack the swimming Beowulf. She has no identity at all, in other words, other than one dependent on her son. (What if Grendel were regularly referred to as Old Mere-Wife's Son?)

Part of this same relationship to Grendel, and one that gives her a major borrowed importance in the story, is that she has the perfectly acceptable obligation to avenge his death (because he is male and thus important). This highly contingent role as Grendel's avenger seems to replace any other imaginable motivations she might feel. Perhaps her notably ferocious defense of her underwater home against Beowulf's invasion is not so much self-defense or even defense of the domestic hearth as it is a defense of the sacred integrity of her son's body, the ritual beheading of which, as much as the killing of the female monster herself, seems to be one chief goal of Beowulf when he plunges into the mere. It is after all Grendel's head he brings back to Heorot, not hers.

Since Grendel's mother has no apparent ancestry, she does not seem to be directly involved in the great feud between Cain's descendants and God. When first mentioned (1258b–65a), she is included among the monsters who have lived on in the "cold streams" ever since Cain killed his only brother, but the poet immediately shifts to retelling how Grendel came to Heorot and was defeated by Beowulf. The total effect of this passage, illogical as it may seem, is to suggest that Grendel is a lineal and faithful descendant of Cain in a way that his mother is not. She is never said to "bear God's anger," possibly because she is beneath God's notice. At any rate, she appears in no theological contexts. Nor indeed is she even dependably human. Animal terms like *brimwylf* (1506, 1599) 'she-wolf of the sea' are often applied to her, though never to the much more humanoid Grendel. This lack of ordinary human features makes her a different sort of "enemy of mankind" (something she is never called) than the classic rebel-figure represented by Satan, Cain, and Grendel. Grendel seems to want very much to stay at night in a human hall he has enthusiastically desecrated, and he is an outlaw as well as a vandal. In both roles he is related, if only by negation, to human society. On the other hand, his mother seems to prefer the company of the mere's sea-dragons, and it may not be only her female lack of strength that keeps her from staying long on her only visit to the men's club at Heorot. Fanatical and vengeful mother-love is her sole human characteristic.

Denied the dubious dignity of that kind of symbolic meaning her son has, she is also robbed of the credit due her for her brave actions. In the narrative itself, it is truly astonishing how little is ever actually said about these actions. When she attacks the hall, the poet insists (1282b–87) that her strength is much less than that of a male and points scornfully at the speed with which she leaves the scene of battle, but otherwise she gets almost no attention. It would be hard to tell from the text that her raid was successful; she did accomplish exactly what she intended. Instead, the poet gives great space to the gallant resistance of the unwary Danes and their grief when they see that Æschere has been carried off. In his later lament, Hrothgar talks much more about Grendel than about Grendel's mother. At two points (1334 and 1351) brief mention of her leads him at once to veer off on a longer account of Grendel, much of it recapitulation that is hardly essential. This is exactly the pattern followed by the poet himself when he first introduces Grendel's mother (1258b–78). Before Beowulf dives into the mere to fight her, he also avoids any specific mention of this threatening female. He is not going down to the bottom to fight *her*, but instead considers the risk of meeting *hild* 'battle' or *deað* 'death', more impersonal and generalized opponents. These all seem effective ways of taking her selfhood away from her, or of granting her close to zero-grade existence.

Yet this way of seeing her is obviously untrue. All readers will agree that we carry away from the poem a vivid impression indeed of the dangerous fighting skill of Grendel's mother. This effect again is rather strange, for a close look at the passage describing the fight proper will show that again she is given absolutely minimum space. By contrast, in the earlier fight with Grendel, the narrative focuses intently on Grendel, particularly on his thoughts and emotions. We are made profoundly aware that two persons full of determined intentions are confronting each other. But we are never told anything specific about Grendel's mother's thoughts. We see her clearly enough, sitting on top of Beowulf and stabbing at him with her dagger for a few brief seconds (1545–49), but then we switch entirely away from her and stay with the hero, all the way through the passage until line 1569, by which time she has been beheaded. It is not possible to be beheaded without being mentioned, but the poet does reduce mention of her to a minimum. It is strange too that even in death she does not rate the usual eddying variations of the implications of it (cf. the space given to the dead dragon, for instance): just a severed vertebra and a fall, a terse clinical report. And then at once both Beowulf and the poet forget about her completely and zoom away into an eager search for the body of Grendel, a search that seems just as important as the hard-won victory over the mistress of the house.

It is thus consistent with this ignoring of her as a concrete character with recognizable courage and strength that the hero later comes close to describing for Hrothgar his fight in the underwater hall (1652–70) without ever being specific about just what he was fighting. It is not Grendel's mother he mentions but once again some abstract heroic action (*wigge, guþ, hild*—words for battle), all of them emphasizing only the hero's own behavior as if it took place in a vacuum, or in a mirror. He mentions his antagonist only in the plural phrase *huses hyrdas* (1666) 'the guardians of the house', and that phrase lumps her together with her son and virtually implies th Beowulf killed both of them at the same time during the mere fight. But in justice to Beowulf, one should point to his subsequent fairness to the she-monster. He gives her much more generous space, indeed roughly equal for once to what he gives Grendel, in his report to Hygelac (2115–43). There he even pays a compliment to her courage as avenger by saying she killed Æschere *ellenlíce* ('bravely' 2122) and he admits how difficult the fight was for him. Such a relatively objective version of the story only shows how much unconscious distortion was applied to it previously.

Engrained and unconscious assumptions of male superiority, especially in the realm of physical combat, reveal themselves almost amusingly in these passages. If the desired effect was to put Grendel's mother firmly in her place as an inferior antagonist, however, it has scarcely been attained. The sharp and uncomfortable disparity between the stereotype of female weakness and the demonstrated energy and power of her actions in the fight only increases our interest in what turns out to be many readers' favorite monster. One would like to believe (against all likelihood) that the *Beowulf*-poet had some awareness of this ironic tension.

Another character entitled at least temporarily to the label of female monster appears briefly in the poem in the person of Thryth (1931–62). She is described as being furiously intent on commanding the death of any man bold enough to look at her. Since it is evident that these men are innocent victims of her accusations, she is manifesting an outrageous abuse of royal power and queenly practice (*cwenlic þeaw* 1940), analogous to King Heremod's monstrous abuse of the privileges of his throne in killing his own hearth-comrades (1709b–22a).

But all is well. The exertions of a strong-minded husband can bring Thryth back to her proper role. Women can be forced to behave themselves, as a man like Heremod cannot be. His subjects seem quite helpless to remedy their plight, like the miserable subjects of Eormanric in *Deor* who can only wait until "it was overcome in regard to that kingdom."[27] When she is at last functioning correctly as Offa's loyal wife, Thryth becomes famous for her goodness and for her deep love for her husband. But this secondary kind of fame is obviously limited, and the spotlight has been switched from her to Offa by the end of the episode, just as the spotlight switches from Grendel's mother to Grendel. She is now one of the adornments that go to create his worldwide reputation, and his taming of her violent habits becomes merely another of his lordly exploits, one more monster-trophy to hang on the wall. Male superiority has been harshly reasserted.

Though Hrothgar's queen Wealhtheow has not usually been clas-
sified as a female monster, some have felt that in power and position she at least partly transcends the conventional limits of the
woman's role. I mention here Helen Damico's recent attempt to
portray her as a figure of commanding authority, rather than as the
helpless and thus tragic queen described in most recent criticism,
including my own.[28] The elaborate analogies Damico tries to estab-
lish between Wealhtheow and strong female figures in Germanic
legend and mythology like Yrsa or certain Valkyrie types will persuade only those willing to tolerate the severe strain such analogies
will exert on a number of customary readings of the text. I find the
strain much too great. Even if queens like Wealhtheow can be seen
as descendants of some almost goddess-like prototypical figure of
Germanic legend, she has been thoroughly adapted and shaped to
a dignified but fundamentally pathetic role in *Beowulf*. She is certainly a strong woman gifted with insight that her aging husband
seems to lack. One could even rephrase this more tellingly: she *is*
the prophetic insight that Hrothgar lacks. But her actions are cru-
elly limited by the very necessity of the traditional story itself to ve-
hement but vain pleas and exhortations. They will not change the
story's plot.

When she first appears (611–41), she is the embodiment of ceremonious decorum and thereby plays a recognized female role. She
moves slowly around the hall to greet individuals and offer them
drink, first to the king and last to the guest Beowulf. Her expression of confidence in the providential coming of the hero helps
move the demoralized Danes psychologically from Unferth's en-
vious snarls toward more positive forms of willing and hoping.
Beowulf takes cue and cup from her and makes a formal boast. In
this scene, as Damico reminds us, she is reminiscent of the women
of Icelandic literature who refuel a warrior's resolve with similar
rituals.

But the decorous ritual of this scene sets up a contrast for her
second appearance, when she surely tests and perhaps exceeds the
boundaries of "proper" queenly behavior in her anxious and forceful speeches to deaf ears. She dominates the scene. Hers is the only
voice we hear during the entire banquet. She progresses in to the
stately beat of hypermetric verse (1162–68), a distinction rare
in this poem. Nonetheless, despite all this heightening of her role,
she cannot transcend the limits of the situation and remains a conscious but helpless victim of it. But why find a deficiency in this
strong and tragic character? Should we labor to convert a finely-

drawn Cassandra into a Medea (or an Achilles) alien to the context of this story?

It is appropriate to end this discussion of the ways characters blend into their conventional contexts by citing the most thoroughly embedded of them all, the young warrior Wiglaf who helps Beowulf kill the dragon. As I once noted, the first mention of him identifies him strikingly as one central point within a complex network of relationships and obligations.[29]

Wiglaf wæs haten,   Weoxstanes sunu,
leoflic lindwiga,   leod Scylfinga,
mæg Ælfheres;   geseah his mondryhten
under heregriman   hat þrowian.   (2602–05)

(He was called Wiglaf, son of Weohstan, a much-loved shield-warrior, lord of Scylfings, kinsman of Ælfhere. He saw his own lord enduring the heat under his war-helmet.)

As has often been pointed out, the story about his father's sword which follows further suggests family and national loyalties inherited from the past. All these relationships that surround Wiglaf remain in neutral or potential form unless they make him able to respond to the emergency. That response will not occur automatically, ensured by the social context, but will occur only if the novice warrior wills it, or re-wills it. Then he embeds himself in that world by his own choice.

So now he moves forward to offer his life in the service of his lord, the infinitely dear *mondryhten,* the *freodryhten.* The strongly willed action reconstructs the heroic framework, pumps vital blood into it, changes it from what is decoratively potential to what is superbly actual. Not only his courage in the fight but all that he later does makes and repeats such a statement of purpose. He speaks the right words to his peers—first words of earnest evocation and entreaty, then words of anathema when they have exercised their own options to desert the heroic system. He hovers lovingly over his dying king, trying to hold life in him. Out of this attitude of grief and devotion grow the right orders (perhaps the first orders Wiglaf has ever given) for the right actions: to send the Messenger to tell the waiting nation of the death and to evaluate the tragic meaning of Beowulf's last embrace of fate; to pass on the king's wishes to his people; to take the lead in organizing the funeral rituals, once all have been made emotionally ready to take full part in it. Once the action has become wholly communal, Wiglaf promptly disappears into the collective body he has reconstituted—that body from which he was constituted—and is never mentioned again. But he has fully demonstrated how the heroic ideal is passed down by example and by reenactment. That is his chief role as character. We need not worry about whether he is actually Beowulf's heir or his successor as king of the Geats. In an important symbolic sense he has become his kinsman's heir and his nation's king.

NOTES

1. See Robert E. Bjork, "Unferth in the Hermeneutic Circle: A Reappraisal of James L. Rosier's 'Design for Treachery: The Unferth Intrigue'," *Papers on Language and Literature* 16 (1980), 133–41, for a recent summary of the decades of controversy over Unferth. Rosier's article appeared in *PMLA* 77 (1962), 1–7. See also Ida Masters Hollowell, "Unferð the þyle in *Beowulf*," *Studies in Philology* 73 (1976), 239–65, for a capable defense of Unferth's much maligned character.

2. *A Reading of Beowulf* (New Haven, CT: Yale University Press, 1968), 66–76.

3. R. W. Chambers, *Beowulf: An Introduction*, 3d ed. with supplement by Charles L. Wrenn, Cambridge: Cambridge University Press, 1959, 29) and Arthur G. Brodeur (*The Art of Beowulf*, Berkeley: University of California Press, 1959, 153) are two critics who tend to view Unferth as the evil counselor. Gerald Morgan, "The Treachery of Hrothulf," *English Studies* 53 (1972), 23–39, does not believe in the treachery of Unferth—or, for that matter, in the treachery of Hrothulf. Fred C. Robinson reviews the Unferth problem in "Elements of the Marvellous in the Characterization of Beowulf: A Reconsideration of the Textual Evidence," in *Old English Studies in Honour of John C. Pope*, ed. Robert B. Burlin and Edward B. Irving, Jr. (Toronto: Toronto University Press, 1974), 119–37.

4. See W. W. Lawrence, *Beowulf and Epic Tradition* (Cambridge, MA: Harvard University Press, 1930), 153–54, and Adrien Bonjour's article retracting his earlier attempt at rehabilitating Unferth (*Twelve Beowulf Papers: 1940–1960* [Geneva: E. Droz; Neuchâtel: Faculté des lettres, 1962] 129–33). The evil Unferth is, however, still alive and thriving in David Williams, *Cain and Beowulf: A Study in Secular Allegory* (Toronto: University of Toronto Press, 1982), 87–88.

5. Carol Clover, "The Germanic Context of the Unferþ Episode," *Speculum* 55 (1980), 444–68. Two recent articles by Ward Parks ("Flyting and Fighting: Pathways in the Realization of the Epic Contest," *Neophilologus* 70 [1986], 292–306, and "The Flyting Speech in Traditional Heroic Narrative," *Neophilologus* 71 [1987], 285–95) continue to explore the convention along similar lines. The wit of the exchange is emphasized by Roberta Frank, "'Mere' and 'Sund': Two Sea-Changes in *Beowulf*," *Modes of Interpretation in Old English Literature: Essays in Honour of Stanley B. Greenfield*, ed.

Phyllis Rugg Brown et al. (Toronto: University of Toronto Press, 1986), 153–72.

6. While I think the emphasis on Danish drinking has some significance, I may be exaggerating its importance, in view of the lack of evidence from any similar poems. T. A. Shippey (*Beowulf* [London: Edward Arnold, 1978], 9) argues sensibly for a simple cultural gap between our modern view that drunkenness is wrong and the Anglo-Saxons' acceptance of it as normal behavior. The Church's attitude was probably different. Hugh Magennis points out in a note that later homilists like Ælfric omitted or toned down references in their Latin sources to "spiritual drunkenness," apparently for fear of encouraging excessive drinking ("The Exegesis of Inebriation: Treading Carefully in Old English," *ELN* 23 [March 1986], 3–6).

7. I can understand recent attempts to soften the last prediction of damnation but cannot accept them as persuasive arguments. Charles Donahue's assertion (*"Beowulf* and Christian Tradition: A Reconsideration from a Celtic Stance," *Traditio* 21 [1965], 92) that Beowulf here means not hell but merely Hel, the morally neutral Germanic death-world, seems unlikely in view of the fact that such specifically pagan places and concepts are no visible part of the poem elsewhere. Robinson's very tentative suggestion ("Elements of the Marvellous," 130) that we might read *healle* 'hall' for *helle* creates a combination of words much less plausible than what we have in the text. See Thalia Phillies Feldman, "A Comparative Study of *Feond, Deofl, Syn* and *Hel* in *Beowulf*," *Neuphilologische Mitteilungen* 88 (1987), 159–74, for a recent consideration of the problem of how much Grendel is Christianized.

8. Chapter 119 of *Njal's Saga*.

9. James L. Rosier, "Design for Treachery: The Unferth Intrigue."

10. Robinson ("Elements of the Marvellous," 131–32) suggests, though with some skepticism, that Unferth might be a coward "regenerated" by Beowulf, like certain characters in the Icelandic sagas.

11. Morton W. Bloomfield, *"Beowulf* and Christian Allegory: An Interpretation of Unferth," *Traditio* 7 (1949–51), 410–15, thinks the name implies "discord." For the contrary view, see Fred C. Robinson, "Personal Names in Medieval Narrative and the Name of Unferth in *Beowulf*," in *Essays in Honor of Richebourg Gaillard McWilliams*, ed. Howard Creed (Birmingham, AL: Birmingham Southern College, 1970), 43–48. See also Jane Roberts, "Old English *Un-* 'Very' and Unferth," *English Studies* 61 (1980), 289–92. She argues plausibly that the name might be commendatory, if its meaning is to be taken as significant at all. *Unferð* could mean 'greatness of heart' if the prefix is the rare but attested intensive prefix *un-*. On the other hand, R. D. Fulk, "Unferth and His Name," *Modern Philology* 85 (1987), 113–27, offers considerable evidence to support his view that the name had no special meaning for Anglo-Saxons, emphasizing that "the name cannot mean 'not-peace', or reflect in any other way on Unferth's

character" (113). He regards Unferth as a round character rather than an allegorical figure of malice, in any case. John C. Pope's careful study of a disputed word in the passage introducing Unferth (*"Beowulf* 505, 'gehedde,' and Unferth," *Modes of Interpretation in Old English Literature: Essays in Honour of Stanley B. Greenfield*, 173−87) leads him to translate 503−05 as "for he would not grant that any other man on earth could ever, under the heavens, care more for glorious deeds than he himself did" (180). He sees Unferth as a normal heroic figure, "a respected fighter among the Danes as well as a privileged spokesman" (183), a view which parallels my own.

12. Rosier, in the article cited above, brings forward evidence from glosses and Old Norse literature for a pejorative sense of *þyle / þulr*, but the evidence has not been generally accepted as proving his point beyond dispute.

13. For a good general view of the subject, especially the tensions between hero and king, see W. T. H. Jackson, *The Hero and the King: An Epic Theme* (New York: Columbia University Press, 1982).

14. *The Battle of Maldon* may be found in *The Anglo-Saxon Minor Poems*, ed. E. V. K. Dobbie, Anglo-Saxon Poetic Records VI (New York: Columbia University Press, 1942), and in a recent separate edition by D. G. Scragg (Manchester: Manchester University Press, 1981).

15. John D. Niles, who generally takes a view similar to mine on this matter, remarks that Hrothgar "appears as only the shell of a good king" (*Beowulf: The Poem and its Tradition*, 110). Nancy Rose, "Hrothgar, Nestor, and Religiosity as a Mode of Characterization in Heroic Culture," *Journal of Popular Culture* 1 (1967), 158−65, draws some parallels I make, though I do not at all share her opinion that Hrothgar is seen as responsible for the Danes' heathen worship. His religiosity is certainly conspicuous, but it is Christian rather than heathen. Straightforward and unqualified praise of Hrothgar is found in Henry B. Woolf, "Hrothgar," *Louisiana State University Studies*, Humanities Series, 5 (1954), 39−54, and that is the usual view taken by critics.

16. Marie Nelson, "It is More Honorific to Give . . . ," *Neuphilologische Mitteilungen* 74 (1973), 624−29, properly points out that the gift-giving passage after the Grendel-fight (lines 1008−49) is to be understood as celebrating Hrothgar's generosity rather than Beowulf's achievement.

17. The reference is to the last 5 lines of the poem. *The Wanderer* is found in the Exeter Book (*Anglo-Saxon Poetic Records* III), and in separate editions by T. P. Dunning and Alan J. Bliss (London: Methuen, 1969), and R. F. Leslie (Manchester: Manchester University Press, 1966).

18. See my article, "The Nature of Christianity in *Beowulf*," especially pages 9 and 14−15.

19. See "The Nature of Christianity in *Beowulf*," 18, for some figures on the dramatic drop-off in the number of Christian references in Part II.

20. Ong, *Orality and Literacy*, 45−6.

21. His special relation to Hygelac all through the poem is well brought out by Arthur G. Brodeur in *The Art of Beowulf*.

22. An excellent brief essay is Peter Clemoes, "Action in *Beowulf* and Our Perception of it," in *Old English Poetry: Essays on Style*, ed. Daniel G. Calder (Berkeley: University of California Press, 1979), 147–68.

23. See John M. Hill, "Beowulf and the Danish Succession: Gift Giving as an Occasion for Complex Gesture," *Medievalia et Humanistica*, n.s. 11 (1982), 177–97.

24. See my article, "Beowulf Comes Home," in *Acts of Interpretation: Essays . . . in Honor of E. Talbot Donaldson*, ed. Mary J. Carruthers and Elizabeth D. Kirk (Norman, OK: Pilgrim Books, 1982), 129–43. See also Samuel M. Riley, "The Contrast Between Beowulf and Hygelac," *Journal of Narrative Technique* 10 (1980), 186–97. This article, which I had not seen when writing mine, makes a very similar point: that Beowulf is obliged to reply to Hygelac's implied charges in a testing scene resembling the Unferth confrontation.

25. *A Reading of Beowulf*, 112–115.

26. For a thorough historical survey of the place of women in Anglo-Saxon society, see Christine Fell, *Women in Anglo-Saxon England* (London: British Museum Publications, 1984). Richard J. Schrader discusses the characters in *Beowulf* specifically in *God's Handiwork: Images of Women in Early Germanic Literature*, Contributions in Women's Studies, No. 41 (Westport, CT: Greenwood Press, 1983). He sees Grendel's mother as an embodiment of revenge, in her fury forsaking the natural peacemaking role of the female. See also Jane Chance Nitzche, "The Anglo-Saxon Woman as Hero," *Allegorica* 5 (1980), 139–48, and her more recent *Woman as Hero in Old English Literature* (Syracuse, NY: Syracuse University Press, 1986).

27. *Deor* is found in The Exeter Book and separately edited by Kemp Malone (London: Methuen, 1933; 4th ed. 1966).

28. Helen Damico, *Beowulf's Wealhtheow and the Valkyrie Tradition* (Madison: University of Wisconsin Press, 1984). Elaine T. Hansen, "Women in Old English Poetry Reconsidered," *Michigan Academician* 9 (1976), 109–17, states more accurately that in *Beowulf* "the female becomes a poetic voice for all lonely and innocent victims of fate, and an apt symbol, for the most skillful poets, of the weakness inherent in the human condition" (117). See also Bernice W. Kliman, "Women in Early English Literature, 'Beowulf' to the 'Ancrene Wisse'," *Nottingham Mediaeval Studies* 21 (1977), 32–49, and the works cited in note 26 above.

29. *A Reading of Beowulf*, 154–58.

THREE

Style and Story: Narrative Modes

In this chapter I want to examine some of the principal ways poetic story-telling works in *Beowulf*, in part at least on the sound principle that by learning how things are being said we understand better what is being said. If there is a single word applicable to most of what I will discuss, it is "interlace," a word borrowed from art history and given wide currency among literary critics by John Leyerle's 1967 article, "The Interlace Structure of *Beowulf*."[1] What Leyerle presents there as a general statement about the poem is true and still useful, still indeed insufficiently exploited by Leyerle himself and by subsequent critics. It is also adaptable to the more recent ideas about the nature of oral-based poetry touched on in the first chapter.

Leyerle summarizes his description of the poem as follows:

The themes [he has been describing monsters, fighting, the death of kings, and treasure as separate themes] make a complex, tightly-knotted lacertine interlace that cannot be untied without losing the design and form of the whole. The tension and force of the poem arise from the way the themes cross and juxtapose. Few comments are needed from the poet because significance comes from the intersections and conjunctions of the design. To the *Beowulf* poet, as to many other writers, the relations between events are more significant than their temporal sequence and he used a structure that gave him great freedom to manipulate time and concentrate on the complex interconnections of events.[2]

Calling attention in this way to the thick interweavings and complicated balances and contrasts that characterize the style of *Beowulf* has permanent critical value, a value still not entirely realized. In fact, his own theoretical approach does not always produce acceptable results in Leyerle's own account of the poem. He arrives at several questionable conclusions. For example, he blames Beowulf for personal vanity and insufficient attention to his people's needs, maintaining that Beowulf brings "dire affliction" upon them by his unnecessary death. This is a way of distorting meaning by implying the presence in the poem of options that do not exist, either in this particular story or in the heroic system as a whole that underlies it. Talk of the hero's personal vanity belongs to another realm of discourse, not the heroic one; in the heroic world what might be called personal vanity is more likely to be admired than reproved. And it is the iron destiny of heroes that compels Beowulf to make his nonetheless wholly free choice to fight the dragon, a creature already actively engaged in bringing "dire affliction" upon his people. Necessary is precisely what Beowulf's death is.

Leyerle is even farther off the mark when he dismisses as "useless" the funeral treasures seen in Scyld's death-ship and on Beowulf's pyre, together with the golden torque presented to Beowulf by Wealhtheow and later taken by the Frisians from Hygelac's body. If the funeral treasures, placed there by the mourners to show the deepest honor to the dead, are useless, then so are the funerals and the men they celebrate, and in the end the social world they live in. In such lead-footed moralizing attitudes, Leyerle betrays a crypto-Christian approach that cannot disguise its blanket disapproval of heroes as heroes, an approach that denies the worth of the poem's secular ideal.

Yet, in a more general way, Leyerle is basically right about the way the poem sounds and looks. To spend a few minutes looking at the specimen illustrations of carvings and manuscript carpet-pages that accompany his article is to see a little distance into the exuberant yet severe convolutions of the barbarian mind. Something of the same effect can be gained by inspecting closely a small-scale "carpet-page" of text from *Beowulf*.

For this purpose I choose a passage of stylistic interlace of above average density, though not one of great complexity of meaning. It is a passage describing the dragon's first arrival at the barrow and its subsequent anger at being robbed of an item of treasure by a human intruder. I have here marked the text with simple symbols, each standing for a particular associative cluster (or, very loosely, a theme or an idea) that is connected here and elsewhere with some of the major symbolic preoccupations of Part II. As we will see later in this chapter, the same themes also make highly significant interpenetrations on a much larger scale of measure.

KEY

A (9 occurrences in this passage)—*Aggression:* hostile behavior, fire, flame; the fear of these.

T (8 occurrences)—*Treasure;* gold, hoard.

M (7 occurrences)—*Man,* mankind.

E (6 occurrences)—*Earth;* grave, barrow (as container).

O (4 occurrences)—*Old;* age, long time.

H (2 occurrences)—*Holding,* guarding.

T
Hordwynne fond

O A	E	
eald uhtsceaða	opene standan,	
A	E A	
se ðe byrnende	biorgas seceð,	
A	A	
nacod niðdraca,	nihtes fleogeð	
A	E M	
fyre befangen;	hyne foldbuend	
A	A	
[swiðe ondræ] da [ð].	He gesecan sceall	
T E	M T	
[ho]r[d on h]rusan,	þær he hæðen gold	
H O		
warað *win*trum frod,	ne byð him wihte ðy sel.	
M A	O	
Swa se ðeodsceaða	þreo hund wintra	
H E	T E	
heold on hrusan	hordærna sum,	
eacencræftig,	oððæt hyne an abealch	
M	M	
mon on mode;	mandryhtne bær	
T		
fæted wæge,	frioðowære bæd	
	T	
hlaford sinne.	Ða wæs hord rasod,	
T		
onboren beaga hord,	bene getiðad	
M		
feasceaftum men.	Frea sceawode	
M O T		
fira fyrngeweorc	forman siðe.	(2270b–86)

(The old dawn-raider found hoard-joy standing open, the one who burning looks for barrows, naked wicked dragon who flies

at night, fire-seized; truly earth-dwellers dread him. He is compelled to seek out the hoard in earth where, ancient in winters,
he will guard heathen gold, no whit the better for it. That is
how the people-killer gripped a mighty hoard-house of immense strength in the earth for three hundred winters—until
one man enraged his heart, a man who carried off a plated cup
to his own master and asked the lord for a peaceful settlement.
Through this, the hoard was invaded—that ring-hoard was
lessened!—the favor granted to the destitute man. The lord
examined the ancient work of men for the first time.)

The passage describes the horror of a dragon's coming to the
world of human beings. *Draconitas* is something vividly and implacably anti-human. Fire, hatred, and inexplicable compulsions are
not hard to identify here, but the alien nature of the dragon, and
also of the dead hoard-world he covets, is expressed as well by the
suggestion of enormous time-spans. The mentality of pre-literate
man cannot cope with such numbers; they overload his capacities
of normal memory. To those without the documents, measures and
calculations that give us the illusion of some control over the im-
mensities of space and time, three hundred years might as well be
three million. The cup the lord examines embodies the sickening
stretch of years from *fyrn* 'long ago' to *forman siðe* 'now for the first
time'. And over these near-geological time-spans dragons "hold" a
hoard, hold it, that is to say, out of use and really out of time,
weight it down with their sheer dead mass, turn it into the rotting
furnishings of a death-house. Though originally creatures of fire
and air, dragons seem to want to drive themselves downward and
to become torpid earth-creatures, happiest never to emerge from
their barrows and burrows for three hundred years, or a thousand.
Though we are later informed of this dragon's great joy in flying,
the nearby Geats have never noticed him before and we must assume it is because he stayed in his barrow. Only when dragons are
disturbed in their crazy rage for torpor will the destructive fire
flame out.

It will be seen in the quoted passage that the few key images are
wound tightly together, virtually braided and locked into place by
heavy and intricate repetition. What some might well see as the
weakness or dullness of this repetitious style, with its "lack of steady
advance," and its compulsive backtrackings and burgeoning variations, can also be seen as its strength. The severely limited lexicon
(note, for example, that the element *hord* occurs as often as five
times in this brief passage) keeps pushing us back to the same

words and the same ideas and images. The effect in this particular case is to make the poet seem just as magnetized by the hoard as the dragon is. At the same time, the requirements of alliteration and of metrical variation keep forcing the verse outward, away from mere repetition into variation. The movement is thus not at all a "steady advance" along a line but a circling that is constantly incremental. Ideas and images rotate away and then come back with some new accretion of meaning, new brush-strokes, new angles of view.

This very high redundancy ensures that even the most inattentive listener must gather from the steady pound of these drumbeats some elementary and elemental message, pointed and paleolithic: An Old, a Hostile One of Fire, Holds Hoard in Earth till Man disturbs. Perhaps we take this in somatically in the form of heavy rhythms; perhaps it all seeps in through the pores, the interstices between the grids of rationality we erect to scan our world. It is fundamentally *emotive* information that is conveyed to us (the only interesting kind in poetry), and it is conveyed to us in a way typical of the oral style.

Though this passage does not make the point, other passages show another important effect of the heavy rhythms and over-determined statements. Their focus on the already mentioned and the wholly predictable allows for the possibility of effective sudden surprise when the unexpected is abruptly introduced. We can be jolted violently from our half-mesmerized brooding over the implications of some set of significant objects. This passage describing the dragon's coming is slow, muffled, intense—but such style prepares us for highly dramatic changes of pace. It can and does build toward an explosion of action in the narrative present.

Another example of narrative interlace, on a somewhat larger scale this time, is the much-discussed account of the Danes' ride back from the mere, during which journey Beowulf's victory over Grendel is praised.[3] The passage can be roughly outlined as follows:

A. 837–52. *Collective experience* (opening of frame). The Danes first assemble at Heorot to visit the *wundor*, and then track Grendel to the blood-stained mere. Clear evidence of his death, confirmed by the narrator (who, unlike the Danes, can see below the mere's surface).

B. 853–67a. *Collective response*. Many praise Beowulf's achievement during the ride back. The Danes race their horses.

C. 867b–74a. *Individual performance*. A *cyninges þegn* who remembers old songs celebrates Beowulf in a new song. (Unless the Sigemund and Heremod stories that follow make up part of this song, its details are not furnished.)

D. 874b–97 (or to 900?). *Individual performance* (by the king's thane or the narrator?). The story of Sigemund's exile and dragon-slaying (probably as an implicit comparison with and celebration of Beowulf's similar exploit? Less likely, a "forecast" of Beowulf's own future dragon-slaying?).

E. 898 (or 901?)–915. *Individual performance* (by the king's thane or the narrator?). The story of Heremod's disastrous decline from early promise. Explicitly stated to be in contrast with Beowulf's virtuous and successful career.

F. 916–20a. *Collective experience* (closing frame, echoing A and B). Racing of horses and visiting the *wundor*, in the reversed order typical of epic "ring structure."[4]

Praising Beowulf by placing him in the already existing pantheon of traditional heroes seems to be one main purpose of this difficult passage. Precisely how this is done is still puzzling. The transitions seem jerky and abrupt, even if the preceding outline furnishes some rationale for them. For one thing it is not always clear whose voice we are hearing. Probably early audiences had few problems with identifying the speakers, since a performer could make the distinction between voices plain enough by intonation, gesture, or timing. It may also be that the audience felt that the praise of Beowulf was what mattered, and that who was doing it was of much less importance. Any individual's voice was merely a form of collective statement.

Even if we cannot answer the questions we ask about this passage, we ought to go over them in search of shadowy answers, if nothing better. Is the *cyninges þegn* a tribal historian or an officially designated *scop* or an amateur and part-time poet, or do none of these categories fit what he is? Does he in fact improvise (as he rides) one long and rather oblique encomium of Beowulf, most of which is taken up with celebrating the old hero Sigemund and with disparaging the criminal Danish king Heremod, thus placing Beowulf within the framing context of one positive and one negative instance? Or does he first compose a song about Beowulf, and then (for an encore?) perform another song about Sigemund, and then yet a third about Heremod? Or (as seems most plausible to me) does the Christian narrator himself come in to append the heavily moralized exemplum about Heremod to the fictional poet's songs of Beowulf and Sigemund?

Supporting evidence for this last view is slight. It may mean something that the same story about Heremod is later repeated in Hrothgar's very decidedly moralized sermon (1709a–22a). And there is on the other hand a frail link connecting the stories of Beowulf and Sigemund in the mention of memory, an idea which may link them more directly to oral Germanic tradition. The words *gemyndig* (868) and *gemunde* (870) point to memory as one of the thane's chief qualifications; it is just this capacity that reveals itself in his feat of being first able to retrieve obscure or little-known (perhaps shady?) details about Sigemund's early life, before he eventually comes (884b–97) to what everyone knows about that hero, his killing of a dragon, the event that makes him not obscure but *wide mærost* (898) 'most widely famous'. In the Heremod passage, on the other hand, this theme of fame and memory is not made explicit.

For all these difficulties, in a general way the idea of fame and its spread dominates and unifies the diverse strands of the passage through interlacing. The defeat of Grendel and what that implies about Beowulf's prowess is new information that we see spreading. It spreads to the many (838, 918) who have come from far and near over distant roads to look at ripping claw and bloody track; across generations, to the old and to the young (853–54); out of the immediate present to the presumed future of Beowulf as potential king (860–63, and the entire comparison of Beowulf with the failed king Heremod); into the traditional repertory of praise-songs, to which Beowulf is now added as subject of a new song; to the small elite of major legendary heroes, among whom Beowulf is now placed. If the method is the expected one of parataxis—laying strand A beside B beside C and letting them make their combined statement without explanatory comment—the various contiguous parts lie within a guiding and informing pattern that is always clear and boldly drawn. Emotion unifies the passage. It is the central emotion of excited gratitude, with the several varying modes of praise or the alternating voices subtly quickened by the vigorous movements of the racing riders, and all of it focused on a poetic articulation of feeling, and perhaps capped at the end by a half-pious amen of crypto-Christian thanksgiving, gratitude that the virtuous hero does not share any of the damned Heremod's sinfulness.

Another pattern of similarly intricate interlace, here involving chiefly the alternation of action with authorial comment, can be found in the narrative describing the killing of the dragon. I will take here only one brief passage, deferring a fuller examination of the larger patterns of this kind until later in the chapter. In the passage I examine now, 2669–2723, we see the narrator taking few chances that we might miss the point of the action we are being shown.

The dragon's furious second attack, from lines 2669 to 2687, during which Wiglaf's shield is burned up and Beowulf's sword fails finally, ends with the poet's coming in to explain the sword's failure in terms of Beowulf's excessive strength. Then the third and last onslaught is beautifully blocked out and filled in. Even small details, like making the fight one between a *þeodsceaða* (2688) 'people-enemy' and a *þeodcyning* (2694) 'people-king', serve to heighten our sense that we witness a "national" emergency. Lines 2688 to 2693 are purest action, with 9 verses allotted to the dragon and his attack, and 3 verses to Beowulf's being desperately wounded. Even in such terms of quantity the hero is shown as being overwhelmed.

Then these three lines of comment, interrupting the torrent of action at a moment of great suspense:

Ða ic æt þearfe gefrægn   þeodcyninges
andlongne eorl   ellen cyðan,
cræft ond cenðu,   swa him gecynde wæs.   (2694–6)

(Then I heard that the warrior by the side of the people's king at the time of his great need made known his courage, his strength and boldness, as it had been bred into him.)

I once suggested that here alliteration, enjambment and juxtaposition create "a tightly woven super-formula of six verses, stating with intensity and economy the need in time of trial for making public show of physical strength and courage, because it is the traditional behavior of a hereditary warrior caste."[5] The very length of this paraphrase or of my translation above, for all their wordiness falling short of representing the packed meaning of the Old English, should make plainer the fine density of the original. Here I call attention to the placement of this ethical gem within descriptions of violent action, for what follows immediately after depicts Wiglaf's right action, without which the ethical statement alone cannot long sustain any force. He hurls himself forward in total recklessness, oblivious of the gaping jaws and burning pain, to pierce the dragon with all his strength in the first vulnerable spot he comes to in his rush.

This headlong action gives Beowulf time to regain his balance.

Þa gen sylf cyning
geweold his gewitte,   wællseaxe gebræd

biter ond beaduscearp,   þæt he on byrnan wæg;
forwrat Wedra helm   wyrm on middan.   (2702b–05)

(Then still the king himself recovered conscious command,
drew his dagger, biting and battle-sharp, that he wore on his
mailshirt; the protector of Weders slashed the dragon apart in
the middle.)

Comment is really woven into this action passage. Note that *as* he
acts, through the very process of acting decisively, Beowulf *becomes
sylf cyning* and *Wedra helm,* and then ideal king and ideal thane can
be linked together in praise in another terse 3-1/2 line summary by
the narrator:

Feond gefyldan   (ferh ellen wræc),
ond hi hyne þa begen   abroten hæfdon,
sibæðelingas.   Swylc sceolde secg wesan,
þegn æt ðearfe!   (2706–09a)

(They felled the enemy—courage drove out his life—and they
both then had succeeded in destroying him, those noble kinsmen. That is how a fighting-man should be, a retainer in time
of need!)

This exultant comment assures us that the two fighters are now
united in a single *ellen,* a common courage, and thus create once
more a staunch community of *sibæðelingas,* with each man taking a full part in destroying their nation's enemy. Sounding out
loudly the names of the dignities and the relationships—*sylf cyning,
þeodcyning, Wedra helm, andlongne eorl, þegn æt ðearfe*—asserts in its
own way a social structure completely revitalized by the strenuous
action that surrounds this discursive statement.

Yet this finely fulfilled moment of glory flickers by in an instant,
for the king feels the poison working in his body. He walks to a seat
nearer the barrow where he can look at the ancient stones of the *ece
eorðreced* (2719), the eternal earth-hall which is the image of his
own death. As he stares at this near prospect (near both in time and
space), Wiglaf looks at him and lovingly tends to his needs as best
he can.

Hyne þa mid handa   heorodreorigne,
þeoden mærne,   þegn ungemete till
winedryhten his   wætere gelafede,
hilde sædne,   ond his hel[m] onspeon.   (2720–23)

([I translate this very literally to preserve the word-order, with words referring to Beowulf in italics]: "*Him* then with hands *drenched-in-blood, the famous prince* the indescribably good thane *his friend-lord* bathed with water *battle-sick* and unlaced his helmet.")

The inflections of Old English permit a word-order that lets us here see Beowulf as object, as an array now of displaced accusatives, all being acted upon earnestly and compassionately by the thane whose merciful actions and loving hands are completely interlocked with the syntax of the sentence. This tight lock of subject and object, love and loyalty, is representative of the style to which the term interlace might most appropriately be applied, where syntax and word-order themselves seem to make a form of ethical statement.

Under the same heading of interlace we could also include the familiar stylistic feature of advancing the story by contrast. In an earlier study I discussed one form of this habitual procedure, the use of negative statements closely coupled with the positive statements and serving to define the positives more clearly and dramatically, more agonistically, to use Ong's word.[6]

Hrothgar's first speech to Beowulf (457–90) offers a compact example of this kind of contrast within one character and one utterance. It is basically a contrast between active and passive. Up until line 472, Hrothgar describes things he *did* as a young king. Events take place, and time moves on in an assured and confident narrative sequence heavily marked by temporal conjunctions: *ða, þanon, ða, ða, siððan*. He explains that Beowulf's father once came to Denmark as a fugitive from a blood-feud. At that time Hrothgar ruled (*weold*) the Danes and held (*heold*) the kingdom; the rhyme stresses these two verbs of power and authority. As strong ruler he acts at once to settle the feud by wergeld payment (470: the active verbs are *þingode* and *sende*) and in return is offered grateful oaths of allegiance by Ecgtheow. He decisively achieves something clear and definite.

But at line 473 we shift dramatically to the passive. Achievement ends. Now Hrothgar finds it painful even to tell anyone what Grendel *has done to him*. His *fletwerod* (476), his hall-company, *is . . . gewanod*, is diminished. Fate has taken them off, though God could stop Grendel. Now we can see that Grendel, fate, God, death take whatever actions are taken. The Danes who stay are killed (death takes them), and Hrothgar is left passively doing nothing, merely ironically "owning" the fewer loyal men. There is an evident contrast between his forcefully "holding" the kingdom in his youth and this wretched form of possession.

The syntactic contrast between active and passive underlines exactly that split in Hrothgar's personality discussed in the previous chapter, the terrible gap between youth and age, between his onetime strength and present helplessness. In terms of the dynamics of the general plot, the contrast heightens our sense of Grendel's tremendous power, a power that can drive a previously strong and confident nation to its knees.

The extent and nature of Grendel's power can also be seen in another passage, describing his first attack on Heorot, a passage which provides an example of a different kind of contrast, this time one involving interesting distinctions between parts of speech. By first mentioning Grendel and his anger at line 86 and taking the time to describe his background and ancestry at some length before the angry monster actually comes to attack the hall (115), the poet of course creates one of his more effectively suspenseful "retards." During this delay Grendel is being defined largely in terms of his home (and Cain's home): hell, borderlands, moors, fens, giants' country—all localities we think of as existing at a considerable distance off in time and space, *mancynne fram*, well away from where mankind lives. The whole race of Cain, like Cain himself, has been forcibly pushed away from humanity when sent into exile. With Grendel's return, it springs back with terrible rebounding force, as strong as the force that once banished it, a vicious striking out of long pent-up violence.

What then comes to Heorot's door—perhaps, dramatically, it is all the astonished and doomed Danes have time to notice—is a furious onslaught of the *adjectives* that describe Grendel. Sleeping trustfully after their feast, the Danes wake to nightmare. I here put the adjectives and modifying phrases in italics.

> Fand þa ðær inne   æþelinga gedriht
> swefan æfter symble;   sorge ne cuðon,
> wonsceaft wera.   Wiht *unhælo*,
> *grim* ond *grædig*,   *gearo* sona wæs,
> *reoc* ond *reþe*,   ond on ræste genam
> þritig þegna,   þanon eft gewat
> *huðe hremig*   to ham faran,
> mid þære wælfylle   wica neosan.   (118–25)

(Then he found inside a host of noblemen sleeping after the feast; they knew no sorrow, the bad luck of men. The creature of evil—grim and greedy, was at once ready, savage, ferocious—and took from their beds thirty thanes; then went away from there exulting in plunder journeying home, visiting his house with his fill of corpses.)

Note how vague the noun *wiht* is, just as the exact nature and identity of the attacker is vague. The unhelpful noun is set off against the adjectives, those terrifying clangs of the tocsin. The astounded Danes were not briefed as we were on Grendel's nature and background. Then the clangs fade away again toward silence as Grendel goes quietly home with his booty, as he came stealthily to the hall and took them by surprise when he came.

But after this first adjectival unleashing of attributes of horror, the poet shifts to verbs in describing Grendel. The verbs say: he comes, he keeps coming, he is *always* coming to the hall. They are verbs suggesting a continuous state of action, perhaps something like a state of war, rather than any specific incidents: *wan* (144), *wan* (151) (and the related noun *gewin* 133 and 191) 'fought'; *heteniðas wæg* (152) 'carried on hostile attacks'; *ehtende wæs* (159) 'kept on persecuting'; *fela fyrena . . . / oft gefremede* (164–65) 'often committed many crimes'; *seomade ond syrede* (161) 'lay in wait and ambushed'. Many references to the long duration of time reinforce this impression of tireless and incessant pressure: *longsum* (134, 192) 'long-lasting'; *wæs seo hwil micel* (146) 'that length of time was great'; *XII wintra tid* (147) 'the space of twelve years'; *hwile* (152) 'a long time'; *fela missera* (153) 'many half-years'; *singale sæcce* (154) 'perpetual fighting'; *singala seað* (190) '[Hrothgar] seethed perpetually'.

Instead of being a sudden bursting in of threats Grendel now becomes an institution of ongoing terror. On the other side of the picture, the only verbs available for the Danes are passive and ironic: they busy themselves with weeping, sitting, idolatry, suffering. Hrothgar suffers in two verbs in one line: *þolode ðryðswyð, þegnsorge dreah* (131) 'the brave man suffered, suffered sorrow for thanes'.

Some Danes make arrangements to get farther away and sleep elsewhere.

Þa wæs eaðfynde   þe him elles hwær
gerumlicor   ræste sohte,
bed æfter burum,   ða him gebeacnod wæs,

gesægd soðlice   sweotolan tacne
healðegnes hete.   (138–42a)

(Then it was easy to find someone who sought a bed elsewhere
where it was more spacious, a bed in the sleeping-building,
when it was signalled to him, said truly, with a clear sign—the
hall-thane's hate.)

Attempted escape is a way of describing their strong psychological
resistance to accepting the frightful reality. The long sentence itself
dramatizes the process by placing the dire word *hete*, the violence
of Grendel's hostility, only at the very end of denial, after a long
fending-off of the evidence. We can also see a later movement from
the *hwil micel*, the defined and limited twelve years of the monster's
depredations, toward a more indefinite and thus more despairing
series of references to time, as it becomes clear to the Danes that
the attacks have no foreseeable end. The world knows

þætte Grendel wan
hwile wið Hroþgar,   heteniðas wæg,
fyrene ond fæhðe   fela missera,
singale sæce, . . .   (151b–54a)

(that Grendel fought a long time against Hrothgar, he carried
out furious attacks, crime, feud, for many years, an eternity of
onslaught . . .)

To those trapped inside this unrelenting horror there is no longer
any way to number or measure these years.

A second scene showing Grendel coming to Heorot, the fully developed occasion when he encounters the waiting Beowulf, shows
how an epic event—which I define here as one that transcends any
previous experience of the participants—can be effectively described through intricate interlacing of points of view, contrasts of
inner with outer experience, and definition by the use of negatives.
In an earlier study I stressed how Grendel's greedy expectations of
feasting were built up in order to show their subsequent frustra-
tion.[7] I did not take up there, however, the step-by-step order of
the approach and the fight itself.

In the fight, the mammoth central fact is Beowulf's hand-grip.
The rhythm of the passage keeps circling back to it, and then going
outward again to explore varied reactions that surround it. Even
the following crude outline sketch will bring out this striking interlace pattern.

748a–49:   Initial *GRIP* imposed by Beowulf on Grendel
  750–57:   Grendel reacts to the *mundgripe*
  758–59:   Beowulf remembers his vow
760–61:   *GRIP* intensified by Beowulf, now standing
  762–64a: Grendel reacts
  764b–65a: *GRIP* described
  765b–88a: Long view: reaction of the Danes witnessing the
               fight from outside the hall. The hall is damaged
788b–90:   *GRIP* described
  791–94a: Beowulf's intention
  794b–808:   Beowulf's men's intentions
  809–12:   Grendel's realization of doom
813–15a: *GRIP* described
815b–18a: *Grendel's gripping arm comes off*
818b–36:   Radiating implications of Grendel's defeat, reach-
               ing a climax in the display of Grendel's own "grip"
               as trophy:

                          Þæt wæs tacen sweotol,
syþðan hildedeor   hond alegde,
earm ond eaxle   (þær wæs eal geador
Grendles grape)   under geapne hrof.   (833b–36)

(That was a clear sign, when the brave one laid down the
hand, arm, shoulder (Grendel's grip was all together),
under the spacious roof.)

Before this happens, Grendel has been launched into a world of
novel experiences, described typically in negative statements. *Never*
on earth, he discovers, has he met a greater hand-grip; *never* in his
life has he been treated like this; he *cannot* flee no matter how much
he would like to. The last insight the heroic grip forces upon him is
that his body is no longer willing to hold up (*him se lichoma læstan
nolde* 812). He knows now he will die (821b–23a).

The epic event shocks others into new perceptions as well. The
Danes think it a great miracle that Heorot does not collapse during
the fight. They have seen stresses that none of its designers could
have imagined possible. And Beowulf's men confidently attack
Grendel with their swords in the old approved manner, only to discover that Grendel has made himself invulnerable to such weapons. They find too that their leader's hand-grip is stronger than all
their swords.

Everyone is surprised by something, except for Beowulf. This fact in itself sets him off effectively. He is not even shown as thinking about what he is doing, except for one brief reassertion of the resolution he had already expressed in his "evening speech." Let others have mental and emotional reactions. He thinks with his hand, *in* his hand. It is the hot and centered focus of terrific intent.

We are shown Grendel's pain, the severing of his sinews as his arm is torn loose, and then later we see the arm produced as evidence of victory, once Beowulf has at last released his fearsome grip. In between, the poet flashes away to collect reaction shots. The ripped-off arm is final. It makes the victory actual and concrete. To Beowulf it means assured and incontrovertible glory; Unferth cannot question this achievement. To Grendel, it means nothing any longer, as he takes his flight toward certain death. To the Danes, it is the fulfillment of their wish and the vindication of their years of suffering. Hrothgar's hall is now cleansed and exorcized; Beowulf's promise to them has been carried out. As in the fight itself, in this aftermath there is a deliberate radiating outward from the physical event or the physical object (which is described minimally) toward the emotional effects generated by it, and toward striking contrasts between these various effects. Such a pattern, perhaps a variation of the "ring" construction, is typical and seems likely to have been derived from an oral style of narrative. A simple example might be the Three Bears' serial reactions to Goldilocks's depredations, responses which (as any parent knows) are the vital core of the tale.

Several of the same features appear in an intricate envelope pattern describing the arming of Beowulf before he goes down into the mere (1441b–72).[8] This passage was discussed in terms of character in Chapter 2; here we take up its formal rhetorical structure. The passage begins and ends with the formulaic idea, "Beowulf was not afraid to lose his life in this venture." At the outset this is stated positively:

> Gyrede hine Beowulf
> eorlgewædum,   nalles for ealdre mearn.   (1441b–42)

(Beowulf dressed himself in warrior-garments, in no way did he worry about his life.)

At the end a similar statement is made in negative form, in terms of the contrast between Unferth's reluctance to fight and Beowulf's bravery:

> Ne wæs þæm oðrum swa,
> syðþan he hine to guðe   gegyred hæfde.   (1471b–72)

(It was not that way with the other [Beowulf], after *he* had dressed himself for battle.)

Between these framing statements, the passage falls into three parts of roughly equal length. (1) describes Beowulf putting on mailshirt and helmet (1442–54); (2) describes Unferth's sword Hrunting (1455–64); (3) is a statement that Unferth was afraid to go down into the mere (1465–71a). (1) is a clearly positive action by the hero. (2) makes a transition to Unferth and to the more problematic matter of his sword (see the discussion in Chapter 2). (3) is a strong negative instance like the Heremod passage mentioned earlier, a counter-example of cowardice to bring out more sharply what Beowulf's courage means.

The statement that Beowulf is not afraid to lose his life is not a mere rhetorical gesture. It in no way suggests that he really thinks he will survive. If he dives into the mere we have just seen, aswarm with ravenous sea-monsters, he will probably lose his life, and he knows this. To go to the edge of this terrible mere and stand there is an act of courage. To plunge beneath its surface is an act of heroism that seems simple lunacy to non-heroic minds. How do the techniques of the traditional oral style define the nature of this situation?

First of all, at the start of the passage, movement is set in contrast with the lack of movement. Beowulf's steady and intent activity (arming himself, without assistance) is played against the lounging of the Danes, seen as a group of zoo-visiting tourists at the mere. At the end of the passage the now ready Beowulf is contrasted with the hesitant and unheroic Unferth. Rhetorically speaking, a brave man needs such cowardly bystanders in Old English poetry, where few assertions are likely to stand alone without being buttressed by counter-statements or negative instances. In this respect the style is like that of a painter who works habitually with the contiguous edges of boldly contrasting color-masses. But in practical life a brave man needs brave neighbors rather than cowardly ones. In this severe challenge Beowulf really needs some help, help he cannot get from those around him. This may be why the poet expands the concept of neighbors or comrades back into the past and out of the scene to include those anonymous artisans, probably now all long dead, who once crafted his armor. Their artefacts live on beyond them and go with the hero to guard his life.

Yet, while the descriptions of byrnie and helmet provide this kind of firm reassurance (reassurance perhaps needed by the hero, certainly needed by the audience), their details also amplify our sense of danger, and with that our awe at Beowulf's courage. The mailshirt will protect the delicate bones of his body from *hildegrap* and *eorres inwitfeng*, but battle-grip and the savage clutch of a furious enemy are brought into our awareness as live threats by this very mention of them. The helmet will guard his head so that swords cannot bite it; but swords do bite. Unferth's venerable sword has never yet failed; but swords do fail. The flower safety and the nettle danger grow from the same stem. The hero is protected by a trim set of negatives warding off all evil; but it is a frail structure, one of hope, chiefly, one of relying on past performance and probabilities. What matters in the end is the man, not his hopeful armor. But in the end one must say that there is some odd if slight circularity or overlap in this passage that eludes exact defining. It can only be lamely stated along lines like these: Beowulf puts on armor because he does not fear for his life because he puts on armor.

How then does the fight come out? It starts very badly. We find Beowulf assuming attitudes of inert passivity strangely uncomfortable for him and alarming to us. He can only allow his trusty comrade-armor to protect him as he is dragged, unable to move, down to the bottom. The armor does work, but other assumptions he had made turn out to be quite wrong. He had thought he could use weapons to defend himself during the swim down, but he cannot. Probably he thought he had reached greater safety when he came out into the hall on the bottom where no water could hurt him, but it was not at all safer there. He assumed the sword Hrunting would work when he needed it, but it does not. He assumed his special strength in wrestling would serve him well, but Grendel's mother throws him easily, beating him at his very own game. It is in fact only his armor, the work of those ancient remote smiths, the symbol of human *communitas*, that lets him survive at all.

Thus the progress into the fight is an elaborate stripping away of defenses, real and symbolic. Past performance can be discarded; it means nothing. He has a new kind of opponent, and is in a new world without stable and predictable rules. What is left, when all the weapons and all the assumptions have been tossed aside, is the naked will: being *anræd, nales elnes læt* 'single-minded, not slow in courage' (1529), and not caring any more about your life. If this naked will is already large enough, larger than any other man's, then and only then God sees to it that a giant sword, larger than any other man can lift, is placed ready to his eye and hand, so that the purifying act of divinely-sanctioned violence can now be consummated. Nowhere else in *Beowulf* do we seem to hear so clearly the full-throated roar of the crowd; nowhere else are we made so aware of the traditional warrior-culture massed for centuries behind this poetry and pervading every word of it. Early audiences must have felt ecstasy in vicariously living out these high fantasies of combat, when one good stroke can save the world.

If we look more closely at the physical details of this fight in the mere-hall, we notice a form of interlace in the blocking of the scene, the placing and movement of characters. In line 1492 Beowulf hurries to leave the upper world, here defined suggestively as the world of human speech (*æfter þæm wordum*), for a new world of brute silence. He begins to float erratically in the paralyzing grip of vast energies not his own. First *brimwylm onfeng* / *hilderince* 'the sea-surge grasped the battle-warrior' (1494b–95a). Presumably the hero does at first swim downward of his own volition, but the act of swimming is not described, as it is described vividly in the Breca swim, for example. What is described instead is Grendel's mother's violent response to seeing a human being invade her alien sanctuary. As in the fight with Grendel, there is great stress on the act of gripping, but Beowulf here does not take part in it. She instantly seizes him (*gefeng*), but is unable to penetrate (*ðurhfon*) his armor with her claws.

Grap þa togeanes,   guðrinc gefeng
atolan clommum.   No þy ær in gescod
halan lice;   hring utan ymbbearh,
þæt heo þone fyrdhom   ðurhfon ne mihte,
locene leoðosyrcan   laþan fingrum.   (1501–5)

(She then gripped out toward him, seized the warrior in horrible claws; none the sooner did she penetrate *into* [*in* stressed by alliteration] the intact body; rings guarded it from outside, so she could not grasp through that war-coat, that lock-linked body-shirt, with hating fingers.)

In its thick detail the passage surrounds Beowulf with fierce, piercing aggression in the gripping and probing claws, against which his defenses seem stubborn but frail. The last line neatly opposes the fingers that once fashioned the beaten links of chainmail to the fingers that now seek to rip it apart. It is a precarious contest.

Once in the mere-hall, Beowulf, now freed from his cramping restraint, at once takes the initiative and rushes on Grendel's mother, but his sword as promptly fails. Without pausing, he then goes on to grip her (*gefeng þa be eaxle* 'seized then by the shoulder' 1537a) and to hurl her to the floor. This ought to be the fight's end, on the basis of past performance, but her terrible grip once again overpowers him: *andlean forgeald / grimman grapum ond him togeanes feng* 'she paid him back his reward with grim grips and seized him' (1541b–42). Again he is made passive and helpless; again it is his armor that barely saves his life (*þæt gebearh feore / wið ord ond wið ecge* 'that guarded life against point and edge' (1548b–49a). He is unable to regain any control of this fight until at last he breaks free somehow and glimpses the giant-sword, which he quickly "seizes" (*gefeng*) and uses to "grasp" (*grapode*) her by the neck and behead her. The language, with its many repetitions and variations of the words *fon* and *feng,* seems to exult in the swift reversals of position. Beowulf provides the final "counter-grip" that succeeds at last in penetrating (*ðurhwod* 1567) her body, as his own was never penetrated.

Language like this points in one direction. Critics have recently done well to remind us that any violent hand-to-hand struggle between male and female can scarcely avoid sexual implications.[9] That we are here invited to observe (and disapprove of) a scene of rape or sadism seems unlikely, however. Yet it must be true that awakened sexual responses must add some dimension of interest and intensity to the fight. From the heroic point of view—ordinarily a wholly sexist one, as we saw when the denigration of Grendel's mother was discussed in Chapter 2—to be blocked from any free action by a female monster must seem more frustrating and humiliating than to be blocked by a male. But perhaps such a feeling of blocked action has as its ultimate basis a human experience common to both sexes, the struggle of all infants against their monster parents, especially their mothers.

In this fight there is, in other words, a powerful and effective contrast between Beowulf's explosively vigorous actions and the severe constraints placed on him during the descent and the first stages of the encounter. When this physical energy at last explodes outward, the audience shares his feeling of release. But we should also note that in this fight in its later stages both combatants move freely. In the first fight Grendel was able to move only within the very narrow limits of Beowulf's hand-grip. It is free and open movement that gives the fight with Grendel's mother its distinctive quality, making it more dangerous, more unpredictable and more excitingly vivid.

We find similar free movement, emphasized by similar temporary impeding of the action, elsewhere. One instance is the account of the battle between Swedes and Geats at Ravenswood, described by the messenger at the end of the poem (2922–98). First the Geats are trapped by the furious old Swedish king Ongentheow, who rages like Grendel's mother outside the armor-like forest of Ravenswood where they hunker down and hole up for the night (2928–45). The dashing arrival of Hygelac to rescue them (analogous to Beowulf's spotting the giant-sword) frees the Geats from their enforced passivity. They burst forth with pent-up violence to drive Ongentheow to bay in his turn and hack him to death. In another instance, the dragon's awesome potential for violence is dramatically throttled back for the length of time he must wait for nightfall before loosing his blasting flame of hatred against the human race that has robbed him of a bit of his hoard (2302b–09a).

Indeed we can identify a similar pattern of contrast between action and inaction in the large-scale structure of Part II as a whole. Even though the battle of Ravenswood is certainly doom-laden, accompanied as it is with explicit predictions of future vengeful attacks by the Swedes on the kingless Geats, it is also felt as brilliantly distinct in the vitality of its action. This vitality is in striking contrast with the generally catastrophic entropy of Part II, its consistent movement out of activity toward inertia and death. This downward movement begins when the Last Survivor lays down the heavy weight of his nation's hoard and history, far down in the earth's embrace (2231b–70a). Life itself comes to seem too heavy for men to hold any longer: *duguð ellor sceoc* 'their strength has gone elsewhere'. It is true that later, after the tremendous exhilaration of the dragon-fight, the figure of young Wiglaf is still seen in clear movement (2752–87), tending his dying lord and entering the barrow to bring out treasure, but that movement only sets off the frozen scene of death and immobility he returns to.

Immobility is stressed through the figure of earth as a terminus. Beowulf is *on eorðan . . . lifes æt ende* 'on earth . . . at the end of life' (2822–23), and so is his slayer, the *eorðdraca* (2825), the earth-dragon. Once a *widfloga*, a far flier, now the dragon has fallen on earth (*hreas on hrusan . . . eorðan gefeoll* 2831–34, the phrase significantly repeated in varied form). For the remainder of the poem all actions are slow and deliberate, half-drugged with sorrow or remorse, often moving in the measured tempos of ritual: the retainers sidle back wretchedly to endure their rebuke from Wiglaf;

the massed Geats sit in grief and apprehension to hear the messenger's prophecies; stately movements of funeral preparations and the slow ceremonial ride around the barrow conclude the story.

On this same large scale, carried out by means of massive scenes and major actions, the interlacing of Beowulf with the dragon can be said to dominate Part II, in the form of an immense moving icon. In its dynamic intricacy it calls to mind those medieval initial letters in the tradition of Hiberno-Saxon and Viking art that show a vulnerable man wholly entangled in the coils of a malevolent though decorative reptile. So, in their reciprocally significant actions and in the symbolic tableaux that enclose them, the dragon and Beowulf constantly interact and intertwine. The great icon warrants examination in detail.

Symbolically we can speak of two distinct worlds impinging on each other, occasionally invading each other, and always defining each other with an interface of sharp clear edges, through the usual contrastive method of oral poetry. One is the world of man, *humanitas,* and the other is *draconitas,* the world of the alien and everlasting worm. Only if we follow the narrative order of Part II, at some risk of treading once again over familiar paths, can we detect and trace this interaction. Ordinary far-ranging methods of analytic criticism must necessarily miss much of this important linear dimension in time. But it must always be borne in mind that an audience listening to a performance of the poem could only receive it consecutively.[10]

Part II begins, traditionally at line 2200, with an assertive and resounding declaration of *humanitas.* Actually such a declaration occurs in the end of Part I just preceding as well, where we respond to the emotion surrounding the reunion of the triumphant Beowulf with his uncle, a satisfying fulfillment of the desire for family recognition. Lines 2200–10a are a furious burst of complicated human history. Of course they serve a narrative purpose in filling in the background and explaining how Beowulf came to be king of the Geats, but they also have strong symbolic meaning in the kind of binary opposition we are observing. The world of *humanitas* shown here is above all else concerned with history, family, dynasty, continuity, and transitions in the urgent time-world. Such a concern is a dominant feature of oral narrative, dating back to the time when it was the only available preserver of such history.

But in line 2210 this absorbing sequence of history is abruptly broken by the savage incursion of the dragon: "until in the dark nights a dragon began to rule." For dragons are implacably dedicated to the obliteration of all history and of all meaningful conceptions of time. We come up hard and jarringly against the dragon when he interrupts the fictive time suggested in narrative sequence, the quick flashing by of history. In a spatial sense, we then also move close to this dragon-world, suddenly and frighteningly, when we accompany the grave-robbing intruder who audaciously steps "near the dragon's head" (2290), drawing us after him.

The discovered world of *draconitas* has no names, no orderly successions, no dynasties, no society at all, none. It is here typically represented in the metaphor of the "earth-house" of oblivion where memory flickers out and human artifacts lie heavy till they rot. We have seen how the Last Survivor of the nation that has perished serves as a final voice for these dead, asking the earth to keep the hoard (of social function, history, memory, these human things) ironically safe. This lugubrious responsibility is quickly assumed by the dragon when he moves into the barrow, the earth-world. The "earth-dragon" is virtually a personified earth, given just enough bare mobility to carry out the functions of holding, keeping, guarding from any intrusion. He presides over a world we would like to think is infinitely remote from and alien to any world we know, but it is only a few feet or a few seconds away, interlaced with us, interfaced with us intimately, like those genes for death which some think nowadays are built into our very cells from birth.

These are merely thoughts we might have. Of course by their very nature dragons have no such thoughts. The rudimentary thoughts a dragon might have about treasure are the thoughts a crocodile has about a fish, though doubtless even less rational and easily explained. Dragons must remain quite opaque to our insistent question: *why* do they . . . ? No answer exists. Insight is useless. We are all rendered fumbling behaviorists, crippled outsiders, in our dragon studies. By contrast the Grendel family seem like reasonable schemers with transparent motives.

What is it we can gather by observing dragon behavior? The poet first shows us the barrow being disturbed when we enter it with the human intruder, who creeps furtively in to commit his theft, but then the poet returns to the incident later to replay it once again, this time from the inside, as we watch the dragon responding with vast energy to this affront. The words *hordweard* (2293), *hordweard* again (2302), and *beorges hyrde* (2304), massed in close succession, stress that what the dragon is doing is the same as what he is being: a guard. He guards. In a frenzy of searching for the intruder, he goes out, comes back, runs around the barrow, goes back into it, and waits tensely for nightfall. After waiting in angry misery for his revenge, he flares out his rage in flames toward those who robbed him. It is fire against people. Alliterations make this point, jumping the gap like electric sparks: *landwara / lige befangen* (2321) '[he had] gripped the folk in flame', *ligdraca leoda fæsten* (2333) 'the fire-dragon [had destroyed] the fort of the people'. Having been first deeply penetrated by the human invader, the death-world of the dragon now bulges out in its turn to invade and coil menacingly around the living world outside and to seek to destroy its heart, the most important symbol of social life, the king's hall.

The poet's omniscient voice is heard just at this point (2309b–11). He watches from a distance that allows him to see both the first shock of impact on the victim (*se fruma*) and the anticipated but certain result, Beowulf's death (*sare geendod*), both viewed with equal clarity by the poet's vatic eyes. But that dire future he sees is not visible to the Geats reeling under dragon-fire; they can only register the fire-storm's power. Then the dragon shoots back into his barrow with the same terrible speed with which he came out. Once again the same strand of interlace appears: the poet intervenes to foresee the future, this time the future for the dragon, whose faith in the security of his barrow-fort will turn out to have little foundation (2321–23). The poet's prophetic power moves us back, at a cool distance from the dragon's lightning motions. We are thus made ready for what we will see. Now that what will happen is clear enough, how it will happen is what must engage our interest.

Furthermore, both the formal symmetry of the narrative order and the poet's predictions invite us to observe and reflect on the contrast between the dragon's convulsive reaction to what it considers outrage and Beowulf's human response to the dragon's attack. We begin with a similarity that sets up the contrast. Both these old treasure-guardians feel the stab of having their inner space violated. The news comes to Beowulf.

Þa wæs Biowulfe broga gecyðed
snude to soðe, þæt his sylfes ham,
bolda selest, brynewylmum mealt,
gifstol Geata. (2324–27a)

(Then horror was quickly, truly, broken to Beowulf—that his own home, that best of buildings, had melted in surges of burning, the gift-throne of the Geats.)

Note how the word-order of the variational phrases shows movement from immediate personal shock at the destruction of a man's own home to the quick realization of national calamity, the loss of the tribal gift-throne. The king is first stricken briefly with guilty fear, thinking he might somehow have caused this onslaught on his people by violating some "old law." But then the situation facing him is restated in a résumé entirely characteristic of the oral style, which never hesitates to repeat a passage if it seems important to keep the emotional facts squarely before our eyes.

> Hæfde ligdraca leoda fæsten,
> ealond utan, eorðweard ðone
> gledum forgrunden; him ðæs guðkyning,
> Wedera þioden, wræce leornode.
> Heht him þa gewyrcean wigendra hleo
> eallirenne, eorla dryhten,
> wigbord wrætlic. (2333–39a)

(The fire-dragon had destroyed by flames the fortress of the people, the sea-coast from outside, the earth-stronghold; the war-king, prince of Weders, thought of revenge against him for that. He thereupon ordered made (that protector of warriors, that lord of men) a marvelous shield, all iron.)

The people's king, as war-king, must respond by putting aside any over-scrupulous broodings and by preparing at once for a new kind of battle. A tool-using creature, a rational human being, he thinks of a plan to have a special fireproof shield made. Both of Beowulf's responses are distinctively human, the guilt and the rational technology.

The two enemies are linked again, for once more the poet speaks in gloomy tones of prophecy, this time foretelling the deaths of both Beowulf and the dragon.

> Sceolde lændaga
> æþeling ærgod ende gebidan,
> worulde lifes, ond se wyrm somod,
> þeah ðe hordwelan heolde lange. (2341b–44)

(The prince noble-in-the-past was fated to live to see the end of transient days, of life in the world—and the dragon along with him, even though he may have long ruled the hoard's wealth.)

Past goodness, past power, past wealth now mean nothing, either to hero or dragon. So icy a doom-statement denies that anything can be generated or extrapolated forward out of the past. Thus what follows is unusually effective, because it gainsays and is in the strongest contrast with so negative an assertion.

Oferhogode ða   hringa fengel
þæt he þone widflogan   weorode gesohte,
sidan herge;   no he him þa sæcce ondred,
ne him þæs wyrmes wig   for wiht dyde,
eafoð ond ellen,   forðon he ær fela
nearo neðende   niða gedigde,
hildehlemma . . .   (2345–51a)

(The lord of rings then scorned to seek the ranging flyer with a military force, a great army; in no way did he feel any dread of that battle, nor account the dragon's fighting or strength or courage worth anything at all, *because* he had once survived many attacks, risking tight places . . .)

Oferhogode: Beowulf scorned, literally over-thought, or out-thought, the doom-statement, brushed it away in his own burning intensity of will, denied its denial. This tough old king is in command of time. He can make the past work for him still to strengthen his resolve and justify his confidence. The interweaving of viewpoints and implications through this part of the poem is subtle. As when Homer places us up among his gods so that we can watch with their calm knowledge and yet with our own human pity and pride the small tormented figures below, so here we have a true double vision: watching the doomed hero feed deep on his own stories of survival and victory in the past. Even though the poet's intervening omniscience sounds a tragic note here, what the hero is reenacting in his own person is what the oral tradition of narrative poetry itself tirelessly reenacts: the recollecting and retelling of old stories in order to fortify listeners whose existence draws most of its meaning from this nurturing tradition.

Three stories from Beowulf's past are here remembered. The first is so vivid in the audience's memory that it need only be mentioned: his spectacular cleansing of Hrothgar's hall from the pollution of the Grendel-race. The other two stories are more complicated stories of survival in difficult and tragic situations, where the opposing monsters are not gross trolls but armies and intractable political tangles.

From 2354b to 2368, the poet describes Hygelac's death at the hands of the Frisians repelling his invasion of their country. The killing takes ten verses to accomplish, and ends with the brutal *bille gebeaten* (2359), 'beaten down by sword'. The poet hovers over this event, as the poet of *The Battle of Maldon* hovers over the death of Earl Byrhtnoth; he is at the same time preparing for and deliberately delaying Beowulf's impressive response to seeing his king and kinsman felled. If we were ever permitted to think in objective terms about this battle, we could only see it as a severe defeat for the Geats, one that perhaps even weakens them permanently and leads to their disappearance from history.[11] But we rarely have any historical objectivity of this kind in *Beowulf*. The way the story is told here is plainly distorted and partial, stressing Beowulf's survival through his individual fighting prowess and his incredible strength in swimming home. His crushing vengeance on the enemy Hetware is framed between two sentences celebrating his escape from the field. The art is to make a major defeat, from which apparently only one single Geat ever returned home, sound like a victory—at least for the hero. Few (that is, none) of the enemy who met Beowulf returned home either. Rhetoric can make it seem that Beowulf was able to draw a great personal victory out of national calamity. But "national" and "personal" are very modern terms after all; the Anglo-Saxons may not have thought in those ways.

In the third story (2369–96), Beowulf agrees to become regent until Hygelac's young son Heardred grows up. Later Heardred assumes the throne and is killed by Onela, king of the invading Swedes, for having given asylum to one of Onela's refugee nephews. Onela then permits Beowulf to hold the Geatish throne, and returns home, presumably in triumph. Beowulf supports Eadgils, the surviving nephew of Onela, in his revenge against his uncle and his recapture of the Swedish throne. In short, the same obvious pattern of defeat as in the previous story of Hygelac's raid is repeated: in the irresistible attack that overwhelms the Geatish force, a Geatish king is killed,—but Beowulf survives the attack and is able to obtain his private vengeance. He salvages glory from a set of unpromising circumstances.

If we assume, as almost all readers do, that the Danish hall Heorot which Beowulf saved has only a short life ahead of it (that it will burn is pointed out immediately after we are told it has been built, 81b–85), we may wish to include the first story among the national catastrophes that Beowulf escapes, albeit unconsciously. If we do so and mass together these three instances of past survival, we may still feel that the defeats themselves are so tainted with hints of coming disaster that they hardly outweigh, as a way of bolstering confidence, the grim odds of the dragon-fight. We can say that Beowulf's "heroic self" is forcefully reexpressed in the *quality* of such past actions, because that is after all probably the point of bringing them in. We should resist any temptation to simplify the matter by taking the defeats as total defeats and by calling Beowulf arrogant and going on to associate his *oferhogode*, that defiant stance that is his legacy from his past, with the serious Christian sin of pride (*oferhygd* or *ofermod* in Old English). If we make this latter judgment, we must blame him for scorning any help and for risking all on the chance of one more survival in a lucky lifetime series. If we are to take this pattern of behavior in a Christian context at all, it is more likely that the poem is suggesting that he was allowed, by some higher power, perhaps even by the Christian God himself, to survive those earlier tight places, the threatening *nearo*, the enveloping destructive coils, in order to win his last fatal victory.

The poet's quiet voice states the paradox, as all this wild rush of violent history once more crashes against the "until" of present and terminal reality:

> Swa he niða gehwane   genesen hæfde,
> sliðra geslyhta,   sunu Ecgðiowes,
> ellenweorca,   oð ðone anne dæg
> þe he wið þam wyrme   gewegan sceolde.
>   (2397–2400)

(That is the way he had survived every assault, every cruel
battle, every act of courage, the son of Ecgtheow—until that
one day he was fated to fight against the dragon.)

The careful picking out of the individual strands braided into the great twisted rope of Beowulf's life had to be done in order to show us the sources and evidence of his strength, but even this long excursus into his past survivals cannot gather quite enough momentum to carry him on beyond this ultimate barrier.

What then is this dragon, this fate he must endure? The passage from 2401 to 2416 moves us toward the dragon in more senses than one, step by step, as Beowulf and his men walk slowly and cautiously forward. The verse now restates the cause and the initial intensity of the dragon's fury. The very man who robbed the hoard, the cause personified, now guides them to the barrow. Thus we are reminded of the *fæhð*, the *bealonið*, the *orleg*—all that unappeasable anger the robbery set in motion, the fire that Beowulf will soon meet. As he did in earlier life, Beowulf must now win vengeance against an overwhelmingly powerful enemy, one that has already in a sense defeated his people. But we recognize this enemy as the ultimate one. Now Beowulf's slow walk to the seat near the barrow is a movement, willed and deliberate, toward death, as well as a movement toward the heroic vindication of his people.

The passage has its share of everyday feelings. The robber of the hoard is full of sadness, humiliation, and fear. The world of such common emotions as these moves toward the ominous death-world, where Beowulf himself seems to be feeling "normal" sorrow and disorientation. His spirit is in some turmoil, *wæfre ond wælfus* (2420) 'wandering and on the point of death', as he comes to the "immeasurable" nearness of his fate. Perhaps he guesses at that nearness. The poet is certain of it.

> . . . wyrd ungemete neah,
> se ðone gomelan   gretan sceolde,
> secean sawle hord,   sundur gedælan
> lif wið lice,   no þon lange wæs
> feorh æþelinges   flæsce bewunden.   (2420b–24)

(. . . *Wyrd* immeasurably near, which was to greet the old man, seek his hoard of soul, cleave asunder life and body: the life of that noble man was to be enclosed in flesh for only the short-est time.)

Only at the end of his long speech does Beowulf mention his own death explicitly, but he is in its world already.

But as we come closer to his death we come much closer to his life as well. We come to know him better than we have known him be-fore. His speech is an even more elaborate flashback into the far past, more intimate and more profound than the poet's flashback since it is in Beowulf's own words. It is a new regrouping of his thoughts and faculties, a new redirection of his stored energy and will. What gives unity to the speech is a tense incompatibility (at least so modern readers must see it) between *sibbe* (love, security, kinship, the world of peace) and *nið* (violent battle-action), an in-compatibility that is resolved, so far as human beings can resolve it, only in the person of Beowulf himself, first through the vengeance he takes, out of his deep love, for Hygelac's death, and second through his behavior in the present situation where he stands alone to face the dragon before the witnessing people he loves so well, better than they love him. The mixture of love and killer-fury was not so evident in the earlier Danish scenes where the love he felt was much less intense. In Denmark Beowulf showed personal pride and/or public-spirited altruism, but not personal love for any of the Danes. This basic difference in emotional intensity is an im-portant distinction between the two parts. It should constitute a strong argument that Part II is in no sense an emotional anticlimax.

The old king goes very far back—is it seventy or eighty years?—

to explore the origins of this deep love, all the way back to a child's earliest feelings of security first threatened and then restored. While scholarly commentators are quite right to explain to us the universality of the medieval custom of fosterage, that social phenomenon ought not to obscure in mere historicism the more timeless and obvious truth that poet and audience knew well how a seven-year-old child taken away from his father (and presumably his mother) feels, and what delight this frightened child knows when he finds that he has not really lost any of his security, because his grandfather holds him safe and loves him.

> Heold mec ond hæfde   Hreðel cyning,
> geaf me sinc ond symbel,   sibbe gemunde.
> Næs ic him to life   laðra owihte,
> beorn in burgum,   þonne his bearna hwylc,
> Herebeald ond Hæðcyn   oððe Hygelac min.
>
>   (2430–34)

(King Hrethel held me and kept me, gave me treasure and feast, bore our kinship in mind; I was in life to him in no possible way more hateful a man in hall than each of his sons, Herebeald and Hæthcyn and my own Hygelac.)

Though the deep feelings of kinship-love that permeate Hrethel's household are here typically expressed in ironically cautious Anglo-Saxon terms, they are nonetheless strong. Terms of kinship run all through this passage: *fæder, sibbe, bearna, Hygelac min, mæges, mæg, broðor.* It is exactly the strength of this love within the family that heightens the horror of the accidental killing of one brother by another. To the Germanic mind, this violation of *sibbe* might be eased or expiated by some form of remedial action, of *nið;* but here there is no mechanism available to treat the bereaved father's pain. The ensuing "Homeric" simile of the old father whose son has been hanged enlarges and explores more lyrically the misery of such final disruption of the kinship-bond. This is the greatest of human afflictions. What can dragons know of things like these?

It is thus only to be expected that Beowulf, raised in so warmly nurturing an atmosphere, grows into the perfect retainer to his uncle Hygelac and suffers greatly when Hygelac is killed on his continental raid. But Beowulf is able to survive Hygelac's death in a way that old Hrethel cannot survive his son's death, because Beowulf is allowed to act out a heroically proper response to it by taking vengeance. It takes the peculiarly satisfying form of squeezing Hygelac's Frankish slayer Dæghrefn to death, an action strange and violent enough to seem some aberrant manifestation of the close embrace of love. Both before Hygelac's death and after it Beowulf pursues his career of personal and devoted service.

> Symle ic him on feðan   beforan wolde,
> ana on orde,   ond swa to aldre sceall
> sæcce fremman,   þenden þis sweord þolað,
> þæt mec ær ond sið   oft gelæste.
> Syððan ic for dugeðum   Dæghrefne wearð
> to handbonan,   Huga cempan.   (2497–2502)

(Always I wanted to go before him in the warband, alone at the point—and in just the same way I will always go on fighting as long as this sword lasts that has held up for me early and late. Afterward I was killer of Dæghrefn, the Franks' champion, in public combat.)

Here he is talking simultaneously about now, the present of the imminent dragon-fight, and about a time sixty (?) years ago, when he fought Dæghrefn, but it is all one unbroken service. Will, dedication and the durable sword that symbolizes them remain the same, early or late, *ær ond sið*. He would hug the dragon to death now if he could get close enough to it.

"Always I wanted to" (*symle . . . ic wolde*) and "still I want to" (*gyt ic wille* 2512) give hard verbal point to his assertion of unslackening determination, but now the poet drops in the two quiet but devastating phrases *niehstan siðe* (2511) and *hindeman siðe* (2517), 'for the last time', tolling their doleful fatal bell. Once again the hero's untarnished brightness of will, growing and glowing as we have seen out of the depths of a child's affection, is held up against the dark doom of the poet's and audience's foreknowledge. And just at this point the special difficulties of this fight come to the fore. There is a little faltering, or at least a deflection or readjustment, of the hero's planned purpose. He almost apologizes. He must now accommodate to the terms of a new struggle: use an iron shield, and no wrestling this time. Yet, no matter, it is still the grand Heroic Dual (*unc, unc, uncer twega* 2525–32), only the two-of-us together at the wall, alone together in the intimacy of death and the judging eyes of God or Wyrd, whatever it is.

Beowulf is not "foolish" or "arrogant," though some have called him those names, to tell his men to wait well out of range of this battle. He is quite right to do so; they are out of range. It is not their *sið*, not their adventure; it is one that belongs only to the dragon and himself, a dual and not a plural. As he makes his final vow (2535b–37), Beowulf may sense that both the alternatives he contemplates will come true: he will win the gold by his courage *and* death will take him. But the pull of fate on the authentic hero is far stronger than the pull of gold could ever be. The challenge is exhilarating, irresistible, an integral and inseparable part of the life-story we have just heard reviewed—and no one else's business. Though he walks toward the dragon-barrow because he loves his people, he walks alone, to die alone, to move temporarily outside the bounds of community toward a final sacrificial solitude.

As he walks forward, *humanitas* now pushes aggressively forward into the deadly dragon-world. Beowulf moves as close to the barrow as he can get before being blocked by the fire-stream that pours out of it along the ground. The two worlds I have been sketching confront each other directly, and now make contact through characteristic modes of expression: speech against flame. When Beowulf's voice, the telltale articulateness of human words (*mannes reorde* 2555), pierces the barrow's interior, the dragon's automatic reaction of hatred roars out like fire. It *is* fire; no metaphor, no words. Symbolically the hero's voice speaks all we have heard built up through the two long surveys of his past. It is as well the voice of mankind and of a culture carried in voice and in memory through many generations, now put at risk in one moment of resolute willing in the face of an exterminating flame that represents no counter-culture but an adamant countering of all cultures.

The fight does not go well. The dragon's shield-like hide protects him from the king's mighty sword-strokes, but Beowulf's own shield keeps him less safe. One sentence dramatizes this. It begins confidently enough in 2570b with *scyld wel gebearg* 'the shield protected well', but then weakens in its progress and ends in a prediction of disaster. Beowulf's sword weakens too in a way that defies expectation: *sio ecg gewac* (2577), *guðbill geswac* (2584). This *sið* he is undertaking, it becomes rapidly clearer as the action proceeds, is not so much an exploit as a death-journey. The communal supports a man can expect in life are vanishing. Shield and sword both fail him, and his retainers fail him too by suddenly taking flight into safety. Beowulf feels the sense of abandonment that Everyman suffers when he sets out on his long journey. Dragon-fire is about to incinerate all the remembered values of the past, that stock of memories (and even an ancient sword is a strong memory) one fights with. Here is the poem's true crisis: the stripped-down scene where all is at stake for the lonely old figure outlined against fire, not only his individual life but the very value its society gives it.

Beowulf can do no more. The crisis is met not by him but by the warrior Wiglaf who resists the general stampede to the safe forest. He remembers.

Nealles him on heape   handgesteallan,
æðelinga bearn,   ymbe gestodon
hildecystum,   ac hy on holt bugon,
ealdre burgan.   Hiora in anum weoll
sefa wið sorgum;   sibb æfre ne mæg
wiht onwendan   þam ðe wel þenceð.   (2596–2601)

(The hand-comrades, sons of noblemen, in no way stood around him in war-troops; no, they turned away into the forest, saved their lives. In one of them spirit welled up against sorrow. Nothing can ever change kinship in a person with the right thoughts.)

What elicits this manifestation of kinship-love is the threat of imminent obliteration by the dragon's death-world, which has now pushed its way far forward into the world of the living. *Sibbe,* what is seen in the poem as the essential value of *humanitas,* has always been Beowulf's most central motivation, and now it becomes Wiglaf's as well. The urgency of Beowulf's present peril triggers the conversion of Wiglaf's memory into action.

This process interests the poet. Wiglaf's "right thoughts" are not to be divided from his right actions, we are told. A series of verbs with the perfective prefix *ge-* express his decisive response: *geseah* 'saw and understood'; *gemunde* 'remembered'; *gefeng* 'took hold (of his shield)'; *geteah* 'drew (his sword)'. As Wiglaf draws the sword he draws out with it its memory, its personal life-history and its past, the account of how his father first won it and how he left it hopefully to his son. Like the men who wield it, the sword derives its power from its early nurture in kinship and heroic history, just as the poem's traditional language draws its power from the same ancient sources. With this revelation of a new, or renewed, force, the counter-attack on the dragon symbolically begins. It is an attack launched against the inhuman and timeless world of empty *draconitas,* a world where there is no such bequeathing and no such obligation to the past.

Obligation is the theme of the crystal-clear paradigm of ideal behavior that Wiglaf delivers to the runaways.[12] They are free to carry out the obligation he reminds them of. We know they could do so, for Wiglaf does so, but they choose not to. So he leaves them behind (they will be left behind forever) and moves up onto the line himself. There he gives Beowulf the only appropriate counsel, a reminder fully consonant with the poem's stress on a consistency of human behavior based on memory: *go on acting as you have always acted in the past* (to summarize lines 2663–68), thereby echoing and reinforcing the theme of Beowulf's own long retrospective and preparative speech.

They now form an intimate pair, cooperating to a point where they combine and fuse to form a new single warrior, fighting behind a single shield to meet the shock of the dragon's third assault. Beowulf's moment of terrible loneliness has ended.

> Byrne ne meahte
> geongum garwigan   geoce gefremman,
> ac se maga geonga   under his mæges scyld
> elne geeode,   þa his agen [wæs]
> gledum forgrunden.   (2673b–77a)

(His mailshirt could not act to help the young spear-fighter, but the young man went bravely behind his kinsman's shield when his own was destroyed by fire.)

Repetition in consecutive lines of the word for "young" seems to suggest both Wiglaf's rashness and his fresh energy. Beowulf's final tremendous stroke (perhaps given extra impetus now by the new need to protect Wiglaf) shatters his sword on the dragon's head; *geswac æt sæcce . . . gomol ond grægmæl* (2681–82a): "it failed in the fight . . . old and grey-patterned." In their suggestion of age, the adjectives foreshadow Beowulf's death. The dragon-jaws close on his unprotected neck, and the dragon reaches his farthest point of advance in the rapid to-and-fro shifting of this interlace of violence.

But now Wiglaf meets the demand for total action, the demand expressed in the phrase "not caring about your life." He risks simply everything, and is rewarded by victory. The kinsmen-warriors work together in their miniature community, sharing their common shield, to show that a human society still survives, as they destroy that society's enemy. Even if Beowulf must die in this fight, the heroic values live, and will live. They live because he and Wiglaf were both absolutely ready to die for them. This all must puzzle dragons.

After the dying Beowulf gives the dragon the coup de grace, the dynamic interrelation between the two contiguous worlds changes.

The frontier between them is no longer an active combat zone, bulging and fluctuating with strenuous incursions and penetrations. The barrow is no longer the threatening fortified outpost of some invading power. It becomes just a grave in the earth, very soon to be a robbed grave, a thing of merely everyday meaning. The war is over. But Beowulf sits wearily and stares at what the barrow has now become for him; perhaps it is a new frontier, his own eternal death-hall, *ece eorðreced* (2719).

The two voices up till now heard separately, the narrator's voice and the hero's, have been approaching each other gradually and now merge in unison, blending toward one flat statement of accepted inevitability.

> Wisse he gearwe
> þæt he dæghwila   gedrogen hæfde,
> eorðan wynne;   ða wæs eall sceacen
> dogorgerimes,   deað ungemete neah.   (2725b–28)

(He knew surely that he had lived out his space of days and joy on this earth. Then the number of his days had all gone by, and death was inconceivably near.)

The first of the two sentences paired here in mournful duet fashion tells what Beowulf knows; the second, in a psalm-like paraphrasing restatement, is the poet's voice.

In the new knowledge he has gained Beowulf speaks once more, now in the past tense, reviewing what he had done in his now-ended life. It is not only in the Christian tradition that Death and Judgment are close companions. At the moment of death, every life crystallizes, sets, locks itself beyond further change into final form and opens itself naked to assessment. Earlier Beowulf had reviewed his still-living past in order to generate from the review a continuity of energy and to make it available for a still-living present where it was urgently needed. Now the past is stilled and terminated, with no future except what may be hinted at in his dimly Christian allusion to God not being able to reproach him with killing kinsmen (2741–42). (The judging God is Christian, but killing kinsmen is a Germanic deadly sin.) The present has come to a virtual stop. The blunt honesty of Beowulf's summary of his life, its level-eyed facing of won and lost, good and bad, is moving. It is good he ruled well for fifty years; it is bad he has no son to leave hopes and war-gear to. True, as for most of us, there is a cruel contrast between what he would have liked (*wolde*) and what he got (*gifeðe*), but the final tone is one of courageous acceptance.

Now any activity must be delegated to Wiglaf, who is urged to hurry into the barrow to bring out treasure for the king to see before he dies. Perhaps this suggests that, as designated surrogate, he must now carry out the task of the heroic dragon-slayer that ought properly to have been Beowulf's: to enter the now unguarded mound and loot it freely as Sigemund looted his dragon-hoard, *sylfes dome* 'at his own judgment' (895; 2776). Wiglaf enters to stare in awe at the riches the greedy dragon wanted no human eye ever to see. In thus entering Wiglaf represents *humanitas* recovering something of its own out of this alien place, this old giant-work. He moves briskly into the interior, his bright youth exulting in victory and his battle-shirt (now worn for the first time) in apt contrast both with the "dead" heaps of rusty armament within and the doubly dead presence of the dragon just outside, the dragon who had first "killed" this treasure by hoarding it out of use and who now himself lies massively and helplessly dead across the entrance he once jealously guarded. *Hord ys gesceawod,* as Wiglaf later remarks: 'the hoard is looked-at' (3084). We can enjoy a little revenge on the dragon simply by looking at what he tried so hard to hide from us.

A far past too dead now to be articulated in memorial language, a past with no names left, one just beyond our recovery, glitters and glows in the exquisite objects of the hoard, objects that force on us, as always, images of those hands and fingers (now dust and bones) that once crafted and cherished the artifacts.

> Geseah ða sigehreðig,   þa he bi sesse geong,
> magoþegn modig   maððumsigla fealo,
> gold glitinian   grunde getenge,
> wundur on wealle,   ond þæs wyrmes denn
> ealdes uhtflogan,   orcas stondan,
> fyrnmanna fatu   feormendlease,
> hyrstum behrorene;   þær wæs helm monig
> eald ond omig,   earmbeaga fela
> searwum gesæled . . .
>   segn eallgylden
> heah ofer horde,   hondwundra mæst,
> gelocen leoðocræftum.   (2756–64a; 2767b–69a)

(Exultant in victory, the brave kin-thane saw then, as he went by the seat, many rich ornaments, gold glittering close to ground

and wonders on the wall, and the den of the old dawn-flyer, the
dragon; saw plates standing, vessels of long-ago men, now without polishers, their decoration crumbling; there was many a
helmet, old and rusty, many an arm-ring, cleverly twisted . . .
an all-gold banner high over the hoard, greatest of hand-
wonders, linked by finger-craft.)

Part of the treasure has rotted away into ghostlike traces; part of it
(the gold) survives and even lights up the barrow's dark interior.
The sight compels us to think of the time it must have taken to
amass such a vast hoard of "culture," this painfully assembled heap
of loot and exploits and artistry and butchery and generosity, as
well as the time it has taken for it to become corroded, crumbled,
and forgotten. The attempt of those who made and collected the
hoard, perhaps to project their identities beyond death thereby,
has failed for lack of maintenance: the treasure has not been cleaned
and polished, the names and stories have not been remembered
and repeated. The failure reminds us that this poem strives to be
a more lasting memorial; this same treasure can go on rotting
uselessly when it is transferred to Beowulf's own barrow, so long as
the barrow is *named and remembered.* That the poet gives us a relatively long description of the hoard is a way of saying that his character Wiglaf looks at it for a significantly long space of time, and
that we should do so too.

Exactly how Wiglaf looks at it is in some dispute because of a textual problem that has busied the critics for many years. The passage in question is this:

> Sinc eaðe mæg,
> gold on grund[e],   gumcynnes gehwone
> oferhigian,   hyde se ðe wylle.   (2764b–66)

We can easily translate all this except for the troublesome *oferhigian,*
found only here, the meaning of which is unclear: "Treasure, gold
in the ground, can easily —— everyone of mankind, let him hide
it who wishes to." [13] Left unemended, *oferhigian* might (on the model
of *oferirnan* 'overrun, outrun') mean 'outhurry, outrace'. This might
be an odd way of saying that treasure can beat us in the race, i.e.,
get the better of us. Another possible reading (also rather odd) is to
emend the word to *oferhiwian* 'transfigure' or 'change the appearance (*hiw*) of'. This would be telling us that treasure alters a man's
appearance, no matter how hard he tries to hide his reaction.

These tentative readings and others that have been proposed still seem to have little specific appropriateness to Wiglaf, if they suggest that the treasure changes him in some important way. There is surely no indication elsewhere that Wiglaf has been seized by cupidity of some serious kind, whatever transient and normal feelings of gratification, greed or surprise he may experience in the barrow. If he has any such feelings, they constitute only a brief and temporary counter-pull to the very strong pull of the love and obedience he owes his king. What he is interested in is not enriching himself but getting back to Beowulf while the king still lives. He snatches up a few specimens because his master had asked to see them.

Looking at these precious objects as he once again speaks, Beowulf thinks of two legacies for his people (*minum leodum* 2797): the treasure, and the memory of who he was. I thank God, he says fervently, that I can leave this wealth to my people for their use. I suspect modern readers have often taken this sentiment too literally. Beowulf could hardly be envisioning a truly practical use for the treasure, such as building up the war-chest of national defense against future invasions. The passage should be quoted, since it has been interpreted and misinterpreted in more ways than one.

> Ic ðara frætwa   frean ealles ðanc,
> wuldurcyninge,   wordum secge,
> ecum dryhtne,   þe ic her on starie,
> þæs ðe ic moste   minum leodum
> ær swyltdæge   swylc gestrynan,
> nu ic on maðma hord   mine bebohte
> frode feorhlege.   Fremmað gena
> leoda þearfe;   ne mæg ic her leng wesan.
>   (2794–2801)

(I say in words thanks to the Lord, to the King of glory, to the eternal Ruler, for all these treasures that I here look upon, [thanks] that I am allowed to acquire such [riches] for my people before my death-day, now that I have paid for this hoard of treasures with my old allotment of life. Keep on attending to the people's needs. I cannot be here any longer.)

Editors usually attach the *nu-* clause in 2799 to the imperative statement that follows, to make the point that the wealth will indeed help the Geats cope with their future emergencies, but such punctuation may merely be determined by a customary interpretation. It seems better semantically, and perhaps syntactically as well, to attach the clause to what goes before.[14] Beowulf is explaining how he got the treasure he is bequeathing.

He has paid for it with his life. He wishes to leave that life behind him as his second legacy: a sharp clear memory of what he was and how he acted, embodied in a towering new barrow they will build on the same high sea-cliff from which the dragon is to be dumped into oblivion. It will be an immense aide-mémoire, for sailors to point to in years to come. The example of his calm courage and devotion will be the Geats' most valuable treasure in the ordeals they face.

In his very last action and last words, Beowulf specifies a third and possibly equally important legacy. The scope of vision narrows down dramatically. We move in closer to catch those last words, move away from large words like mankind and nation, for we move now to the clan, back to the Wægmundings, *usses cynnes,* our family. And he takes off gold ring and mailshirt to place them in the hands of that young kinsman who came to help him. This act is not what it is sometimes taken to be, a formal ritual of passing on the royal succession. That point would have been made very emphatically indeed. But, for whatever reason, the poet never hints that Wiglaf becomes king, nor indeed does he ever mention any other successor to the Geatish throne. It is often overlooked that the plural imperatives *fremmað* (2800) and *hatað* (2802) cannot properly be addressed to Wiglaf, but to the collective nation via the young warrior who will relay the message.[15] Beowulf's action in giving Wiglaf his own personal possessions is rather something intimate and affectionate within the bounds of a small warm family. We return to the family feeling Beowulf knew at seven years of age. And now the old king falls into line in the procession of his ancestral kinsmen out of life, perhaps to rejoin the family at the end of the journey. Everything he had he has now given away, *and to other people,* not to the barren earth as the Last Survivor had to do. In its simplicity, Beowulf's *ic him æfter sceal* 'I must go after them' (2816) makes his death seem, like Scyld's funeral voyage, a majestic journey, a journey he accepts and wills. His body "chooses" the fire of cremation (2818b–19a).

Suspense in Part II is not about whether Beowulf will die, or even really about how he will die, but about how others will respond to his death. At first the world he has left simply stops momentarily. A scene of mournful, brooding stasis ensues, for the participants perhaps a little like our modern ritual of a viewing. This stopped world is dominated physically by a giant corpse, the fifty-foot bulk of the stopped dead dragon, and emotionally by Wiglaf's stopped and as yet unexpressed grief. The poet registers no positive or approving comment on that transfer of treasure from one corpse to another that seemed, a moment before, so important to accomplish. What commands attention now is that the price paid for this hoard was the lives of both immense figures.

In line 2845, movement begins to return to this frozen tableau in the slowly moving shapes of the men who had run from the fight. They edge back to contemplate their fallen lord. But this movement is partial, muted, limited; none of them speaks, none is identified. In silent shame they watch Wiglaf going through the motions, a set of ritual gestures, of trying to revive his king. His active figure is seen as still struggling against fate. The runaways never struggled so stoutly with what they must have seen looming as their own fate, the onrushing fire-dragon. They took to their nimble heels to avoid it. By staying to fight, Wiglaf went "beyond [his] measure" (*ofer min gemet* 2879). They stayed comfortably within theirs.

Now a burst of movement, after this effectively slowed pace of action. Wiglaf comes violently to life, as he finds emotional release in his furious outburst at the deserters. His angry speech culminates in a withering statement, perhaps a curse, at its end. The cowards are essentially dead now themselves, or will wish they were. The functioning society they once took part in, or pretended to take part in, is now a stopped world for them, symbolically as dead as the scene we saw before they came back, and it has been stopped partly through their actions.

> Nu sceal sincþego   ond swyrdgifu,
> eall eðelwyn   eowrum cynne,
> lufen alicgean.   (2884–86a)

(Now taking of treasure and giving of swords, all joy in one's country, all love, will lie still for your race.)

Such a passage comes close to making this statement: life in heroic society resides in fellowship and courage, and in losing those qualities the runaways have lost life itself.

After this fiery blaze of anger, the poem reverts to frozen scenes, now described from the viewpoint of the Messenger who rides up the hill to where the Geatish host has been sitting "the morning-long day" in anxious suspense over the outcome of the fight. Their immobility makes a frozen scene and, as the Messenger begins to speak (2900), he pictures for them the scene at the barrow: Beowulf fast in his death-bed (*deaðbedde fæst*), the dragon hugely inert beside him, Wiglaf keeping "head-watch" over both. The frozen tableau delivers visually the appalling news of the king's death, he who was *wilgeofa Wedra leoda, / dryhten Geata* 'generous giver to the Weder people, lord of Geats' (2900–1). Their protector's death sets the right keynote for a speech that will mercilessly dramatize Geatish vulnerability. Some, showing the plain common sense of literate readers, have pointed out that the Messenger has forgotten about Wiglaf's vigorous speech of rebuke, and with telling logic have insisted that the Messenger must of necessity have been one of the fugitive cowards himself.[16] These are irrelevant observations, however. In oral-derived verse we watch what we are shown at the moment of performance, and what we are meant to respond to here is the helpless grief and the fear triggered by this silent death-scene.

It is a poetry, as we have seen, of boldly juxtaposed sharp edges. At line 2910, without warning, the frozen tableau explodes into rapid movement and strong emotions of another kind; the Messenger voices "hot" passages of anger and violence. These are forecasts of political turmoil occurring on a much larger scale than the personal behavior rebuked in Wiglaf's bitter prophecy, and are perhaps to be thought of as an expansion or variation of Wiglaf's remarks, a farther development of the theme of the fatal aftermath.

The Messenger predicts the Franks and Frisians will react with fury to the news of Beowulf's death. This fury, long repressed, will be a delayed reaction to an earlier violent impact upon them in the form of Hygelac's plundering raid.

> Wæs sio wroht scepen
> heard wið Hugas, syððan Higelac cwom
> faran flotherge on Fresna land. (2913b–15)

(That conflict was set going hard against the Franks, when Hygelac came sailing with his armed fleet into the Frisians' land.)

The phrase *heard wið Hugas* comes like the smack of a fist, and elicits the same outrage. In their anger at the invasion, the Franks counterattacked, killing Hygelac and all but one of his men, creating one more silent death-field. This battleground was described ironically earlier in the poem: *Geata leode / hreawic heoldon* 'the Geatish people held the corpse-town' (1213b–14a). But, despite their victory over Hygelac, Frankish resentment of the affront of this pirate raid seems never to have abated, and may never be ap-

peased until the Geats can be repaid in kind by a Frankish invasion
of their country.

Another Geatish raid, here at least definitely presented as a similar marauding expedition northward into Sweden, drew similar
fury from the Swedes and will likewise cause more trouble in the
future. The Swedes' anger in this case is brilliantly personified, as
we saw earlier in this chapter, in the fierce old king Ongentheow
who battles the invaders of his country and the abductors of his
wife. The battle of Ravenswood is an extremely "hot" narrative of
see-saw combat that ends in Ongentheow's gallant death.[17] It is
made so vivid to us that we can be sure the memory of the old man's
death must still be fresh in Swedish memories even after some seventy years.

The fearful imminence of such retaliatory attacks by vengeful
neighbors places the scene taking place in the poem's present in a
new context, as we see in this difficult transitional passage.

> Þæt ys sio fæhðo   ond se feondscipe,
> wælnið wera,   ðæs ðe ic wen hafo,
> þe us seceað to   Sweona leoda,
> syððan hie gefricgeað   frean userne
> ealdorleasne,   þone ðe ær geheold
> wið hettendum   hord ond rice
> æfter hæleða hryre,   hwate Scildingas,
> folcred fremede   oððe furður gen
> eorlscipe efnde.   Nu is ofost betost
> þæt we þeodcyning   þær sceawian
> ond þone gebringan,   þe us beagas geaf,
> on adfære.   (2999–3010a)

(That is the feud and the enmity, deadly violence of men, so as
I expect, with which the Swedish people will seek us as soon as
they hear our lord is dead, the one who had protected hoard
and kingdom against enemies after the fall of warriors,
[protected?] the brave Scyldings, the one who had executed
wise policy and, even more, had acted like a hero.—And now
haste is best, that we look at the nation's king there and bring
the one who gave us rings to the funeral pyre.)

One large mystery of the poem is what happens during that space
of time or leap of thought some editors represent typographically
by a dash placed before *nu* in the middle of line 3007 (as in my
translation here). It links the Messenger's assertion that the Swedes

will surely attack with his suggestion that the Geats should quickly
go look at Beowulf's body and carry it to the pyre. He must be implying that they have to hurry; with the enemy at the gates there is
little time for leisurely ceremonies. He seems to be calling for two
major efforts from them: self-defense and the carrying out of the
funeral rites. Are they in some sense the same effort? He reminds
the Geats that the parties in hall are over and the peacetime world
is dead; hence placing the treasure on the pyre is a symbolic re-
nouncing of the joys they had known. But he issues no invitation to
langorous melancholy but a call to arms. They need to summon
enormous strength to face this future, an effort all the greater since
they are disheartened by the loss of their king. Confronting this
dragon-fire of the future is no matter of pleasurable apocalyptic
frissons, but a wretched business of picking up ice-cold spears morning after morning and fighting blindly to some unknown end.

The effort to defend themselves and the effort to carry out the
funeral rites are blended in another way as well, in an image. The
birds of prey mentioned at the end of the Messenger's speech have,
as I once suggested,[18] their familiarly passive roles as funeral atten-
dants in a world where all human beings seem to have died (the
"twa corbies" motif), but they are also closely related to those
alarm-sounding, action-provoking birds and beasts used so tellingly as stimuli by Hnæf in *The Fight at Finnsburg*, when he calls urgently to his men to rise, arm, and hold the hall against sudden
night-attack.[19]

When at last the Messenger's impassioned voice falls silent, we
hear the poet's voice, solemnly and earnestly sanctioning the ac-
curacy of all that was said.

Swa se secg hwata   secggende wæs
laðra spella;   he ne leag fela
wyrda ne worda.   (3028–30a)

(In such a way that brave man kept making hateful statements;
he didn't lie much in facts or words.)

Now the weeping Geats move in a mass to look at the *wundor*, and
we go back one more time, after all the told-of violence, to the same
frozen scene where Beowulf lies in "wonder-death" (3037) and the
dragon, having made his last use of earth-caves, is stretched out
deaðe fæst (3045–46). Geats and audience are forced, through the
circling movement back to this grim *compositio loci*, to share in yet
one more intent meditation on death, one that leads on to thoughts

about the treasure and its history, about the curse once laid on it, and about the reconciling of Beowulf's sacrificial death with the real needs of his bereft people.

The hoard now lies open and unprotected; the dragon no longer guards it and it has not been kept intact by the curse once imposed on it.

> Þonne wæs þæt yrfe,   eacencræftig,
> iumonna gold   galdre bewunden,
> þæt ðam hringsele   hrinan ne moste
> gumena ænig,   nefne god sylfa,
> sigora soðcyning,   sealde þam ðe he wolde
> (he is manna gehyld)   hord openian,
> efne swa hwylcum manna   swa him gemet ðuhte.
>
> (3051–57)

(Then [300 or 1000 years before?] that legacy, enormously powerful, the gold of men of long ago, was wrapped round with a spell, so that no man could be allowed to touch the ring-hall, unless God himself, the true king of potencies, granted permission to the one he wished—he is the protection of men!—to open the hoard, to whatever man seemed suitable to him.)

Unless we have lost something said about a curse in the text of the damaged folio 179 of the manuscript (a slight but real possibility, since that is where dragon and hoard are first described), this is the first mention of one, and it comes very late in the poem. This curse was placed on the hoard by unidentified princes (þeodnas mære 3070) at some time in the vague far past. Introducing the curse here seems to be a notable nonce-effect, one that does not have to be related to other parts of the story, since it is intended for an immediate atmospheric effect in a narrow context. We should not be too logical therefore. There is not the least need to connect the curse with the Last Survivor (himself a nonce-effect, most probably), who seems in any event too self-absorbedly passive and fatalistic in his lament to be concerned about imposing curses. If he asks earth to hold the treasure, it is so that he can lay it down and rest at last, not so that other men cannot have it. In its own special context each of these inconsistent stories about the hoard evokes its own appropriate emotion: the tragic sense of communal death and oblivion in the Survivor passage, the concern with the deep mysteries of possession and loss in the passage on the curse.

But modern readers have real problems understanding the purpose of the curse. We must take it as a real and functional curse, not a phantom or an illusion. If the Christian God had not intervened to cancel its operation, we have no reason to assume it would not have continued to be efficacious. Pagan magic was thought to have limited but real powers, as we can see in the spell the "heathen" Grendel has put on swords, for example. Though the passage is not very clear, I think it tells us that God intervenes to break the curse through the agency of his favored hero Beowulf, who by his very victory over the dragon (a kind of ordeal by battle revealing God's verdict) undoes this magic spell and is thus figuratively handed the keys to the barrow. Gaining the treasure, seen this way, is a God-assisted defeat of a heathen power, possibly a power somewhat similar to that represented by the heathen Grendel-race, real enough but of a much lower degree of spiritual reality than the beneficent forces of the Christian universe. Ending the curse would then be a beneficial side-effect of Beowulf's victory, like the cleansing of the polluted hall and mere in Denmark. Justice is carried out. We must therefore conclude that it was wrong (*unrihte* 3059) for the unknown hider to put the treasure under a curse—wrong if only because the trick did not succeed.

Most certainly Beowulf's death is not *caused* by the curse, though some may be tempted to think that it was. That would be to grant much too much power to heathen spell-casters, or else to make the curse God's very peculiar way of punishing Beowulf for his sin of avarice (this latter a curious explanation that has gained popularity in some circles).[20] It must be granted, as lending some color to this latter hypothesis, that the threats of the curse are couched in terms very like those of Christian anathema.

Swa hit oð domes dæg   diope benemdon
þeodnas mære,   þa ðæt þær dydon,
þæt se secg wære   synnum scildig,
hergum geheaðerod,   hellbendum fæst,
wommum gewitnad,   se ðone wong strude.
(3069–73)

(Similarly famous princes put a deep spell on it until Doomsday, those who had put it there, [saying] that that [hypothetical] man who might plunder that ground would be guilty of sins, locked away in heathen shrines, fast in hell-bonds, punished with plagues!)

But Christian anathema was probably simply the cursing register most natural to a Christian poet and his audience. No one would have thought it incongruous that pagan cursers would use such language. It is just possible that this unusually heavy rhetoric may be mocking itself, or at least mocking the old heathen Pooh-Bahs who used it, since all this great piling up of dire consequences no longer means a thing when God has already canceled the curse *in toto*.

In some more general sense, however, the curse may illustrate the common inability of men to project their wishes beyond their own deaths. We are concerned with such failures at this point in the poem. The dragon failed in his intention. The mysterious hider and curser of the hoard failed as well (*se sið ne ðah* 'that attempt did not suceed' 3058). Are we then to raise the question of whether Beowulf also in some way failed? He indeed failed to foresee his own death clearly, and the poet seems to stress this fact, but chiefly with the intention of making Beowulf's death an ultimate mystery.

> Wundur hwar þonne
> eorl ellenrof   ende gefere
> lifgesceafta,   þonne leng ne mæg
> mon mid his magum   meduseld buan.
> Swa wæs Biowulfe,   þa he biorges weard
> sohte, searoniðas;   seolfa ne cuðe
> þurh hwæt his worulde gedal   weorðan sceolde.
>   (3062b–68)

(It is a universal mystery just when a brave man shall travel to the end of his decreed life, when he can no longer live in a mead-hall with his kinsmen. It was this way for Beowulf when he sought out the barrow's guardian and his treacherous violence; he himself did not know how his parting from the world would come about.)

Perhaps, if Beowulf had known about the curse and if it had been operative as originally intended by the curser, he might have been able to predict his own death as he approached the lethal hoard. But even that knowledge was impossible for him to have, since he had never even looked at the hoard before. It is in this context that I take the famous crux in lines 3074–5, taking *næs he . . . ær gesceawod* as being roughly parallel in sense to *seolfa ne cuðe* (3067). I would take the two lines unemended as a separate sentence.[21]

Næs he goldhwæte   gearwor hæfde
agendes est   ær gesceawod.

(He had not very eagerly looked at the gold-bright (?) property of the owner [dragon?].)

But the long meditation on death and its implications ends, and we return to the living Wiglaf in line 3076. Certainly one important implication is that Beowulf's death shatters the sense of stable community that is a principal ideal of the world this poem imagines. John Niles argues at length that the poem's primary focus is in fact on social community, maintaining that "interest centers not on man as solitary hero but on people and what holds them together." [22] Here what has held these people together has been one man, and the disintegrating effect of his death shows itself in several ways. As we have seen, either all action and all interaction stop dead—the whole social machine stops—or else things race wildly and erratically, as in Wiglaf's angry tirade or in the vicious action of the battle at Ravenswood, emblematic of the incessant warfare the Messenger sees ahead of them. The Geats are shown as feeling conflicting and disordered emotions: shame and pride, anger and profound sorrow, love and despair. The accounts of political turmoil are merely images of wild emotions and shocked loss.

Yet at this stage of the poem the poet is working out an interlace of major importance. While things seem to be accelerating their plunge into collapse and entropy, a distinctly positive counter-process is set in motion. Wiglaf is its earliest and most visible representative. His public show of love and courage reasserts an essential minimum of community morale, and plants a seed for future growth. Perhaps we can already detect one form of growth in his second speech to the cowardly retainers. We can see it as an increase in maturity. In his first speech, Wiglaf naively assumed they would all honor their often-expressed promise to help their lord in his time of need. In his second speech, he knew better. But this new bitter understanding does not merely stop at routine cynicism but leads him on to a loftier role as interpreter and mediator, communicating the noble reality of the Beowulf he saw in crisis to a confused and bereaved nation.

Other shifts in emphasis, though slight, reinforce this sense of a positive movement. As we have seen, the Messenger's speech is for most of its length a prospect of disaster, but it ends with a call for resolution and determination in full understanding of the dimensions of that disaster. It is a call, in other words, for a new mature attitude. If the cowardice of some of the Geats was once castigated as an unmitigated failure to meet the standards of heroic behavior, it is now forgotten for the remainder of the poem. Erasing it in this way, reducing it to zero grade, may be one way of saying indirectly that the Geats will no longer be cowards. If we are not made to think about cowardice, there is none; the oral poet must keep his stimulus and his response very close together. His attention now is obviously not on cowardice but on how he can interweave implications, emotional reactions, imbalances, and balances.

Before any reconstruction of true community can take place, the issues must be aired. Wiglaf's important speech begins with a blunt statement of the Geats' situation, and of the facts that have to be talked out and thought through.

> Oft sceall eorl monig   anes willan
> wræc adreogan,   swa us geworden is.
> Ne meahton we gelæran   leofne þeoden,
> rices hyrde,   ræd ænigne,
> þæt he ne grette   goldweard þone,
> lete hyne licgean   þær he longe wæs,
> wicum wunian   oð woruldende;
> heold on heahgesceap.   Hord ys gesceawod,
> grimme gegongen;   wæs þæt gifeðe to swið
> þe ðone þeodcyning   þyder ontyhte.   (3077–86)

(Often many a man is compelled to endure suffering at the will of one person, as has happened to us. We could not by any argument persuade our dear lord, the realm's protector, not to greet that gold-guardian, [persuade him] to let him lie where he had been long, let him live in his house till the world's end. He [Beowulf] clung hard to his high destiny. The hoard is open to view, grimly won. The fate was too strong that drew the people's king toward that place.)

Wiglaf is certainly confronting a problem of emotional response, and the first two lines of this speech may seem to many readers a simple answer to it.[23] We could conclude the the Geatish nation has been ruined because of Beowulf's arrogant folly in daring to fight the dragon. His conceited and inflexible *willa* has destroyed him and with him his people, who were unable to deter him from the irrational venture. But this answer is not acceptable. For one thing, the apparent option of leaving the dragon and his treasure alone is merely a rhetorical and irrational gesture on Wiglaf's part. The option never did exist.[24] We have no guarantee that the dragon will not continue his aggressive nighttime forays. In any event, to leave the dragon alone might be to submit to the conditions of the old heathen curse. If God, as we are told, permits Beowulf to win the gold (3054–57), he may really wish him to win it. To regard Beowulf here as the very same kind of God-directed champion he unmistakably was in Part I is not only to be consistent about him, it is to view his initiative in getting the gold and thus breaking the spell on it as part of his *heahgesceap*, a high destiny that may well have Christian as well as secular meaning (consider the countless uses of *heah* and *heah-* in Christian contexts). But, in the end, deciding to fight the dragon hardly needs any more elaborate justifying than common prudence and self-protection.

When Wiglaf then goes on to discourse at some length about the treasure that was won, he is neither celebrating nor deprecating royal avarice. True, treasure seems to be used here as an image of the object of desire, but the desire exists in a strictly limiting heroic context. In this kind of context, a hero's high destiny is a mysterious fusion of his own freely chosen act, his *willa*, and the fate ineluctably in store for him, the *gifeðe*, the given. That force-field that pulls him on toward doom and glory is much stronger than greed. It is indeed too strong for Beowulf, and too difficult for less heroic natures to understand.

Playing the role of interpreter of the heroic psyche, then, Wiglaf may be using the pull of the treasure to express the pull of destiny. Surely in no literal sense does Beowulf move eagerly toward the gold. He is not raiding and looting some enemy hoard but defending his own honor and his people's lives. But ordinary Geats have to understand this distinction, and perhaps, since they are not heroes, they can sense heroic motivation only in such crass terms: *when you see gold, go for it.* Wiglaf hammers on this very crassness, hovering insistently over the gold. I was actually there, in the barrow, he tells them. I saw all the treasure. I picked some of it up in these hands (*mid mundum* 3091, a gesture), and carried it out to show the king. Now you come look at it too, he insists.

> Uton nu efstan   oðre siðe,
> seon ond secean   searogimma geþræc,
> wundur under wealle;   ic eow wisige,
> þæt ge genoge   neon sceawiað
> beagas ond brad gold.   (3101–05a)

(Now let us hurry one more time to see and seek the crowd of crafted gems, marvels under the wall—I'll show you the way—so you can get your fill of looking at rings and broad gold.)

This is not the only place in Old English literature or in *Beowulf* where gold is used as a measure of heroic effort. Tender-minded moderns, we may prefer to think that Beowulf killed Grendel for reasons other than the money, but surely the original audience would have thought the achievement grotesquely incomplete without the enormous rewards Hrothgar heaps on the young man afterward, not to speak of the near half of a kingdom Hygelac presents him with when he returns triumphant.[25] Beowulf would have agreed. But what now, at the poem's end, can possibly reward the eager hero for his greatest and most difficult victory? Only the poem's most tremendous treasure, the hoard amassed by an entire lost nation, far more than Hrothgar or Hygelac could have given him. There is no king now to give him reward for services performed. The people themselves must partake of royal generosity and place the dragon-treasure on the pyre in a ritual through which they can symbolically reward the hero. It is the same kind of action taken by the Danes long before when they loaded wealth on Scyld's funeral ship. So long as the symbolic nature of the rewarding is understood, we are not likely to see the action in either case as throwing the gold away, any more than most of us would see the posthumous presentation of a medal for valor to a solider's widow as a merely stupid act.[26]

So now, after he relays to the Geats Beowulf's request that they build a barrow in his memory, Wiglaf invites them to come with him to look at the hoard. Clearly this action is viewed as meaningful and necessary. This may be because to look hard enough at this long-hidden and hard-won treasure is to share vicariously in Beowulf's triumph by seeing his reward, and to feel something of the magnetic force that inspired him and drew him there.

Næs ða on hlytme   hwa þæt hord strude,
syððan orwearde   ænigne dæl
secgas gesegon   on sele wunian,
læne licgan;   lyt ænig mearn
þæt hi ofostlic[e]   ut geferedon
dyre maðmas.   Dracan ec scufun,
wyrm ofer weallclif,   leton weg niman,
flod fæðmian   frætwa hyrde.   (3126–33)

(Then they had no need to draw straws to see who was to plunder that hoard, once the men caught sight of any part of it lying unguarded and perishable in the hall! None of them hesitated a moment about quickly carrying out precious treasures. They shoved the dragon, the worm, over the steep cliff, let the wave take him and flood embrace him, that treasure-shepherd.)

The pace quickens rapidly as the Geats rush into the barrow and confidently seize the gold. They seem to swagger. Their contempt for the dragon's failure to guard his hoard is reflected in the way they push his corpse—in the same rude and forceful manner they entered his barrow—off the sea-cliff. These free actions imply a movement out of their emotional paralysis. As the victors now, they are glad to demean the loser by denying him ritual; in the same motion they are reverently carrying the dragon's treasure away toward the lofty ceremony of the king's funeral. Connections between these various sensations and actions are typically intuitive and paratactic. Once the Geats have the proper *feel* of all this, then they will know where the treasure must go now and who should be its present possessor. Wiglaf must orchestrate these impulses of feeling and bring them together. In his relaying of Beowulf's request, he does just this.

> Worn eall gespræc
> gomol on gehðo   ond eowic gretan het,
> bæd þæt ge geworhton   æfter wines dædum
> in bælstede   beorh þone hean,
> micelne ond mærne,   swa he manna wæs
> wigend weorðfullost   wide geond eorðan,
> þenden he burhwelan   brucan moste.   (3094b–3100)

(In sorrow the old man spoke many things and told me to greet you all, asked that you build in memory of your friend-lord's deeds a high barrow in the place of burning, great and splendid, just as he was the warrior most excellent of all men far over earth, while he was allowed to enjoy borough-wealth.)

The personal greeting that comes to the Geats from their king touches them, and that opens a way for them to enter into the hero's will at last, to share it and work within it, to carry it out and expand it finally to a high barrow, the measure and objective correlative of his heroic worth.

And now, his intermediary role fulfilled, after line 3137 Wiglaf vanishes in a way very familiar in Anglo-Saxon poetry. His disappearance leaves all action for the remaining lines of the poem to the collective *Geata leode*, now on their feet and now able to function communally with dignity and confidence. As they come together into a unified group and enact the serene rite of the funeral, they represent a reconstructed community and the final victory of *humanitas*, so far as it can be achieved on this earth and under this sky.

NOTES

1. "The Interlace Structure of *Beowulf*," *University of Toronto Quarterly* 37 (October, 1967), 1–17. See also Lewis E. Nicholson, "The Art of Interlace in *Beowulf*," *Studia Neophilologica* 52 (1980), 237–49. Nicholson's essay traces various images through the poem rather than studying local complexities of texture. See also Brian Stock, *The Implications of Literacy*, 81–83, for an attempt to relate styles of visual art to oral and literate contexts. The term "interlace" is strongly objected to, however, by Morton W. Bloomfield, "'Interlace' as a Medieval Narrative Technique with Special Reference to *Beowulf*," *Magister Regis: Studies in Honor of Robert Earl Kaske*, ed. Arthur Groos et al. (New York: Fordham University Press, 1986), 49–59. He maintains that only in the visual arts can one have the simultaneity that the term implies. A close relative to "interlace" is the narrative technique called "stranding" well described by Carol J. Clover, *The Medieval Saga* (Ithaca, NY and London: Cornell University Press, 1982).

2. "Interlace Structure," 13.

3. See Kemp Malone, "Coming Back from the Mere," *PMLA* 69 (1954), 1292–99. Among the oral-formulaic scholars who have concentrated their attention on the fictional scop's performance are Robert P. Creed, "The Singer Looks at his Sources," *Comparative Literature* 14 (1962), 44–52, and Jeff Opland, "Beowulf on the Poet," *Mediaeval Studies* 38 (1976), 442–67, and *Anglo-Saxon Oral Poetry: A Study of the Traditions* (New Haven, CT: Yale University Press, 1980), 202–05.

4. On ring structure, see Cedric W. Whitman, *Homer and the Heroic Tradition* (Cambridge, MA: Harvard University Press, 1958) and John D. Niles, "Ring Composition and the Structure of *Beowulf*," *PMLA* 94 (1979), 924–35.

5. *A Reading of Beowulf*, 164.

6. *A Reading of Beowulf*, chapter I.

7. *A Reading of Beowulf*, 22–28, 103–04.

8. On the envelope pattern, see Adeline Bartlett, *The Larger Rhetorical Patterns in Anglo-Saxon Poetry*, Columbia University Studies in English and Comparative Literature, 122 (New York, 1935).

9. Jane Chance, *Woman as Hero in Old English Literature*, 102–04.

10. See Robert Kellogg, "Varieties of Tradition in Medieval Narrative," *Medieval Narrative: A Symposium*, ed. Hans Bekker-Nielsen et al. (Odense, Denmark: Odense University Press, 1979), 120–29.

11. Critics who have seen Hygelac as rash and self-destructive include Robert E. Kaske, "*Sapientia et Fortitudo* as the Controlling Theme of *Beowulf*," in *An Anthology of Beowulf Criticism*, ed. Lewis C. Nicholson (Notre Dame, IN: Notre Dame University Press, 1963), 290–92, and F. Anne

Payne, "Three Aspects of Wyrd in *Beowulf*," in *Old English Studies in Honour of John C. Pope*, ed. Robert B. Burlin and Edward B. Irving, Jr. (Toronto: University of Toronto Press, 1974), 28–29.

12. This passage is discussed more fully in Chapter 4, p. 158.

13. The standard editions contain most of the scholarly suggestions on this passage. A recent study is Raymond P. Tripp, Jr., "The Restoration of *Beowulf* 2769b and 2771a, and Wiglaf's Entrance into the Barrow," *ELN* 15 (1978), 244–49. He reinterprets the text in an unorthodox way to show Wiglaf as seriously tempted by greed for the treasure, and takes *oferhigian* as meaning 'overpower'.—The emendation to *oferhiwian* proposed here is suggested in Toller's Supplement to the Bosworth-Toller *Anglo-Saxon Dictionary*, and in W. J. Sedgefield's edition of *Beowulf* (3d ed., Manchester: Manchester University Press, 1935).

14. Bruce Mitchell remarks, in a discussion of *apo koinou* constructions: "The *nu* clause in *Beo* 2799 can be taken both with what precedes and with what follows" (*Old English Syntax* [Oxford: Clarendon Press, 1985], para. 3799 [vol. II, 911]).

15. Bruce Mitchell (*Old English Syntax*, para. 253) also doubts that the imperative plurals can properly be addressed to Wiglaf alone, but tries to solve the problem by a rather strained reading, taking them as indicative plurals, with "treasures" supplied as subject of the first verb and *heaðomære* as subject of the second.

16. Thomas A. Carnicelli, "The Function of the Messenger in *Beowulf*," *SP* 72 (1975), 246–57. He argues that the Messenger, although one of the cowardly runaways, later redeems himself by proposing that the Geats renounce the treasure.

17. The Ravenswood episode is discussed at some length in *A Reading of Beowulf*, 179–91.

18. *A Reading of Beowulf*, 188.

19. The relevant lines are:

Ac her forð berað;   fugelas singað,
gylleð græghama,   guðwudu hlynneð,
scyld scefte oncwyð.

(5–7a; text from E. V. K. Dobbie's edition in *The Anglo-Saxon Minor Poems* [New York, 1942]).

(No, here they carry forth [weapons?]; birds sing, the greycoat [wolf] howls, war-wood resounds, shield answers shaft.)

A few lines later in this speech Hnæf is commanding his men to rise and fight the attackers of the hall.

20. Eric G. Stanley, "Hæthenra Hyht in *Beowulf*," in *Studies in Old English Literature in Honor of Arthur G. Brodeur*, ed. S. B. Greenfield (Eugene, OR: University of Oregon Press, 1963), 136–51, was one of the first to see Beowulf as tainted with avarice. Margaret E. Goldsmith argues throughout her book, *The Mode and Meaning of Beowulf*, that cupidity is one of two major sins castigated in the poem and in the poem's hero, the other being

pride. A sensible description of how wealth is viewed in Germanic society is Ernst Leisi, "Gold und Manneswert im *Beowulf*," *Anglia* 71 (1953), 259–73. Stanley B. Greenfield sees the hero as perhaps humanly imperfect in his judgments, but in no way tainted ("'Beowulf' and the Judgement of the Righteous," *Learning and Literature in Anglo-Saxon England: Studies Presented to Peter Clemoes . . .* , ed. Michael Lapidge and Helmut Gneuss. Cambridge: Cambridge University Press, 1985, 393–407).

21. The major editions, especially Dobbie's, have extensive summaries of scholars' attempts to fit these lines into an uncertain context. Klaeber and others emend *næs he* to *næfne*: the intruder would be damned by the curse *unless* he had been in God's grace (*agendes est*) in some sense. The problem here, however, is really not so much textual as contextual; scholars simply do not agree about the degree or nature of Christian thought we can expect to find in the poem.

22. *Beowulf: The Poem and its Tradition*, 233. Kathryn Hume, "The Theme and Structure of *Beowulf*," *SP* 72 (1975), 1–27, also rejects a hero-centered approach to the poem in favor of a similar interpretation, involving the central theme of "threats to social order."

23. Margaret E. Goldsmith, for example, seems to agree with Wiglaf's censure of Beowulf's rash zeal, at one point stating flatly that "the hero was at the best tragically wrong to suppose that his single combat with the dragon would benefit his people" (*The Mode and Meaning of Beowulf*, 226).

24. John C. McGalliard, "The Poet's Comment in *Beowulf*" *SP* 75 (1978), 243–70, denies that the poet ever blames Beowulf for fighting the dragon and maintains that, if Wiglaf seems to do so, it is only in a moment of grief.

25. On the Old English attitude toward wealth, reward and prestige, see the insightful remarks of T. A. Shippey, *Beowulf*, 18–21.

26. It is true that the poet remarks during the later description of the funeral that the gold is of no use:

Forleton eorla gestreon   eorðan healdan,
gold on greote,   þær hit nu gen lifað
eldum swa unnyt,   swa h[it ær]or wæs.   (3166–8)

(They let the earth hold the treasure of men, gold in the dirt, where it now still lives as useless to men as it was before.)

But this seems to distinguish "gold in the dirt," which is out of circulation now as it was "before" when the dragon had it, from gold functioning normally as stimulus and reward.

FOUR

The Hall as Image and Character

The broad canvas of oral and oral-derived poetry is dominated by strong effects of chiaroscuro and bold contrast. Often these are centrifugal or non-organic nonce-effects, not totally irrelevant to the whole but indulged in for their special effectiveness in a local context. Such effects may be naturalized in the larger poem more through their predictable conventionality, their membership in an entire poetic ("every poem has something like this in it"), than by any tailored fit to some central unity of the poem. Such a centrifugal style can often lead to weak story-plots, particularly to an unstructured and rambling episodic form. Much medieval literature, especially the later romances that still show strong traces of their origins in preliterate poetry, is open to criticism on such grounds. Thus it may be important for an author to provide unity by other means: by a strong and prominent central character, a big and engrossing single action, a compelling theme—or, especially effectively, by a single controlling image that dominates the story.

In his illuminating and now classic definition of the epic genre, Thomas Greene points out that the "arch-image" is one major characteristic of epic poetry.[1] By this term he means those massive symbols that take up so large an area in these poems, symbols like the doomed city of Troy (and its complex of walls, gates, lookout points) in the *Iliad,* or perhaps the narrow frontier pass between paynim Spain and sweet France in *The Song of Roland.* Used in much more "literate" and self-conscious ways, of course, the twin images of the rational city and the passionate fire that consumes the city dominate Virgil's *Aeneid.*

In *Beowulf,* there seems little doubt that the major controlling image throughout the poem from beginning to end is the hall. To trace the ways this centered symbol shimmers in the imagination in various changing lights, as halls are built, attacked, restored, abandoned, laid waste, is to gain sharper understanding of the poem's larger meanings.[2] It is also a convenient way for a critic to try to bring the poem back together into a single focus.

A hall is a mental construct. Before we see an actual hall in *Beowulf*, we must first be made aware of its contents: the feelings and beliefs that are destined to fill and shape it. The poem begins with a rapid series of images that seem at first ill-matched but nonetheless combine in a pattern rich in meaning for the rest of the poem. After the initial three-line summons back to a past of Danish glory, we first see an example of aggressive conquest in Scyld, a king who redeems his suffering people by imposing his fierce will on all his neighbors until they submit to him and pay him tribute. Then, in an abrupt change of pace, we see the welcome arrival of babies who will themselves grow up to become protectors of the nation, thus expanding power in a slower and less violent way, through a dynastic use of natural process. We see finally an elaborate funeral ritual of a strange kind, strange not only archeologically but emotionally, a ritual that evokes surprisingly deep emotions seemingly out of nowhere, since the lead time for them has been so short. The feeling accompanying the funeral is the strong sudden music of a lyric poem rather than the emotion aroused by an ordinary narrative. This may be enough to tell us that the funeral passage, like the sonnet of later centuries, is only truly comprehensible to an audience already familiar with its emotional conventions. Poets composing within such well-established expectations need almost no lead time at all.

If the opening of *Beowulf* makes a lyric poem, what unites its component parts? All these things—weakness and conquest, birth and death, continuity and loss—are brought together in the poet's quick and practised probing literally to the heart of the heroic world, to those profound and warm relationships that arise paradoxically from fear, insecurity, and desperate need, and to that forced interdependence of human beings that, in an implacably harsh universe, is source of both our pride and our vulnerability. Phrases in the funeral passage bring out these close relationships: *swæse gesiðas* (29) 'dear companions'; *wine Scyldinga* (30) 'friend-lord of the Scyldings'; *leof landfruma* (31) 'beloved prince of the land'. No one stands alone in this early-medieval world. All can survive only in a lord's protection or through the ready help of dear comrades. Even the dead King Scyld, himself once the mightiest and most memorable of protectors, Shield of his nation, moves on his stately funeral-ship not ultimately alone but in some other lord's safekeeping, *on Frean wære* (27), in 'the Lord's protection'.

Important as well in such a funeral ritual is our sense that the massive presence of a great king does not disappear at once when he dies.[3] A continuity—real, though expressed in varying ways—exists here. Scyld's death is shown as movement or procession from the first mention of it:

> Him ða Scyld gewat   to gescæphwile
> felahror feran   on frean wære.   (26–27)

(Then Scyld went traveling at the fated time, full of energy, into the Lord's protection.)

To a modern reader, the adjective *felahror* seems strange here. It gives that same impression of being both clumsily inappropriate (i.e., "needed for alliteration") and brilliantly apt which, as we noted before, the Homeric epithet sometimes gives, and probably for the same reason: their common derivation from oral traditions of poetry. *Felahror* vibrates with the peculiar vitality with which a hero seizes his final fate, whether it is Achilles leaving his shelter for the early death he has been told is certain if he ventures out to the field to avenge Patroclus, or the young hero Christ in the Old English *Dream of the Rood,* eagerly climbing up to embrace the cross of torment. So Scyld seems almost to hurry to board his death-ship.

His living presence also persists in the extension of his will beyond death into the obedient actions of his people who carry him down to the shore *swa he selfa bæd* (28) 'as he himself had ordered'. Even the word *selfa* here keeps vivid our sense of his identity, as if we could still hear in the sea-wind some echo of that royal self through those words of command by which he once ruled.

The sense of movement is also implied in the description of the funeral-ship as *fær,* something that travels, something which is personified as *utfus,* eagerly straining to be away, to leave harbor. The word *utfus* is like *felahror* in its strong suggestion of still-living energy. But Scyld cannot set out until his people have, at their own slower pace, honored him as they should. The beloved king they tenderly lay in the ship's bosom was—and still is—*beaga bryttan* (35) 'the dispenser of gold rings', and it is only in proper response to the riches he gave—and gives—that they heap wealth beside him in the ship. As it is his will being acted out, it is his wealth that is being used for the act. Even here the sense of busy movement continues as riches are brought to the harbor over far roads, and hands are in motion arranging armor and weapons beautifully in the ship's hold.

Similar positive responses to the death, besides those hinted at in the funeral, can be detected. Though the funeral itself certainly dominates the tone of the first 52 lines, these lines also include the description of the mysterious childhood of Scyld, when he was sent in a boat as a baby to the rescue of the Danes, and mention of the birth of his son Beow. The lines are then followed by a dynastic passage (53–63) telling how successor kings in turn "awoke," were born to carry on the guardian role. Birth fills as large a space as death, in other words. The space given to birth implies that we are meant to feel there is some normal process of growth and regeneration in the time-world that operates to preserve those relationships so vividly memorialized in the treasures the Danes heap on their dead saviour-king. Scyld's transition from life to death becomes both an accompanied journey and in some special sense an act of birth.

The treasures, emblems of their donors' love, will journey with him:

> Him on bearme læg
> madma mænigo,   þa him mid scoldon
> on flodes æht   feor gewitan.   (40b–42)

(In his embrace lay many a treasure, treasures that were destined to travel far with him into the ocean's possession.)

Translation cannot convey what is suggested by the delicate alliterative stress on *mid:* that, wherever he may voyage, the treasures will stay '*with*' him, will never abandon him. Though his people cannot go with him, they can send the treasures to keep him from being alone and unattended. Scyld seems to come home to his origins in this scene. The image just hinted at here of a child sleeping secure amid its possessions leads naturally to the next picture of that earlier launching of Scyld, when mysterious beings (simply *þa* 'those') sent the infant Scyld out alone over the waves *æt frumsceafte* (45) 'in the beginning', at his beginning, and perhaps in some larger dimension of time, at the world's beginning. Perhaps the whole myth hints at some oversea transhuman world where time is always at a fresh beginning. Perhaps (a large perhaps) the original audiences had a strong sense of such a surrounding outer world of reality, where the gods lived (they must have been well into the process of bringing that outer world into line with Christianity); perhaps they preferred to have their stories composed with a clear relation to such a background. Such a world out of our time is set in contrast with the time-ridden world we know, for the continuity of our time-processes is stated and restated in the many adverbs and conjunctions marking time through this section: *oft, syððan, oðþæt, æfter, ær, lange hwile, eft, þa gyt, þa.* Ultimately this ongoing temporal process, a process of birth and becoming under God's beneficent nurturing, ends with the emotional bonds reifying themselves organically in the form of one single concrete object: a hall.

All this complex of feelings is thus given a symbolic embodiment more durable and more steadily functional than a departing funeral-ship. The hall is a fixed locus where the vital and affectionate interchanges of social solidarity, the giving and taking of rewards and service, responsibility and gratitude, all that constitutes heroic life, can be carried on over a long period of time.

The hall the Danes now build is a named place, and thus itself partakes of the general imagery of birth, for it is christened like a newborn child, given all the power of the naming human word: you are *Heorot.* We may guess at the implications of meaning added through this act of naming, but with no certainty. There is probably some totemic power in the animal name "hart" that we can never comprehend now, but only wonder about and surmise that it *has* some meaning, as we may wonder about the strange horned figures in the Palaeolithic cave-paintings.

Heorot is also a word in another sense, that of a pledged word, a promise, for the hall is the reward promised by Hrothgar to his warriors in return for their loyalty and prowess in his youthful wars. He now keeps his word, his *treow:* he makes it explicit and visible by building his promised hall. Once it has been built, Heorot seems to expand: outward in time, to the limits of human memory (it is a greater building than the sons of men had ever heard of), and also outward in space, to the limits of the known world, *geond þisne middangeard* (75) 'far over this middle-earth', where its fame (which is its self in heroic story) extends. In the poem itself the image of this great hall expands to dominate entirely the first two-thirds. All action takes place in Heorot or focuses on it. The evil outsiders are suddenly stirred to life only when it is built. It is built to show Hrothgar's power, for which the word *word* is also used, in yet one more sense.

> Scop him Heort naman
> se þe his wordes geweald   wide hæfde.   (78b–79)

(He created for it the name Heorot, he who widely had power of his word.)

Against this great word, this heroic assertion, this Germanic logos, instantly spring up opposing forces of wordless destruction: a roaring fire in time to come, that will one day level Heorot in a blaze of sword-hate (81b–85), and, in much closer proximity in space and time, a violent attack by the dumb monster-outlaw Grendel, an embodiment of outer unreclaimed and inarticulate darkness. As has often been pointed out, this darkness gains greatly in vividness through being set in contrast with the story of the birth of the Universe that Heorot's scop sings at the inaugural feast in Heorot, where he tells the Danes of a creation abounding in life and free movement played upon by the lights of sun and moon. Even though the relationship between darkness and creation is stated (as is usual in oral-derived poetry) paratactically and not as a part of a causal relationship, and the theological implications might alarm the orthodox, probably we must feel somehow that the ominous stirring of darkness to swift and murderous action is also a natural growth and movement out of that original creative word, that *fiat lux*. Grendel's sudden motion seems a cancerous twist and thrust of that life-force back against its origins.

Such twisting of good to evil is a pattern in the poem, of course. Hrothgar later (1709b–22a) describes the evil king Heremod as having been set moving firmly in the right direction by God but as then inexplicably choosing to plunge off that high road into the joyless thickets of slaughter and exile. Cain too once lived in a human hall with a family, but chose to sever the holy cords of kinship with that first death-stroke that is consistently represented in *Beowulf* as the true original sin, as it is also in the often cited passage in *Genesis A* (987–1001). There the blow that killed Abel is represented as the "twig" that produced branches and leaves that afflict all mankind with violence and torment to this day.

Like his descendants, Cain is forcibly driven away from *man-dream*, the paradise of joyous human fellowship of which the hall is the symbol. Then, like the Danish Scylding dynasty, the wretched dynasty of Cain also "awakens," though producing not great kings but only its own chaotic progeny of trolls, giants, and the evil hulks of the undead. The Anglo-Saxons may have thought this kind of birth, the generation of evil monsters, to be an unceasing cyclical process, but it happens linearly in the narrative present of the poem. When he hears the poet's song about the way the world was made, Grendel too first "awakens" from whatever muddy stupor he had been lying in before Heorot was built and put to happy use, and he responds by attacking the shining hall.

It is always the hall, this symbolic building, that Grendel attacks. Whatever it stands for, always he is driven to destroy it. Perhaps, when all is said, the hall itself remains the clearest explanation for the puzzling motivation of the Cain-monsters. It is simply not possible for them ever to break their old relationship with the hall. If they cannot live in it, then they must render it unlivable for others. Compulsively Grendel labors to bring its mutually supportive heroic activities, its interchange of dependencies, the circulation of its heart's blood, to a dead standstill. Some cryptic Dark Age theology, perhaps brewed from a blending of Manichean-tinged Christianity with the grim chill of Northern myths, seems to underlie this compulsive opposition. Out of the howling darkness, the frost-giants prowl ever closer to put out our sustaining fires. Grendel's dominant preposition is *wið*, 'against'. He is always the Against, the *Andsaca*, the 'Adversary', all his coarse vitality straining to freeze that vital movement that was first set dancing in God's act of creation. He soon effectually freezes the Danes, who sit, weep, suffer, pray uselessly to their resuscitated pagan gods, shiver and simmer in grief. In all this paralyzed landscape, the only moving thing is Grendel's shape lurching forward again and again in tireless attack and ambush and persecution—never getting his fill of it—over twelve long years.

Beowulf alludes to the Danes' paralyzed condition and the lastingness of their affliction at the end of his first speech to the coastguard when he arrives in Denmark (260–85). If no remedy should appear, he says, the Danes and their king Hrothgar may well remain in wretchedness

> þenden þær wunað
> on heahstede   husa selest.   (284b–85)

(so long as the best of houses remains there, in the high place.)

The "there," stressed by alliteration, would surely have been accompanied in performance or recitation by a broad gesture up toward mighty Heorot. (Such cues for stage-gestures are frequent in *Beowulf*, especially in the speeches. They furnish another kind of evidence for highly dramatic oral performance.) The remark and the accompanying gesture also identify the hall as a cause of afflictions. So long as it remains standing there, Grendel's attacks will never cease. The lines make it plain as well that Heorot's fame has reached Beowulf's country. He is perfectly aware of what he has

come to save, and probably also aware of why it is being attacked—
more than the Danes seem to know.

Beowulf's knowledge and assurance is abundantly evident in the
following passage. He soon sees Heorot for himself as the coastguard leads them up the path from the shore.

> Guman onetton,
> sigon ætsomne,   oþþæt hy sæl timbred,
> geatolic ond goldfah,   ongyton mihton;
> þæt wæs foremærost   foldbuendum
> receda under roderum,   on þæm se rica bad;
> lixte se leoma   ofer landa fela.   (306b–311)

(The men hurried forward, pressed on together to where they
could plainly see the timbered hall, splendid and gold-bright;
that hall was by far the most famous to earth-dwellers under
the skies, where the mighty king was waiting. Its light shone out
over many lands.)

Heorot is never more explicitly described as a center of radiant energy than here. Merely to enter this world-famous building is for
the provincial Geats[4] a major event, given more imposing meaning
by the ringing challenges they encounter and the requirement that
they disarm before coming inside. Yet, once inside "under Heorot's
roof," Beowulf seems anything but provincial. He shows precise
awareness of where he is and of just where the problem for the
Danes is the most painful. The first thing he tells Hrothgar is that
he has heard that this hall (and again he gestures toward what now
surrounds him), this best of all halls, has been made empty and
useless every night because of Grendel's depredations. It is presented as a major international problem. This is the calamitous outcome of *Grendles þing* (409). Beowulf then courteously but very
insistently asks Hrothgar for leave to cleanse Heorot and thus free
it once more to play its proper role. Beowulf makes plain that he
knows all the risks involved in the venture. Grendel is surely as
likely to eat Geats in Heorot as he was to eat Danes there.

In the latter half of his reply (473–90, a passage already quoted
above in Chapter 2 during the discussion of Unferth), Hrothgar
tells how his men tried again and again to stay on after dark in the
hall to defend it against its attacker. In our present context, we
should note the prominence given to the hall in this account. After
Grendel had carried out the inevitable massacre each time, it was to
the same blood-drenched hall (*eal bencþelu blode bestymed, / heall*

heorudreore 486–87a 'all the bench-floor soaked in blood, the hall soaked in sword-gore') that Hrothgar returned the next morning—*this* mead-hall (and now in his turn Hrothgar waves an arm around him dramatically), a mead-hall personified to some degree as a wounded and suffering creature. The suffering is obviously also Hrothgar's since he so deeply identifies himself with his hall. Note the placing of words in this sentence:

> Sorh is me to secganne   on sefan minum
> gumena ængum   hwæt me Grendel hafað
> hynðo on Heorote   mid his heteþancum,
> færniða gefremed.   (473–76a)

(It is sorrow in my spirit for me to say to any man what humiliation Grendel has inflicted on me in Heorot by his vindictive thoughts and sudden violence.)

Me and *on Heorote* are felt to be co-objects in apposition, both suffering the effects of Grendel's attack. Three first-person pronouns occur in the sentence. Later in the poem Hrothgar refers to Grendel as *ingenga min* (1776) 'my invader', *the one who comes into me*, a way of putting the situation that shows equally strikingly the extent to which he takes Heorot to be an intimate part of himself and of his personal space, and shows why he takes Grendel's brutal acts as direct personal affronts as well as desecrations of his nation's sacred place. Even the conventional metaphor for a king, "fence" (*eodor*), reinforces the association of a king with a protective structure, and of Grendel with fence-breaking, as well as the penetrating of bodies.

The context we have been outlining here may offer a little guidance on how to read the difficult two lines that end Hrothgar's speech:

> Site nu to symle ond onsæl [on sæl?] meoto,
> sigehreð secgum,   swa þin sefa hwette.   (489–90)[5]

Adopting one alternative reading of the text, this might be translated as an invitation to Beowulf: "Sit at the feast now and think about happiness and victory for my men, as your spirit urges you on." That is to say, Hrothgar wants the dreary subject changed and the atrocious memory of the blood-smeared hall cleared from his mind by more cheerful thoughts. It might also be possible to read it in another way that would also suit the context, by taking *on sæl meoto* as meaning "think about the hall," think, that is, both about the bloody hall Hrothgar is haunted by and the potentially safe and liberated hall. Possibly the original reading was *on sele meoto* (cf. *on sele wunian* 3128b), metrically better.

After listening to Hrothgar, Beowulf at once commits himself totally to the defense of the hall—so long as he can move and fight—and even to death. In the vow he makes after taking the cup from Wealhtheow (632–38), he swears to kill Grendel or die *on þisse meoduhealle* 'in this very mead-hall', again with a vigorous and emphatic gesture toward the building they are in, keeping the hall's presence always vivid in the audience's imagination. His vow, like the other vows that are exchanged as the feast continues, is a *þryðword* (643) 'a power-word', a charged promise that welds the hero's terrific will to the collective will of Hrothgar and the Danes. But it is a word that must at once be made flesh in action if the desperately wounded hall, that maimed and bleeding Fisher King of this poem, is to be restored to healthy function. Insofar as strong words and sincere rituals alone can initiate a healing process, the rebuilding of Hrothgar's shattered community seems already to have begun as the Geats join the Danes at their feast and combine with them to create a new *duguð unlytel* (498) 'a good-sized host'. As we noted in Chapter 2, any residual intertribal tension then disclosed in Unferth's challenge to Beowulf's credibility and Beowulf's tough reply to it can be harmlessly discharged and dissipated in this newly hopeful atmosphere.

It is just at this point that we realize the fact that, so far in the poem, we have been entirely within Heorot's range and scope, never outside it at all. Heorot stands massively in the human center, assembling and projecting forward all that has gone before in Danish history and pulling inward toward itself both Grendel and Beowulf, its destroyer and its rescuer. This strong sense of centeredness, reinforced by the new and promising alliance of the two nations, is a profound source of unity. It makes us feel that Heorot is indeed the world, or the vital heart of the heroic world, where we find our most deeply rooted communal defenses against the threat of chaos-bringing powers. These rooted defenses are social and familial. Our early childhood sensations of threatened security, exactly those sensations that form the basis of the most powerful and popular folk-tales, are here evoked in multiple ways. Whether identified as cosmic, theological, or Freudian, these threats never seem so pressing to us as now in the poem, when we get just a glimpse of that outside. Hrothgar tells us that Grendel, the dark shape of the Shadow Outside, has had his attention focused all the long day *to þæm heahsele* (647), unswervingly focused 'on this high building', the fury of that obscure menace growing in intensity as the light sinks and man's courage falters. Grendel does not know what has been going on in Heorot. He does not know that Beowulf has arrived. He does seem to know that someone will be staying over in Heorot this particular night, since he hopes for a feast. But it hardly matters to him who is there. He merely comes, as he always comes, is doomed and driven to come, against the hall, to fight the hall.

Now the pace speeds up. It is high time to transfer jurisdiction over Heorot, since Grendel is already on his way. By this time Hrothgar does not need to protract his examination of Beowulf's credentials. He is ready to give him the hall. The confidence he feels in Beowulf's ability to help him (*geoce gelyfde* 608 'he trusted in help'), which Wealhtheow also feels (*gelyfde* 627), leads, with something like word-play, to entrusting (*alyfde* 655) Heorot to him. As we saw earlier, this transfer is a difficult abnegation of the king's authority and responsibility but one he carries out with dignity. That Grendel, *Grendel,* is on his way is what dominates the scene and precipitates such decisions. The function of hall-watch (*seleweard*) that Hrothgar assigns to the young hero in this ceremony of transfer is, a moment later, said to be laid on Beowulf by God himself (665b–68), a measure of its infinite importance in the central myth of the poem's world.

The hall is Grendel's only goal and obsession during the ensuing famous passage describing his approach.[6] While he is still far off, too far for us to make him out clearly, still a dim shadow-walker in the night, we are being shown the threatened and vulnerable hall, with all the Geats except Beowulf now asleep. The outside scene where Grendel is and the inside scene are gradually drawn together until they finally merge. God's anger at Grendel has been made visible in the outside scene, in the forbidding landscape of moors, fens, and misty cliffs to which he has banished the Cain-race. But, like Milton's Satan, Grendel can carry his hellish environment as well as God's anger with him wherever he goes, even when he travels away from home (*godes yrre bær* 711). The poet in fact artfully develops anger as a unifying theme underlying the approach and the fight. It was Cain's anger at his brother that set it all in motion. Now God's anger lies heavy on Grendel, and Grendel's displaced rage swells as he walks toward the hall to meet the angry (*bolgenmod* 709) Beowulf.

In the second of the three *com* passages (710 ff.), we see Grendel only a little more clearly than we did at first. Now he is walking below the mist-cliffs and thinking about trapping some man "in the high hall." At last he comes to a point where he can sense or sniff (probably not see very clearly) the nearness of the glittering gold-hall of men. As the poet earlier described Heorot as wounded and bleeding, here he again personifies it as a victim attacked by Grendel. Through the means of Grendel's own violent assault, the monster completes the personifying of Heorot. It becomes one of the people he attacks and eats. First he touches the hall with his hands, and the door flies open. Then he jams his brutal claws into Heorot's mouth and wrenches it apart—a gross violation of the hall's body as well as an act of sacrilege against the temple-like building. Probably we are to see this particular act of mayhem appropriately avenged later by the violation of Grendel's own body, especially when his ripped-off arm is hung snug up against Heorot's famous golden roof, like some extorted payment of wergeld, quid pro quo, to console the wounded hall for the outrage visited on it. Indeed the ultimate vengeance may come when Beowulf's men dump Grendel's severed head onto the hall floor. It is interesting that both severed parts, arm and head, are offered in atonement directly to the violated hall.

Since in reality the entire fight between Grendel and Beowulf is presented in terms that make it seem to be in very large part Grendel's battle with Heorot, the poet maintains the same device of semi-personification throughout his account.[7] We are shown few physical details of the wrestling-match between Grendel and Beowulf at the time it takes place. It is indeed surprising that our clearest close-up view of the actual encounter comes only after the fight, when Beowulf is describing the action to Hrothgar (958–72a). We should note there that Beowulf has come out of the conflict unbruised, without a scratch, if excited and a little disappointed that Grendel got away, even though without his arm. But this should not be taken to mean that Grendel was incapable of inflicting damage. Clearly what has taken the full impact of the fight has not been Beowulf but the hall itself, now almost completely wrecked. Thus it is fitting that the most vivid part of the fight while it is actually in progress is the account (beginning in line 767) of the Danes observing Heorot from a safe distance outside, wincing in dread of the imminent collapse of their beloved hall, as its iron braces take up the tremendous strains and its mead-benches are torn from the floor and fly in all directions. Only its horn-gabled roof stays firm and rides out the storm within.[8]

Presenting the fight in these curious double terms bears some interesting resemblances to the way the Crucifixion is represented in *The Dream of the Rood*. There Christ can remain the eager, serene, and confident young hero who seems merely to grow "tired" at the end of his ordeal, while it is the Cross itself, standing for Christ's mortal nature, that suffers fearful pain. It reports to us directly how it is pierced with dark nails, drenched in blood, and racked by the tormenting emotions of conflict. Though so full a degree of personification is never matched in *Beowulf*, the comparison suggests that separating the pure essence of heroic will from the ugly physical suffering that is bound to attend its exertion in the real world must have been a way of conceiving such a configuration that was congenial to the Anglo-Saxon imagination. The pain of battered Heorot (if we may use such a phrase) and the real agony of Grendel, voiced at top volume in the horrible screaming of his "terror-song" (786), are set in their extravagant physicality in strongest contrast to the calm and masterful control of everything around him that Beowulf displays all through this violent scene. The control seems manifested in the very style itself. The poet placidly repeats formulas first used when Beowulf was introduced, as if to say the hero has methodically done only what was to be expected of him:

> Heold hine fæste
> se þe manna wæs   mægene strengest
> on þæm dæge   þysses lifes.   (788b–90)

(He held him fast who was strongest in might of any man at that day of this life. [Cf. 196–97])

The same contrast or discrimination between the assertion of heroic will and the physical devastation it causes is echoed in later lines. That Beowulf's exertion of his physical strength is less emphasized than we might expect it to be increases our sense of its staggering moral power. Certainly it effects an instant and permanent change in Grendel's attitude toward the hall he has been plaguing. He has been turned around now. He will never want to attack it again, or even come near it. Indeed, if the hall has now been largely wrecked, that seems to have happened in large part because of Grendel's own galvanic efforts to struggle free from it, to break out through the wrenched door, and go anywhere else in the world, though preferably back to his joyless hideout in the fens "to seek the company of devils" (756). There could be no better evidence for the sheer concentrated impact of Beowulf's adamant nay-saying will than the sight of Grendel's juggernaut hall-smashing force so convulsively reversed in its direction.

After the fight, Beowulf's specific achievement is lucidly spelled out:

Hæfde þa gefælsod   se þe ær feorran com,
snotor ond swyðferhð,   sele Hroðgares,
genered wið niðe.   (825–27a)

(He had cleansed, he who came from afar, wise and strong, the hall of Hrothgar—he had rescued it from attack.)

One can find still more personification lurking in this last phrase. It could equally well have been applied to the rescuing of a friend in battle or other difficulty. The same formula is so used elsewhere in the poetry.[9] Heorot plays the role of fellow-fighter, a warrior like the personified shield in the Shield riddle, who fights on doggedly even though, being a merely defensive weapon, he never deals any blows himself but can only endure endless wounding in all his battles.[10] Battered Heorot is like Ajax in the *Iliad*, always seen in battle as standing off Trojan onslaughts behind his mighty shield rather than as using weapons of offense.

And now there is visible proof of victory:

                    Þæt wæs tacen sweotol,
syþðan hildedeor   hond alegde,
earm ond eaxle   (þær wæs eal geador
Grendles grape)   under geapne hrof.   (833b–36)

(That was a clear sign, when the brave one laid the hand, arm, shoulder—there Grendel's grip was all together—under that spacious roof.)

The image of the two opponents, the great "grip" juxtaposed against the lofty roof, is stressed by the alliterative structure of line 836. This combination is what Hrothgar and his queen now see, and, as he looks at it, the king remembers once more the hall as it was before in its wounded state, 'when the best of houses was blood-drenched, bright with gore' (934b–35). His excitement and relief lead him at once to propose an even more intimate bonding of Beowulf to the hall, for it is now that he suggests the adoption of Beowulf as his son, so that he will become a full member of the hall's own family and not merely Heorot's temporary guardian.

Now Heorot is quickly healed and its wounds bound up, as it is repaired and redecorated by the eager and affectionate hands of Danish men and women who reenact the original creation of the great building. The scene resembles the ritual purification of Odysseus's palace after the slaying of the suitors at the end of the *Odyssey*. In a second more functional sense, Heorot is rebuilt by becoming once again recommissioned as the scene of a feast full of hall-joy, gift-giving, and entertainment by the court-poet.

First Hrothgar makes a formal processional entry into his rehabilitated hall, as if it had just been built for the first time. Then it leaps to full life as the great *werod* of warriors crowd in to surround their treasure-giving king, seating themselves on the newly-righted benches, eating and drinking in company. The exhilaration of this regathering of the tribe is so contagious that even Hrothulf, viewed elsewhere with some apparent distrust by Wealhtheow, can gladly be included among the "friends" who now throng Heorot. In such a context, it is hard to conceive of any lurking irony in the mention of him; the irony of *Beowulf* never lurks. There follows the most elaborate account in the poem of what formal gift-giving can be, as Beowulf accepts a series of immensely valuable presents from the grateful king. This "slow" descriptive passage has probably interested archeologists more than it has literary critics, but we ought to recall that gift-giving was what Heorot was originally built for (cf. lines 67b–73). So full and lingering a depiction of this activity demonstrates and validates the complete restoration to function of the hall, and of its king, who has had little chance to be munificent in the last twelve years. We must assume that the original audience took pleasure in savoring this leisurely ceremony. In *Beowulf*, a hall is really only a shell, a passively potential institution, unless and until, like the characters, it can be made actively functional. It is the wholly functional hero who has enabled the hall to recover its function.

But this celebration of the delights of a hall in proper working-order is only one extreme of a set of long-term pendulum swings in the deeply fatalistic rhythms of the poem. Heorot was built; it was put out of commission for years; it is now refurbished and happily functioning; it will cease to function again very soon. This is the grim parataxis of the way it is in the world. Thus it is not surprising, given such a pattern of thinking, that the official hall-entertainment, the *healgamen* chosen by the Danish scop to please the jovial feasters in Heorot, turns out to be the catastrophic story of what happened in another hall, Finn's hall, Finnsburg.

In this traditional oral story, as we can tell since luckily, for once, we do have another version of it in the Finn Fragment, it is the building itself that is the central focus of a tale of treachery against guests, of a surprise night attack on the hall where the guests are housed.[11] What remains of the Fragment is wholly centered on the memorable and stirring defense of the hall by the Danish visitors. In the version of the story we find in *Beowulf*, we see the same hall still starring in a later stage in the narrative, now with its jurisdiction divided by the terms of the treaty between the surviving Danes and the Frisians. The hall is thus shared by two hostile tribes who are obliged to carry out reluctantly a hollow travesty of allegiance and gift-giving, so different in every way from what has just gone on in the narrative present in Heorot. In Finnsburg the resentful Danes must out of necessity pretend to be part of the loyal retinue of their hated enemy King Finn. With every vibration dissonant, a hall so divided cannot long stand.[12] Its instability as a fatally crippled social unit is implied both in the tortured and precarious intricacy of the treaty's language (1085b–1106) and in Hengest's fierce desire to take himself out of such a situation and such a hall as quickly as he can. No one can be surprised that the hall ends up raped and gutted, ironically redecorated at the end with the blood of more Frisian corpses. That King Finn is abruptly cut down *æt his selfes ham* (1147) 'in his own hall', may earn us a little sympathy for him, as his queen and his treasures are being carried away to Danish ships. Shifting focus from this grim hall-entertainment back into Heorot's present situation can only convey a warning that Heorot itself is not yet wholly safe, nor can it ever be, any more than any hall can be, even though the exultant and relaxed Danes move back into it for the night and sink into contented sleep.

A certain irony invests this scene of the banquet's end, where we suddenly see more homely details of the ordinary prosaic way of life in Heorot than we ever see elsewhere. The poet shows us just what the Danes have now recovered through Beowulf's efforts. Housekeeping details now appear. Floors are cleared and spread with mattresses and pillows. Shields are placed near the sleepers' heads. On the mead-benches helmets and mailshirts are piled ready at hand. The very normality of sleeping arrangements, this mundane and domestic aspect of hall-life, lulls us too. And so of course it is now, when we are all lulled, that Grendel's vengeful mother makes her lightning smash-and-grab raid, loping back afterward to her underwater home with one dead Dane and her son's arm. Vigilance was relaxed too soon. As at Finnsburg, murderous violence can always burst into any hall from the darkness outside.

As Grendel's mother moves away from the hall, the full attention of poet and audience now begins to swing outward with her, directed away from the hall for the first time in the poem. Grendel's mother has no previous record as a hall-raider. So plainly does she reveal no intention whatever of coming back to attack Heorot again that none of the characters even mentions that possibility. She has neatly limited her goal to a simple one-for-one, a head for a head. Now she will have to be tracked down elsewhere, outside Heorot.

After Hrothgar tells Beowulf that his favorite thane has been snatched up in sleep in the newly restored hall, the king's dazed thoughts begin to probe and search falteringly outside the enclave of Heorot:

> Wearð him on Heorote   to handbanan
> wælgæst wæfre;   ic ne wat hwæder
> atol æse wlanc   eftsiðas teah,
> fylle gefægnod.   (1330–33a)

(That wandering murderous guest was his [Æschere's] killer here, in Heorot—but I don't know what direction the demon took, gloating in her prey, sated with food, on her way homeward.)

Then, as memory begins to seep back into Hrothgar's distracted mind, there follows the exploration of that ghoul-haunted "elsewhere," the home of the elsewhere-spirits, the *ellorgæstas,* somewhere in the vicinity of the loathsome mere. To the king at least, the mere is obviously the very opposite of any hall. He describes no buildings there. It is bleakly an outdoor unsheltered place, exposed to winds, wolves and appalling climatic turbulence. Mysterious and repulsive, to men as well as to hunted stags it is above all dangerous, a *frecne stowe* (1378).

Yet, as we saw earlier in discussing the character of Hrothgar in Chapter 2, his active response to the challenge here offered is a great moment for him. To experience yet one more time the deep violation of his hall, and this time in the acute form of the butchery of an old friend, is a fearful shock to the old man after his relief at the apparent salvation of his kingdom. But, at Beowulf's forceful urging, he leaves the precincts of his hall for the only time in the poem to lead both Danes and Geats to the mere. When we next see him, he has returned to his royal domain never to leave again, but in his march out to the mere he shows us how courage and love can once again stir into action the almost obscured heroic qualities of this aged king.

After we actually see the melodramatic horrors of the mere's swirling waters and grotesque monsters, it is strange and surprising that the edifice on the mere-bottom that Beowulf must enter to fight Grendel's mother turns out to be a quite ordinary Germanic hall, described in the usual vocabulary (*hof, niðsele, hrofsele, guðsele, reced, wic, hus*), with a cosy fire burning on its hearth and a bed supporting the body of Grendel. Its conventional domestic decor includes weapons hanging on the walls and much treasure.

It seems fitting, though why that should be is not entirely clear to me, that the dwelling in the mere not itself be bizarre or supernatural (other than in its unusual location) but much like a real hall. We see one hall pitted against another. Furthermore, one effect of describing it this way may be to make Beowulf's invasion of it seem like a rude irruption into a haven of domestic security. Possibly this effect emphasizes the subliminal but somewhat disturbing "rape" associations of this violent assault on a female in her home. There are also chances for irony, not unlike the irony associated with Grendel's "calling" at Heorot. Beowulf too comes calling at the mere-hall, though not treated with much hospitality by the lady of the house or by the ugly and aggressive sea-monsters, defenders of the mere, that try to kill him during his swim down. The hall also makes a suitable and quite normal place for a fight. And it does turn out to be an authentic rough-and-tumble hall-fight, fully exploiting the entire stage-set and properties: floors, lighting, walls, and what hangs on the walls. One almost expects to see the bar-mirror, bottles, and chairs of the Western movie, all ready for the smashing.

After Beowulf has made full use of the props at hand to kill Grendel's mother, and with great difficulty, he carries out the act he really came for. He beheads Grendel, doing it properly in Grendel's own hall and in Grendel's own bed, just as Grendel had once tried to attack Beowulf in his bed in Heorot. The great ravager of halls is himself ravaged in the same way and the same place. The symmetry reminds us of ring-structure and folk-tales. The safe home, the cosy place, that Grendel had so longed to flee to when he felt the exquisite pain of the hand-grip has now in its turn been pierced and neutralized by Heorot's own chosen champion. Thus one hall conquers another. Both halls are now cleansed by this action, as is the evil mere itself, when the hero carries out the ritual killing of the elsewhere-spirit in his very human-appearing home.

The treasure in the mere-hall represents something of an anomaly. Another poet in another version of the story might have done more with it. Unlike Heorot or other Germanic halls, the monsters' hall does not seem to be used for any transfer of treasure, or even primarily for the amassing and hoarding of it, in accordance with the well-established practice of dragons. Neither Grendel nor his mother ever evinces the slightest interest in looting or in protecting treasure. We are not told where the treasure in their hall came from. The one specimen of it we see, the hilt of the giant-sword that Beowulf carries back to Heorot, seems to be a Cain-family heirloom if we take it literally. Since we cannot do so (why would they treasure this hilt with its story of calamity in the past?), it is simply a conventional placard explaining to the audience, extra-dramatically or metatextually, that Grendel's forebears long ago were also hammered by God. The story of the Flood on the hilt makes it more of a portable story than an object of value. For whatever reason, Beowulf himself does not plunder the mere-hall, as one might normally loot a captured hall or dragon-mound.[13]

Perhaps the true treasure that Beowulf brings back is Grendel's head. The odd but compelling relationship between the two halls requires that the Geats now carry the enormous head back again all the way to Heorot, the *goldsele*, the 'gold-hall'. Beowulf's entrance into the hall is a reenactment in triumph of his original arrival in Heorot, except that now all the promises have become actuality and he does not come empty-handed.

> Ða com in gan   ealdor ðegna,
> dædcene mon   dome gewurþad,
> hæle hildedeor,   Hroðgar gretan.
> Þa wæs be feaxe   on flet boren
> Grendles heafod,   þær guman druncon,
> egeslic for eorlum   ond þære idese mid,
> wliteseon wrætlic;   weras on sawon.   (1644–50)

(Then came walking in the lord of thanes, the man fierce in deeds, honored now in glory, the hero brave in battle, to greet Hrothgar. Then by the hair Grendel's head was carried out onto the hall-floor, where men were drinking. It was terrifying to the warriors and to the queen too, an amazing sight. Men looked at it.)

Note how, on the micro-scale, the successive variants here describing Beowulf resonate with more than merely ornamental tones. They mean something in this context. We have just seen and are now seeing Beowulf as lord of thanes indeed, marching at the head of his men after they have (in their finest hour) so loyally waited by the mere's bank for his return. They have earned their place in the story, and march in triumph. And the close-knit interaction between leader and men was never so tellingly suggested before. We see him literally walking through the part of being a lord of thanes; we have just witnessed the specific *dæd* and *hild* that have proven him brave (*cene, deor*) and graced him with deserved honor (*dom*).

The shock to the Danes in this scene is real but salutary. Only when that horrible head is dumped on their floor and the debladed giant-sword handed over to their king are they wholly free and safe in their great hall. It can now be restored to its pristine splendor, having been made as whole and safe as Beowulf can make it. *Reced hliuade / geap ond goldfah:* 'the hall towered high, spacious and bright with gold' (1799b–1800a). By killing the *huses hyrdas*, the two guardians of the underwater hall, he as guardian of Heorot has made it possible for Hrothgar and all his men to sleep secure in their own hall. They will no longer have anything to fear in *that* direction, he assures the king; *on þa healfe* (1675), where the alliteration stresses the limiting of safety to the elimination of only one kind of threat.

As everyone knows, however, this is far from saying that Heorot has now become impregnable. In fact, we are given several very broad hints that this hall's life will be quite brief. One day soon, perhaps in Hrothgar's lifetime, it will go down before that greatest enemy of halls, fire, for it will be destroyed during the war between Danes and Heathobards, despite the peace-making political marriage proposed by Hrothgar between his daughter Freawaru and Ingeld of the Heathobards (81b–85). Furthermore, the family solidarity that is one important value that should be implied by a royal hall will be shattered in some future struggle over succession to the throne, probably involving Hrothgar's nephew Hrothulf in some way.

But it is possible that we tend inevitably to exaggerate the importance of these prophecies of doom. The Germanic mind habitually prophesizes doom. Doom is unavoidable. But the Anglo-Saxons see such events in the future differently, perhaps because of being more time-bound in the present than we are with our trained "historical" imaginations. Whatever interesting shadows they may cast, these future events do not actually ever take place in the poem. They are not foregrounded (with the possible exception of the predicted outbreak of the Heathobard feud) in the way oral poetry gives importance to events. Mention of them adds richness and depth of texture to the story, but Heorot remains unburned and glorious so long as we actually see it in the poem, and is the scene of a final celebration on Beowulf's last night in Denmark. After the feast all at last sleep soundly in it, after so many years. To the extent that Beowulf by his own efforts can ensure Heorot's survival, he is completely and unqualifiedly successful. We need not see his victory as ironically incomplete or temporary, perhaps even pathetic. The image of Heorot we take away from the poem is not one of smoldering ruins but of a majestic palace still casting its bright light over many lands.

The destruction of Beowulf's own royal hall, on the other hand, is no veiled and atmospheric prophecy but a crystal-clear absolute fact, an event we see, indeed virtually the only fact we are ever furnished about it. We really never see this hall. The accounts of Beowulf's gift-giving in his hall with which Wiglaf tries to persuade the runaway retainers to come back are too typical and generalized to be considered truly visualized scenes. It is strange but true that there is never a scene where we are brought in close to see Beowulf enthroned as king in his hall, not once during his fifty-year reign. The hall is burned at the beginning of Part II, the remaining action of which then takes place on the last day of Beowulf's life.

The point should be made, however, that we were once present at a major scene in the Geatish royal hall, though it was before Beowulf became king. It is the setting for the returning hero's report on his Danish adventures, where he is richly rewarded by his uncle King Hygelac (1925–2199). This scene occupies an important pivotal position in the narrative. It comes after the real end of the Danish portion at line 1887 and forms a strong epilogue to that section in its general tone, maintaining Part I's highly social atmosphere and its heavy stress on the royal political activity for which a hall is the proper venue. Beowulf's report is thus the last great hall-scene of the poem. As such, it sets up the usual abrupt contrast with Part II. That treasure-giving scene still shines warm and bright in the imagination when we are suddenly told that that very building has gone, vanished in the surges of dragon-fire.

Where Part I is entirely dominated, as we have seen, by struggles over the possession of a great hall, Part II, without any gradual modulation, at once confronts a world where there is no hall to be struggled for. Since so large a burden of symbolic content has been laid on the image of the hall, making it a center of value for all members of heroic society, this massive contrast forces major questions on us. What meaning can human life have without the hall at its center? Is life even possible outside the limits of the social world the hall stands for? It will be recalled that the poem once defines life itself as "dwelling in a mead-hall" (*meduseld buan* 3065). Bede's myth of the sparrow flying out of the darkness through the lighted hall and out again must come to mind.[14] Your death-day comes when you are no longer permitted to stay in the hall's warm and noisy interior but must go outside to die in the cold and dark. In the figure of the Wanderer in the Old English elegy, we see someone who exists out in this cold and dark, dragging out an existence haunted by agonizing memories and hallucinations curiously like those experienced by a person near death. Separation from the hall-society, whether by disgrace (as in the case of the cowardly retainers) or by accident (the death of the Wanderer's lord), is here not easily distinguishable from death itself.

Another specific connection between the imagery of the Old English elegies and the final part of *Beowulf* suggests itself, leaving aside the many less tangible emotional and stylistic links. After Beowulf's royal hall has been destroyed by fire, all that remains of it seems to be the *haga* (2892). I take this to be the surrounding enclosure of earthworks and/or palisade, within which the main body of Geats sit and wait for news of the dragon-fight and then listen to the Messenger's report and prophecy. If this is in fact what is meant by the *haga*, we would have here the familiar setting of a ruined building such as we find in *The Wanderer* and in *The Ruin*, an appropriate locale for forecasting the ruin of a nation.

Unlike the speakers in the elegies, however, Beowulf is not concerned with coming to terms with his despair about unavoidable loss and deprivation among such ruins, literal or figurative. As we saw in the previous chapter, when he hears his hall has been burned, his first reaction is to wonder why this has happened to him and to assume, at least momentarily and instinctively, that he must somehow have incurred God's anger. That it is *his sylfes ham* (2325), 'his own home', as well as the communal and official *gifstol Geata*, 'gift-throne of the Geats', that has been destroyed makes it seem to him, as earlier to Hrothgar in a similar crisis, a personal blow and a direct insult. As we saw in Chapter 2, Hrothgar's response to invasion was fatalistic and passive, and he drew no inference that he himself might be in any way responsible for it. Beowulf's response, leading to his brief and unusual "dark thoughts" (2332), is more like the puzzled questions of Job: "If I have sinned, how do I injure thee, thou watcher of the hearts of men? Why hast thou made me thy butt, and why have I become thy target?" There are great differences, of course. We have no reason whatever to think that God is punishing or testing Beowulf, and Beowulf's thoughts have none of the aggrieved and self-pitying tone one detects in Job, though it is true that we are told little about his thoughts, other than that they are dark.

His reaction assuredly does not mean that this is a kind of confession by the hero and that therefore we must set ourselves to ferreting out whatever hidden sin he might have committed—avarice, sloth, pride, or something else sufficiently deadly.[15] Affliction by means of monsters I do not believe to be a deserved punishment instigated by God, whether in Denmark or Geatland. It is not that the poet has no interest in right and wrong. He is quite interested in right and wrong emotional responses. Beowulf's is right, though he is at least as innocent as Job. The Geatish king has been dealt a more bitter blow than Hrothgar, in the special sense that his hall has not merely been made temporally uninhabitable, it has been wiped out forever. But I cannot see the destruction of the hall as having any genuine ethical meaning. We must simply accept the fact that it is, mysteriously, time for the hall to go, as it is its chief resident's time to die. They vanish almost simultaneously.

Too much has been made of Beowulf's brief fit of depression, which occupies only a few lines. What matters much more, what matters most of all in this kind of poetry generally, is what the author elects to devote the most space to. And here it is action on Beowulf's part. It is still conceivable, though hardly likely, that his refusal to let any of his men help him in the dragon-fight reflects some lingering idea on his part, even though he cannot fathom why, that he is being held personally responsible for the calamity and wishes to take the consequences squarely on his own aged shoulders. But this is overly fussy. All we can be sure of is that he acts responsibly; that, for the few hours that remain of his life, he behaves with absolute resolution. He is in no way diminished as an individual.

Yet the world in which he must now function is a diminished and devastated one. To the extent that halls are mentioned at all in the rest of Part II, they are likely to appear as structures destroyed, abandoned entirely, or functioning only in some deeply ironic sense. Kathryn Hume's term "anti-hall" is useful to describe this kind of functioning.[16] The barrow or grave-mound where the dragon crouches over his mighty hoard is the chief instance of such an anti-hall. It is called a hall some dozen times, often with ironic reference to its being a kind of residence, essentially a residence for the dead, a grave, an *eorðsele*, an earth-hall. Such terms as these exemplify a common form of irony very explicitly brought out, for example, in the late Old English poem called *The Grave*, where the grave is gruesomely pictured as a cold, cramped, low-ceilinged house one is forced to move reluctantly into.[17]

The dragon's barrow is also called a hall with reference to its containing treasure, its being a *hringsele* 'a ring-hall'. The broader term "ghost-hall" might include both these ironies and also suggest the way some memory of a real hall lingers over the structure and its contents from the time when the Last Survivor of the long-forgotten people that buried the treasure first introduced us to its history (2244–66).

He laments the loss of *seledream*, the joy of communal pleasure in the hall, and catalogues in his mournful series of negatives the vital activities that once took place there, and were seen and heard there, and have gone: ceremonial eating and drinking, the polishing and donning of armor and weapons, the sound of harps and pounding of horses' hooves. All these objects that stood for that life have been placed in the barrow, now felt to be a house of death precisely because it so insistently reminds us of a lost life. When Wiglaf enters the barrow after the dragon has been killed we are again reminded of this in a description quoted and examined in another context in Chapter 3. I cite only the beginning of it here:

> Geseah ða sigehreðig,   þa he bi sesse geong,
> magoþegn modig   maððumsigla fealo,
> gold glitinian   grunde getenge,
> wundur on wealle, . . .   (2756–59a)

(Exultant in victory, the brave kin-thane saw then, as he went by the seat, many rich ornaments, gold glittering close to ground and wonders on the wall . . .)

The passage goes on to describe the cups and vessels of the "long-ago men." It is unclear whether the *sess* of line 2756 is a seat located inside the barrow-hall or the bench outside the barrow where the dying Beowulf sits (*gesæt on sesse* 2717), but the former seems more likely, since Wiglaf is already inside the barrow (*under beorges hrof* 2755). If this latter reading should be accepted, the "ghost" appearance of a hall arranged with seats and perhaps with dishes standing on tables, as if for the living, something in the nature of Miss

Havisham's wedding-breakfast in *Great Expectations,* would be even more strongly suggested. Even if visualization this detailed is not in the text, we can be sure nonetheless that not even the three hundred years of silence and moldering decay, during which time its sole inhabitant never stirred from his anti-hall (so far as we are told), have erased the strong memory of these ghosts of long-ago men.

A similar effect is also achieved in Beowulf's own exemplum of hopeless grief, the description of the father whose son has been hanged (2444–62a). This passage needs closer examination from the thematic standpoint than it was given earlier in the context of Beowulf's entire speech and character. The father tries first to express his pain and helplessness in "painful song," but then the focus shifts to a hall.

> Gesyhð sorhcearig   on his suna bure
> winsele westne,   windge reste
> reote berofene.   Ridend swefað,
> hæleð in hoðman;   nis þær hearpan sweg,
> gomen in geardum,   swylce ðær iu wæron.
> Gewiteð þonne on sealman,   sorhleoð gæleð
> an æfter anum;   þuhte him ealle to rum,
> wongas ond wicstede.   (2455–62a)

(He stares in dazed grief at his son's chamber, at the devastated wine-hall, at the windswept bed bereft of joy. Riders sleep, men under grave's cover; there is no harp-sound there, no joy in the palace as there was once. He goes then to his bed, he sings a sorrow-song, alone for the one alone; all of it seemed to be too much space, the fields and dwellings.)

What we respond to in this moving passage is the father's agonized sense of a vacant space in his life. In the lines just before this, there are still a few quick details of normal reality in an ordinary time-world (the reminder of loss each morning at least implies mornings; the abandoned plans for a new heir at least imply some notion of the future and its plans), but now the intensity of the father's suffering not only pictures the son's chamber and bed as empty but goes on to empty out the entire wine-hall and to leave it ruined and abandoned to the wind, with all riders and harpers immobilized and silenced. More than that—for we suddenly realize they are all long gone, like the long-ago men in the dragon-barrow, where time itself has also been emptied out. Meaning and value are so drained from this ruined place and this ruined life that the bed the father at last makes his stumbling way toward (himself a last survivor) is plainly nothing but a grave. To move toward death is also to move completely out of the normal world of linear time. The very process of emotional "ruining" has been depicted memorably for us.

In a more complex way, the memory of Beowulf's own hall which is, as I pointed out above, very briefly revived for us in Wiglaf's two speeches to the cowardly retainers, is an image that also moves toward an emptying out of meaning, at least as this process takes place in Wiglaf's angry mind. In his first hortatory speech (2633–60), as he steps forward to help Beowulf fight the dragon, he recreates the Geatish royal hall momentarily for his immediate polemic purposes. It is a scene standing for any number of similar scenes in the past, when retainers once pledged their loyal services to their king as they received their gifts of weapons from him—*these weapons*, Wiglaf keeps shouting and pointing, weapons they hold in their hands, weapons that should in themselves bring back the sharpest memories of their lord's love and their own obligations. The very syntax of Wiglaf's speech keeps tying lord and men, members of the comitatus, into close possessive collocations: *ussum hlaforde, minne goldgyfan, hlaford us.* Subjects of sentences alternate to create a further interlacing or interdependent effect: we drank mead, we promised; he gave rings we would repay him for, he needed help, he chose us for war, he thought us worthy, gave treasures, rated us good warriors. Now this rapid exchange and interplay has ended; the responsibility rests solely on them; it is their turn now. *Nu is se dæg cumen* (2646). 'that day has now come'.

Even if the hall in which this interchange once took place is gone to ghostliness, the weapons and their obligations are still here. Heroic life goes on. In his second speech (2864–91), after Beowulf's death, Wiglaf once again recalls such scenes of gift-giving in the hall, but now in tones of savage contempt. The hope or the faith has by this time died, whatever it was that once gave meaning to such scenes. Let it all burn now, the tradition of obligation along with the hall. The acts of giving and taking will now "lie dead" (*alicgean* 2886). We have come to another ruin and another grave, a mass-grave now. In Wiglaf's eyes, like the Last Survivor and the Old Father, these Geats can now only move out of the ghostly tatters of their once-noble hall and the ruins of their once-noble lives toward a world of death, though a death in their case at least marginally better than a life of total disgrace, or so Wiglaf claims.

Beowulf's hall is symbolically burned yet once more, at the end of the Messenger's speech.

> Ne scel anes hwæt
> meltan mid þam modigan,   ac þær is maðma hord,
> gold unrime   grimme gecea [po] d,
> ond nu æt siðestan   sylfes feore
> beagas [geboh] te.   Þa sceal brond fretan,
> æled þeccean,   nalles eorl wegan
> maððum to gemyndum,   ne mægð scyne
> habban on healse   hringweorðunge,
> ac sceal geomormod,   golde bereafod,
> oft nalles æne   elland tredan,
> nu se herewisa   hleahtor alegde,
> gamen ond gleodream.   (3010b–21a)

(Not a part only ought to melt with that great-minded one, but there is a full hoard of treasures there, uncounted gold bargained for grimly and now, at the end, rings purchased at the price of his own life. Fire shall eat those, flame enfold them; no warrior shall wear an ornament in his memory, no beautiful woman have a precious ring around her neck—no, grieving and stripped of gold, she shall tread a foreign land often, not merely once, now that the leader of our army has laid down laughter, mirth, and joy.)

Part of what the Geats will carry and commit to the pyre will be memories: the memories of their life in the hall, thoughts that cling persistently to the objects of the hoard. As these objects melt and are eaten by fire, so too the social relationships once centered in the hall and relying on communal memory will disintegrate and collapse. Links will be broken. Warriors will no longer carry precious things that remind them of the giver; beautiful women will be forced outward, away from the old center, exiled or enslaved far away from their native land and the source of their wholeness.

The final scene of the Messenger's speech, in which men are being suddenly awakened to seize their "morning-cold" spears, might be intended to remind us of a hall-scene just before an attack (like the one in the Finnsburg Fragment), but more likely it is imagined as taking place in a military bivouac, an exposed outdoor locale, where the hunted campaigners are now on a level with the beasts of prey who talk above their heads. Only the barely audible ironic ghost of harp-song hovers over this bleak tableau and again evokes a ghost-hall.

> Forðon sceall gar wesan
> monig, morgenceald,   mundum bewunden,
> hæfen on handa,   nalles hearpan sweg
> wigend weccean,   ac se wonna hrefn
> fus ofer fægum   fela reordian,
> earne secgan   hu him æt æte speow,
> þenden he wið wulf   wæl reafode.   (3021b–27)

(And so many a spear will be morning-cold, grasped tight, lifted in hands—in no way will the sound of a harp wake warriors, but the dark raven eager over the doomed will speak volubly, tell the eagle how well he did at feasting when he competed with the wolf in savaging the dead.)

If halls exist any longer in the post-holocaust world envisioned here, they may serve as temporary shelters in some endless war but surely no longer as centers of *gamen* and *gleodream,* the warm happiness they once stood for. What the poem has defined as civilization has here become a ghost.

Yet, striking as they are, these images of the ruining and burning away of halls and the collapsing of their values are not the final images of the poem. As we saw in Chapter 3, memory is not totally destroyed. We are not at the end of things, for work remains to be done, and can be done. To speak in terms of the specific imagery we have been following through the poem in this chapter, still to be constructed out of all these ruins is a new fabric of memory, one that reminds us of a hall and yet converts the newly made image into something else, something more like the image of Scyld's funeral-ship. The structure that will be made is intended to stand in full view, but also to be buried for resurrection, a time-capsule concentrating and preserving values perhaps for use at some unknown time in the future. As so many have noted, at the poem's end we come full circle. In place of Scyld's treasure-laden ship, and evoking it, we see Beowulf's grand barrow, built on the ashes of the pyre of destruction. Those who build it, the Geatish community of Last Survivors, may now seem only a wasted remnant, a *wealaf,* as if their king's titanic self made up the larger part of their nation. They are only the *lastweardas,* the followers and guardians of his track. But to regard them with pity is to lower their dignity and at the same time to give them too much prominence as characters.

They are arranged there to point selflessly toward Beowulf, and we follow their pointing. They are only anonymous choristers leading us in a hymn of praise.

It is part of the responsibility the dying Beowulf laid on his kinsman that Wiglaf must make the Geats ready for their final ceremonial function. It was pointed out in Chapter 3 that the following words from Wiglaf's speech may be misread as a serious and even final condemnation of Beowulf's destructive egotism in daring to fight the dragon:

> Oft sceall eorl monig   anes willan
> wræc adreogan,   swa us geworden is.
> Ne meahton we gelæran   leofne þeoden,
> rices hyrde,   ræd ænigne,
> þæt he ne grette   goldweard þone, . . .   (3077–81)

(Translated above, page 126).

In that earlier discussion the symbolic role played here by treasure was examined, since not understanding how that symbol is used leads to one form of misreading. But there are also other forms.

From a different point of view, in the context of dramatic relevance and character, Wiglaf's words may seem inappropriate to us to the degree that they condemn Beowulf's rashness in a way that the poet himself does not. In a later and more sophisticated poem like *Sir Gawain and the Green Knight,* we would not be surprised to see this kind of condemnation and would have a ready explanation for it. There harsh criticism not only of the hero's rashness but of the silliness of the chivalric code itself can boldly be incorporated; but this is done clearly in order to add comic tension and richness to the story.[18]

As we should realize by now, we cannot apply such literate standards to *Beowulf,* a work where it is enough for the words to fit a local emotional context. They need not fit into some larger context that demands a consistent viewpoint, whether of approval or disapproval or, as in *Sir Gawain,* some neat balance of attitudes. In part at least, what we have in this scene is simply a conventional motif of any action narrative: "his prudent friends try but fail to dissuade the determined hero from reckless action." We have watched such a scene on stage and screen many times: loyal friends cling to each brawny arm, while one hisses, "it's certain suicide to go in there!" Indeed what we may call (thinking of the prudent co-hero of *The Song of Roland*) the same "Oliver motif" was used earlier in the poem, and in a similarly inconsistent way. In two places (202–04, 415–18) we are told that the Geats had actively urged Beowulf to go to Denmark to fight Grendel, whereas later Hygelac says he had pleaded with his nephew *not* to go and had advised him to let Grendel be (1994b–97a). But whether he is being urged or not urged really matters little; the point in either case is to direct attention to the hero's bravery. In each case the nonce-effect is what matters most.

But in another way this passage is not merely a routine narrative device but an eloquent way of showing how Wiglaf voices, for himself and for his nation, deep and irrational grief in a form we can recognize as psychologically exact, a form that sounds much more like anger than like anything else. The death of those we love infuriates us. It is easy to turn our rage against them for their cruel folly in dying and abandoning us. For a moment at least, the Geats cannot forgive Beowulf.

In the larger final context of what follows in the poem until its conclusion, however, Wiglaf's idea of all suffering "at the will of one" can be given more positive meaning. The shared emotion brings the community together; it introduces the communal mourning ritual. Earlier we quoted the passage in which Wiglaf passes on Beowulf's dying instructions to his people.

> Worn eall gespræc
> gomol on gehðo   ond eowic gretan het,
> bæd þæt ge geworhton   æfter wines dædum
> in bælstede   beorh þone hean,
> micelne ond mærne,   swa he manna wæs
> wigend weorðfullost   wide geond eorðan,
> þenden he burhwelan   brucan moste.   (3094b–3100)

(Translated above, page 129).

A closer look at this passage shows it to be a model in its stylistic detail, and a crucial step in shifting the tone from negative to positive. It builds the barrow for them, shows them how: it moves up, from *hean* 'high' to *micelne ond mære* 'great and famous', then bursts free into the superlative of *weorðfullost* 'most full of honor', before mortality (*þenden* 'so long as') sets its time-limit on the expansion one life is permitted. The passage expresses in small space the epic poet's vision of a hero who almost transcends the bounds of mortality.

Most of all Beowulf wanted them to hold fast to his memory and never to let him slip away from them into the forgetting that is the real death. In an oral world that knows no other records, a barrow on a prominent sea-cliff, like a notch on a stick, a knot in a string, a narrative poem of praise, is a mnemonic device.

Now the new burning, this time a deliberately willed one and not a calamity from outside, must take place. The Geats Wiglaf sends off to fetch firewood must truly understand what they are doing. Wiglaf tries to make it plain.

> Nu sceal gled fretan,
> weaxan wonna leg   wigena strengel,
> þone ðe oft gebad   isernscure,
> þonne stræla storm   strengum gebæded
> scoc ofer scildweall,   sceft nytte heold,
> feðergearwum fus   flane fulleode.   (3114b–19)

(Now fire shall eat and dark flame fatten on the ruler of fighters, that man who often endured iron showers, when the storm of arrows impelled by bowstrings surged over the shield-wall, as the eager shaft did its job, bristling with feathers.)

The brief speech insists on realism and harsh finality. No matter what roaring storms of arrows Beowulf once stood bravely against, the fire will eat him now. It will eat their good king who survived so long. Not only must they accept this, they must make sure it takes place. Fire must eat their king, as it has already eaten his hall, and as it will very soon eat what is left of their property and their lives, when the fatal predictions of the Messenger come true. They must accept it all.

The Geats respond to this severe command by generously heaping the pyre with weapons taken from the dragon-hoard. It is true that they are complying with Beowulf's own wish (*swa he bena wæs* 'as he had asked' 3140), but their compliance is made to seem their own spontaneous wish and an expression of their own feeling, at the same time a submission and an initiative. Their impulse holds nothing back: they give all they have to the pyre, so that it will not be feeble or half-hearted (*ad on eorðan unwaclicne* 'pyre on earth not weak' 3138).

Now smoke, flame, weeping, aroused emotions swirl and rise together in strong confusion, as the fire "breaks the bone-house" *hat on hreðre* 'hot in the breast' (3148). The last phrase unites the king and his mourners even more closely, unites them in a kind of pun. With frank realism it describes the cremation of the body at the same time that it alludes to the mourners' painful sorrow, like all strong emotions in Old English thought of as "hot." Undisguised feelings of apprehension are expressed by a designated speaker, a woman who dreads slavery and humiliation for herself, now that their protection has gone. Surely she voices fears endemic in the community, but her feelings are not allowed to divert communal feeling into unrestrained self-pity. Nor is hers the last voice we hear at the funeral, as this fire of passionate grief burns itself out. Her outcries go up to heaven with the towering smoke-plume as we move on to a final stage.

What all need in order to allay such profound dread of annihilation is renewed courage and dignity, gained not at all by self-concern but by putting attention outward, wholly on Beowulf, by a heroic act of memory. The second phase of the funeral constructs a new emotional balance, largely suggested by stable images of craftsmanship and building rather than of destroying and swirling flames. The Geats make a walled barrow, built high and broad. It is like a new hall in the way it stands visible to many over a great distance and in the way it carries a known name on into the future.

> Hi on beorg dydon   beg ond siglu,
> eall swylce hyrsta,   swylce on horde ær
> niðhedige men   genumen hæfdon,
> forleton eorla gestreon   eorðan healdan,
> gold on greote,   þær hit nu gen lifað
> eldum swa unnyt   swa h [it ær] or wæs.   (3163–68)

(They put in the barrow rings and brooches—indeed all those treasures warlike men had taken from the hoard; they abandoned that wealth of men to the earth to hold, gold in the dirt, where it will still go on living as useless to men as it was before.)

The act of abandonment is itself dramatized in the course of the sentence, which begins with the familiar litany of precious objects and ends in useless dirt. Such a progression, as we saw in our earlier examination of the symbol of treasure, is not intended to cast scorn on the Geats or on their king. The Geats freely give the treasure back, give it back to Beowulf, who had given it to them, and give it back to the earth where it is robbed of value because it will not be used. Giving it up is possibly to be seen as a kind of potlatch, a conspicuous wasting of wealth meant to honor the king's memory—but that is to give it too much prominence. By now, dealing with the treasure is not at all an act they brood over or regard as all-important. The poet has abandoned the treasure too. It is a distraction they can place away in the earth and forget about. Its final uselessness may reflect its inadequacy as a mode of symbolic expression.

More expressive of symbolic meaning is the fact that the barrow resembles a hall or a model of a hall, and the fact that the twelve riders who orbit its center when it has been completed are a brilliant adumbration of a rebuilt *werod*, a new body of retainers and hearth-companions, now expiating any disgrace they may have incurred and any unworthy self-pity they may have been guilty of by dwelling once again in reconciliation, in a temporary ritual community of right feelings and right words.

Not treasure but their words will convey their meaning. Treasure vanishes from the poem after line 3168. Instead there are many words about language and speaking: *cwiðan, mænan, wordgyd wrecan, sprecan, eahtodan, demdon, wordum herge, begnornodon,* and the last word in this series, *cwædon.* Since up until now we have always been able to watch with our own eyes what Beowulf has been doing, we have never had to take anyone else's word for him. Now we take their words for him. His most lasting barrow will be his people's words. It is *gedefe,* altogether fitting and proper, that men and women tell how they feel when their friend-lord, their *winedryhten,* has to be led from his body, because they have been his hearth-comrades, *heorðgeneateas,* who shared the warmth of his hearth and his affection. At the end, in the closing lines, they say they remember not his battles but the warm love for others that led him to fight those battles.

> Swa begnornodon Geata leode
> hlafordes [hr] yre, heorðgeneatas,
> cwædon þæt he wære wyruldcyninga
> manna mildust ond mon [ðw] ærust,
> leodum liðost ond lofgeornost. (3178–82)

(This is how the people of the Geats, the hearth-comrades, lamented the fall of their lord; they said he was of all world-kings the most merciful of men and the gentlest, the kindest to his people, and the most eager for praise.)

God has no hall in *Beowulf,* though in other Old English poems he is sometimes said to live in one, the great mead-hall of heaven where his comitatus of saints gathers in joy. Here at the end of this poem there is only the structure men make, a frail shell around their solidarity, fated to have only a brief space of time before the final burning. It is a boundary situation. If the hero's barrow imitates, or at least makes a gesture toward, the image of a human hall, it also stands on the edge of the sea of the unknown. It both towers high and is invisibly small. We feel this because the Geats' riding and their speaking of the words of praise draw the audience into the poet's circle of human solidarity. We too can see and honor, always against the terrible darkness, Beowulf's qualities: strength, mercy, gentleness, and above all an unquenchable passion for glory.

NOTES

1. "The Norms of Epic," *Comparative Literature* 13 (1961), 193–207; in slightly different form this essay forms the first chapter of *The Descent from Heaven: A Study in Epic Continuity* (New Haven, CT: Yale University Press, 1963).

2. See Kathryn Hume, "The Concept of the Hall in Old English Poetry," *Anglo-Saxon England* 3 (1974), 63–74, and the brief but pithy remarks of T. A. Shippey on halls in *Beowulf*, 21–24. In Freudian terms, the hall as "erection" is seen as the central symbol of the male warrior class by James W. Earl, "The Role of the Men's Hall in the Development of the Anglo-Saxon Superego," *Psychiatry* 46 (1983), 139–60.

3. An excellent article by Thomas D. Hill, "Scyld Scefing and the 'Stirps Regia': Pagan Myth and Christian Kingship in *Beowulf*," *Magister Regis*, ed. Arthur Groos (New York: Fordham University Press, 1986), 37–47, emphasizes the pagan symbolism of kingship and its continuity in this proem, seeing the myth of Scyld as a divine sanction (probably invoking Woden) of the kind that must have been hard for the Christian missionaries to suppress.

4. Kemp Malone's argument that the Danes are seen as an important nation in the poem while the Geats are a relatively weak and obscure one seems persuasive ("Symbolism in *Beowulf*: Some Suggestions," *English Studies Today*, 2d series [1961], 81–91).

5. Earlier scholarly interpretations are summarized in Dobbie's edition. Like many others, Dobbie takes *meoto* to be a noun and *onsæl* to be a verb, translating the general meaning as "Sit down now to the feast and tell us about yourself, as your mind may inspire you." One real objection to this reading is that Beowulf does not respond to the invitation.

6. The approach of Grendel to Heorot has been studied in detail by, among others, Arthur G. Brodeur, *The Art of Beowulf*, 90–92, Alain Renoir, "Point of View and Design for Terror in *Beowulf*," *Neuphilologische Mitteilungen* 63 (1962), 154–67, and Stanley B. Greenfield, "Grendel's Approach to Heorot: Syntax and Poetry," in *Old English Poetry: Fifteen Essays*, ed. Robert P. Creed (Providence, RI: Brown University Press, 1967), 275–84.

7. John D. Niles, who interprets the fight in terms of oral ring-composition around a central core, concludes: "All the details of the fight radiate about a single kernel, the moment of extreme violence when Heorot itself seems about to fall" (*Beowulf: The Poem and its Tradition*, 154).

8. Arthur G. Brodeur sees this oddly disjunctive account of the fight in somewhat different terms, as a chance for the poet "to convey the power and menace of Grendel's gigantic strength without permitting him a moment's advantage over the hero" (*The Art of Beowulf*, 58).

9. *Genere me wið (fram) niðe* occurs as a prayer several times in the Paris Psalter and the Fragments of Psalms. Cf. also *nergan wið niðum*, *Guthlac* 553.

10. Riddle 5 in the Anglo-Saxon Poetic Records edition of the Exeter Book, Riddle 3 in *The Old English Riddles of the Exeter Book*, ed. Craig Williamson (Chapel Hill, NC: University of North Carolina Press, 1977).

11. *The Fight at Finnsburg* is found in Klaeber's edition of *Beowulf* and edited separately by Donald K. Fry, *Finnsburh: Fragment and Episode* (London: Methuen, 1974).

12. I am assuming that there is only one hall, though the text here (as very often in the Finn Episode) is not entirely clear. Some believe that the *oðer flet* (1086) which the Frisians provide for the visiting Danes is not half a hall-floor but a second hall. The point is discussed at length in the major editions of the poem.

13. Neither does Grettir, in the analogous Sandhaugar episode (Chapter 66) of *Grettir's Saga*. He finds much treasure (*mikit fé*) in the cave under the waterfall, but does not bring any back with him. Could it be dangerous to possess?

14. *Historia Ecclesiastica Gentis Anglorum*, Book II, Chapter 13.

15. Margaret E. Goldsmith may again be taken as representing a certain approach. She observes that the poet "goes out of his way to tell us that Beowulf saw the dragon's attack as a sign of God's anger upon himself," and places this passage within the context of her description of how the hero yields to avarice (*The Mode and Meaning of Beowulf*, 226).

16. "The Concept of the Hall," 68.

17. "The Grave" is a twenty-five-line poem added in the margin of a homily in Bodley 343 (Bodl. 2406, f. 170a), all but the last three lines in a late twelfth-century hand; first published by H. Schröer, *Anglia* 5 (1887), 289–90. For a translation, see Charles W. Kennedy, *The Earliest English Poetry* (New York, 1943), 331.

18. Lines 672–85, where some of the members of Arthur's court complain that Gawain goes off on a foolish and probably suicidal mission merely on a dare.

BIBLIOGRAPHY

Asser. *Alfred the Great.* Translated by Simon Keynes and Michael Lapidge. Harmondsworth, UK: Penguin, 1983.

Bartlett, Adeline. *The Larger Rhetorical Patterns in Anglo-Saxon Poetry.* Columbia University Studies in English and Comparative Literature, 122. New York: Columbia University Press, 1935.

Ben-Amos, Dan. "Folklore in African Society." *Review of African Literature* 6 (1975), 165–98.

Benson, Larry D. "The Literary Character of Anglo-Saxon Formulaic Poetry." *PMLA* 81 (1966), 334–41.

Berger, Harry, Jr., and H. Marshall Leicester, Jr. "Social Structure as Doom: The Limits of Heroism in *Beowulf.*" *Old English Studies in Honour of John C. Pope,* ed. Robert B. Burlin and Edward B. Irving, Jr. Toronto: University of Toronto Press, 1974. 37–79.

Biddle, Martin, and Birthe Kjølbye-Biddle. "The Repton Stone." *Anglo-Saxon England* 14 (1985), 233–92.

Bjork, Robert E. "Unferth in the Hermeneutic Circle: A Reappraisal of James L. Rosier's 'Design for Treachery: The Unferth Intrigue'." *Papers on Language and Literature* 16 (1980), 133–41.

Bloomfield, Morton W. "*Beowulf* and Christian Allegory: An Interpretation of Unferth." *Traditio* 7 (1949–51), 410–15.

———. "'Interlace' as a Medieval Narrative Technique with Special Reference to *Beowulf.*" *Magister Regis: Studies in Honor of Robert Earl Kaske,* ed. Arthur Groos et al. New York: Fordham University Press, 1986. 49–59.

Bolton, W. F. *Alcuin and Beowulf.* New Brunswick, NJ: Rutgers University Press, 1978.

Bonjour, Adrien, *The Digressions in 'Beowulf'.* Medium Ævum Monographs, 5. Oxford: Oxford University Press, 1950.

———. *Twelve 'Beowulf' Papers: 1940–1960, with Additional Comments.* Geneva: E. Droz; Neuchâtel: Faculté des lettres, 1962.

Brodeur, Arthur G. *The Art of Beowulf.* Berkeley and Los Angeles: University of California Press, 1959.

Carnicelli, Thomas A. "The Function of the Messenger in *Beowulf.*" *Studies in Philology* 72 (1975), 246–57.

Chambers, R. W. *Beowulf: An Introduction.* 3d ed. with supplement by Charles L. Wrenn. Cambridge: Cambridge University Press, 1959.

Chase, Colin. "Beowulf, Bede, and St. Oswine: The Hero's Pride in Old English Hagiography." *The Anglo-Saxons: Synthesis and Achievement,* ed.

J. Douglas Woods and David A. E. Pelteret. Waterloo, Canada: Wilfrid Laurier University Press, 1985. 37–48.

———, ed. *The Dating of Beowulf*. Toronto: University of Toronto Press, 1981.

Chickering, Howell, D., *Beowulf: A Dual-Language Edition*. Garden City, NY: Anchor Books, 1977.

Clemoes, Peter. "Action in *Beowulf* and Our Perception of it." *Old English Poetry: Essays on Style*, ed. Daniel G. Calder. Berkeley: University of California Press, 1979.

———. "'Symbolic' Language in Old English Poetry." *Modes of Interpretation in Old English Literature: Essays in Honour of Stanley B. Greenfield*, ed. Phyllis Rugg Brown, Georgia Ronan Crampton and Fred C. Robinson. Toronto: University of Toronto Press, 1986. 3–14.

Clover, Carol J. "The Germanic Context of the Unferþ Episode." *Speculum* 55 (1980), 444–68.

———. *The Medieval Saga*. Ithaca, NY and London: Cornell University Press, 1982.

Cox, Betty S. *Cruces of Beowulf*. The Hague: Mouton, 1971.

Crane, R. S. "On Hypotheses in 'Historical Criticism' : Apropos of Certain Contemporary Medievalists." *The Idea of the Humanities and Other Essays Critical and Historical*. 2 vols. Chicago and London: University of Chicago Press, 1976. II, 236–60.

Creed, Robert P. "The Singer Looks at his Sources." *Comparative Literature* 14 (1962), 44–52.

Crook, Eugene J. "Pagan Gold in *Beowulf*." *American Benedictine Review* 25 (1974), 218–34.

Cross, James E. "The Ethic of War in Old English." *England Before the Conquest: Studies in Primary Sources Presented to Dorothy Whitelock*, ed. Peter Clemoes and Kathleen Hughes. Cambridge: Cambridge University Press, 1971. 269–82.

Damico, Helen. *Beowulf's Wealhtheow and the Valkyrie Tradition*. Madison: University of Wisconsin Press, 1984.

Dobbie, E. V. K., ed. *The Anglo-Saxon Minor Poems*. The Anglo-Saxon Poetic Records, 6. New York: Columbia University Press, 1942.

———, ed. *Beowulf and Judith*. The Anglo-Saxon Poetic Records, 4. New York: Columbia University Press, 1953.

Donahue, Charles. "*Beowulf* and Christian Tradition: A Reconsideration from a Celtic Stance." *Traditio* 21 (1965), 55–116.

Dunning, T. P. and Alan J. Bliss, ed. *The Wanderer*. London: Methuen, 1969.

Earl, James W. "The Role of the Men's Hall in the Development of the Anglo-Saxon Superego." *Psychiatry* 46 (1983), 139–60.

Feldman, Thalia Phillies. "A Comparative Study of *Feond, Deofl, Syn* and *Hel* in *Beowulf*." *Neuphilologische Mitteilungen* 88 (1987), 159–74.

Fell, Christine. *Women in Anglo-Saxon England*. London: British Museum Publications, 1984.

Finnegan, Ruth H. *Oral Poetry: Its Nature, Significance and Social Context.* Cambridge: Cambridge University Press, 1977.

Foley, John Miles. *Oral-Formulaic Theory and Research: An Introduction and Annotated Bibliography.* New York: Garland Publishing, 1985.

——, ed. *Oral Traditional Literature: A Festschrift for Albert Bates Lord.* Columbus, OH: Slavica Publishers, 1981.

Frank, Roberta. "'Mere' and 'Sund': Two Sea-Changes in *Beowulf.*" *Modes of Interpretation in Old English Literature: Essays in Honour of Stanley B. Greenfield,* ed. Phyllis Rugg Brown, Georgia Ronan Crampton and Fred C. Robinson. Toronto: University of Toronto Press, 1986. 153–72.

Fry, Donald K. "Old English Formulas and Systems." *English Studies* 48 (1967), 193–204.

——, ed. *Finnsburh: Fragment and Episode.* London: Methuen, 1974.

Fulk, R. D. "Unferth and His Name." *Modern Philology* 85 (1987), 113–27.

Goldsmith, Margaret E. *The Mode and Meaning of Beowulf.* London: Athlone Press, 1970.

Greene, Thomas. "The Norms of Epic." *Comparative Literature* 13 (1961), 193–207. In slightly different form this essay forms the first chapter of *The Descent from Heaven: A Study in Epic Continuity* (New Haven, CT: Yale University Press, 1963).

Greenfield, Stanley B. "Grendel's Approach to Heorot: Syntax and Poetry." *Old English Poetry: Fifteen Essays,* ed. Robert P. Creed. Providence, RI: Brown University Press, 1967. 275–84.

——. "'Beowulf' and the Judgement of the Righteous." *Learning and Literature in Anglo-Saxon England: Studies Presented to Peter Clemoes,* ed. Michael Lapidge and Helmut Gneuss. Cambridge: Cambridge University Press, 1985.

Greenfield, Stanley B., and Daniel G. Calder. *A New Critical History of Old English Literature, with a Survey of the Anglo-Latin Background by Michael Lapidge.* New York and London: New York University Press, 1986.

Hansen, Elaine T. "Women in Old English Poetry Reconsidered." *Michigan Academician* 9 (1976), 109–17.

Hart, Thomas E. "Tectonic Design, Formulaic Craft, and Literary Execution: The Episodes of Finn and Ingeld in *Beowulf.*" *Amsterdamer Beiträge zur älteren Germanistik* 2 (1972), 1–61.

——. "Tectonic Methodology and an Application to *Beowulf.*" *Essays in the Numerical Criticism of Medieval Literature.* Ed. Caroline D. Eckhardt. London and Lewisburg, PA: Bucknell University Press, 1980.

Hill, John M. "Beowulf and the Danish Succession: Gift Giving as an Occasion for Complex Gesture." *Medievalia et Humanistica,* n.s. 11 (1982), 177–97.

Hill, Thomas D. "Scyld Scefing and the 'Stirps Regia': Pagan Myth and Christian Kingship in *Beowulf.*" *Magister Regis: Studies in Honor of Robert Earl Kaske,* ed. Arthur Groos et al. New York: Fordham University Press, 1986. 37–47.

Hollowell, Ida Masters. "Unferð the þyle in *Beowulf.*" *Studies in Philology* 73 (1976), 239–65.

Hume, Kathryn. "The Theme and Structure of *Beowulf.*" *Studies in Philology* 72 (1975), 1–27.

——. "The Concept of the Hall in Old English Poetry." *Anglo-Saxon England* 3 (1974), 63–74.

Huppé, Bernard F. *The Hero in the Earthly City: A Reading of Beowulf.* Medieval and Renaissance Texts and Studies, vol. 33. State University of New York at Binghamton, 1984.

Irving, Edward B., Jr. *A Reading of Beowulf.* New Haven, CT: Yale University Press, 1968.

——. *Introduction to Beowulf.* Englewood Cliffs, NJ: Prentice-Hall, 1969.

——. "Beowulf Comes Home." *Acts of Interpretation: Essay . . . in Honor of E. Talbot Donaldson,* ed. Mary J. Carruthers and Elizabeth D. Kirk. Norman, OK: Pilgrim Books, 1982. 129–43.

——. "The Nature of Christianity in *Beowulf.*" *Anglo-Saxon England* 13 (1984), 7–21.

Jackson, W. T. H. *The Hero and the King: An Epic Theme.* New York: Columbia University Press, 1982.

Kahrl, Stanley J. "Feuds in *Beowulf:* A Tragic Necessity?" *Modern Philology* 69 (1972), 189–98.

Kaske, Robert E. "*Sapientia et Fortitudo* as the Controlling Theme of *Beowulf.*" *An Anthology of Beowulf Criticism,* ed. Lewis D. Nicholson. Notre Dame, IN: Notre Dame University Press, 1963. 290–92.

Kellogg, Robert. "Varieties of Tradition in Medieval Narrative." *Medieval Narrative: A Symposium,* ed. Hans Bekker-Nielsen et al. Odense, Denmark: Odense University Press, 1979. 120–29.

Kennedy, Charles W. *The Earliest English Poetry: A Critical Survey of the Poetry Written before the Norman Conquest with Illustrative Translations.* New York and London: 1943.

Kiernan, Kevin S. *Beowulf and the Beowulf Manuscript.* New Brunswick, NJ: Rutgers University Press, 1981.

Klaeber, Fr. *Beowulf and the Fight at Finnsburg.* 3d ed. Boston: D. C. Heath, 1950.

Kliman, Bernice W. "Women in Early English Literature, 'Beowulf' to the 'Ancrene Wisse'." *Nottingham Mediaeval Studies* 21 (1977), 32–49.

Kroll, Norma. "*Beowulf:* The Hero as Keeper of Human Polity." *Modern Philology* 84 (1986), 117–29.

Lawrence, W. W. *Beowulf and Epic Tradition.* Cambridge, MA: Harvard University Press, 1930.

Lee, Alvin A. *The Guest-Hall of Eden: Four Essays on the Design of Old English Poetry.* New Haven, CT and London: Yale University Press, 1972.

Leisi, Ernst. "Gold und Manneswert im *Beowulf.*" *Anglia* 71 (1953), 259–73.

Leslie, R. F., ed. *The Wanderer.* Manchester: Manchester University Press, 1966.

Leyerle, John. "The Interlace Structure of *Beowulf.*" *University of Toronto Quarterly* 37 (October, 1967), 1–17.

Lord, Albert B. *The Singer of Tales.* Cambridge, MA: Harvard University Press, 1960; repr. 1968.

Magennis, Hugh. "The Exegesis of Inebriation: Treading Carefully in Old English." *ELN* 23 (March 1986), 3–6.

Magoun, Francis P., Jr. "The Oral-Formulaic Character of Anglo-Saxon Narrative Poetry." *Speculum* 28 (1953), 446–67.

Malone, Kemp. "Coming Back from the Mere." *PMLA* 69 (1954), 1292–99.

———. "Symbolism in *Beowulf:* Some Suggestions." *English Studies Today,* 2d series (1961), 81–91.

———, ed. *Deor.* London: Methuen, 1933; 4th ed., 1966.

McGalliard, John C. "The Poet's Comment in *Beowulf.*" *Studies in Philology* 75 (1978), 243–70.

Mitchell, Bruce. *Old English Syntax.* 2 vols. Oxford: Clarendon Press, 1985.

Morgan, Gerald. "The Treachery of Hrothulf." *English Studies* 53 (1972), 23–39.

Nelson, Marie. "It is More Honorific to Give . . .". *Neuphilologische Mitteilungen* 74 (1973), 624–29.

Nicholson, Lewis E. "The Art of Interlace in *Beowulf.*" *Studia Neophilologica* 52 (1980), 237–49.

Niles, John D. "Ring Composition and the Structure of *Beowulf.*" *PMLA* 94 (1979), 924–35.

———. *Beowulf: The Poem and its Tradition.* Cambridge, MA: Harvard University Press, 1983.

Nitzche, Jane Chance. "The Anglo-Saxon Woman as Hero." *Allegorica* 5 (1980), 139–48.

[Nitzche], Jane Chance. *Woman as Hero in Old English Literature.* Syracuse, NY: Syracuse University Press, 1986.

O'Keeffe, Katherine O'Brien. "Beowulf, Lines 702b–836: Transformations and the Limits of the Human." *Texas Studies in Literature and Language* 23 (1981), 484–94.

Okpewho, Isidore. *The Epic in Africa: Toward a Poetics of the Oral Performance.* New York: Columbia University Press, 1979.

Olsen, Alexandra Hennessey. "Oral-Formulaic Research in Old English Studies: I." *Oral Tradition* 1 (1986), 548–606.

Ong, Walter J. *Orality and Literacy: The Technologizing of the Word.* London and New York: Methuen, 1982.

Opland, Jeff, "Beowulf on the Poet." *Mediaeval Studies* 38 (1976), 442–67.

———. *Anglo-Saxon Oral Poetry: A Study of the Traditions.* New Haven, CT: Yale University Press, 1980.

Parks, Ward. "Flyting and Fighting: Pathways in the Realization of the Epic Contest." *Neophilologus* 70 (1986), 292–306.

———. "The Flyting Speech in Traditional Heroic Narrative." *Neophilologus* 71 (1987), 285–95.

Parry, Adam, ed. *The Making of Homeric Verse: the Collected Papers of Milman Parry*. New York: Oxford University Press, 1971.

Payne, F. Anne. "Three Aspects of Wyrd in *Beowulf*." *Old English Studies in Honour of John C. Pope*, ed. Robert B. Burlin and Edward B. Irving, Jr. Toronto: University of Toronto Press, 1974. 15–35.

Pope, John C. "*Beowulf* 505, 'gehedde,' and Unferth." *Modes of Interpretation in Old English Literature: Essays in Honour of Stanley B. Greenfield*, ed. Phyllis Rugg Brown, Georgia Rowan Crampton and Fred C. Robinson. Toronto: University of Toronto Press, 1986. 173–87.

Raw, Barbara C. *The Art and Background of Old English Poetry*. London: Edward Arnold, Ltd., 1978.

Renoir, Alain. "Point of View and Design for Terror in *Beowulf*." *Neuphilologische Mitteilungen* 63 (1962), 154–67.

Riley, Samuel M. "The Contrast Between Beowulf and Hygelac." *Journal of Narrative Technique* 10 (1980), 186–97.

Roberts, Jane. "Old English *Un-* 'Very' and Unferth." *English Studies* 61 (1980), 289–92.

Robertson, D. W. "The Doctrine of Charity in Medieval Literary Gardens: A Topical Approach through Symbolism and Allegory." *Speculum* 26 (1951), 24–49.

Robertson, D. W. *A Preface to Chaucer*. Princeton, NJ: Princeton University Press, 1963.

Robinson, Fred C. "Personal Names in Medieval Narrative and the Name of Unferth in *Beowulf*." *Essays in Honor of Richebourg Gaillard McWilliams*, ed. Howard Creed. Birmingham, AL: Birmingham-Southern College, 1970. 43–48.

———. "Elements of the Marvellous in the Characterization of Beowulf: A Reconsideration of the Textual Evidence." *Old English Studies in Honour of John C. Pope*, ed. Robert B. Burlin and Edward B. Irving, Jr. Toronto: University of Toronto Press, 1974. 119–37.

———. *Beowulf and the Appositive Style*. Knoxville: University of Tennessee Press, 1985.

Rose, Nancy. "Hrothgar, Nestor, and Religiosity as a Mode of Characterization in Heroic Culture." *Journal of Popular Culture* 1 (1967), 158–65.

Rosier, James L. "Design for Treachery: The Unferth Intrigue." *PMLA* 77 (1962), 1–7.

Schrader, Richard J. *God's Handiwork: Images of Women in Early Germanic Literature*. Contributions in Women's Studies, No. 41. Westport, CT: Greenwood Press, 1983.

Schröer, H. Edition of "The Grave." *Anglia* 5 (1887), 289–90.

Scragg, D. G., ed. *The Battle of Maldon*. Manchester: Manchester University Press, 1981.

Sedgefield, W. J., ed. *Beowulf*. 3d ed. Manchester: Manchester University Press, 1935.

Shippey, T. A. *Beowulf*. Studies in English Literature, 70. General editor, David Daiches. London: Edward Arnold Ltd., 1978.

Stanley, Eric G. "Hæthenra Hyht in *Beowulf*." *Studies in Old English Literature in Honor of Arthur G. Brodeur*, ed. S. B. Greenfield. Eugene, OR: University of Oregon Press, 1963. 136–51.

———. "The Narrative Art of *Beowulf*." *Medieval Narrative: A Symposium*, ed. Hans Bekker-Nielsen et al. Odense, Denmark: Odense University Press, 1979. 58–81.

Stock, Brian. *The Implications of Literacy: Written Language and Models of Interpretation in the Eleventh and Twelfth Centuries*. Princeton, NJ: Princeton University Press, 1983.

Tolkien, J. R. R. "*Beowulf:* The Monsters and the Critics." British Academy Lecture, 1936. Reprinted in *The Monsters and the Critics and Other Essays*, ed. Christopher Tolkien (Boston: Houghton Mifflin, 1983).

Tripp, Raymond P., Jr. "The Restoration of *Beowulf* 2769b and 2771a, and Wiglaf's Entrance into the Barrow." *ELN* 15 (1978), 244–49.

Watts, Ann Chalmers. *The Lyre and the Harp: A Comparative Reconsideration of Oral Tradition in Homer and Old English Epic Poetry*. Yale Studies in English, 169. New Haven, CT: Yale University Press, 1969.

Webber, Ruth W. "The *Cantar de Mio Cid:* Problems of Interpretation." *Oral Tradition in Literature: Interpretations in Context*, ed. John Miles Foley. Columbia: University of Missouri Press, 1986. 65–88.

Weil, Simone. "L'*Iliade* ou le poème de la force." In *La source grecque* (Paris: Gallimard, 1953). Tr. Mary McCarthy as *The Iliad or the Poem of Force*. Wallingford, PA: Pendle Hill Pamphlets 91, 1956.

Whitelock, Dorothy. *The Audience of Beowulf*. Oxford: The Clarendon Press, 1951.

Whitman, Cedric W. *Homer and the Heroic Tradition*. Cambridge, MA: Harvard University Press, 1958.

Williams, David. *Cain and Beowulf: A Study in Secular Allegory*. Toronto: University of Toronto Press, 1982.

Williamson, Craig, ed. *The Old English Riddles of the Exeter Book*. Chapel Hill, NC: University of North Carolina Press, 1977.

Woolf, Henry B. "Hrothgar." *Louisiana State University Studies,* Humanities Series, 5 (1954), 39–54.

Wright, Herbert G. "Good and Evil: Light and Darkness: Joy and Sorrow in *Beowulf*." *Review of English Studies*, n.s. 8 (1957), 1–11. Reprinted in *An Anthology of Beowulf Criticism*, ed. Lewis E. Nicholson. Notre Dame, IN: University of Notre Dame Press, 1969.

INDEX

University of Pennsylvania Press
MIDDLE AGES SERIES
Edward Peters, General Editor

F. R. P. Akehurst, trans. *The* Coutumes de Beauvaisis *of Philippe de Beauma-noir.* 1992

Peter Allen. *The Art of Love: Amatory Fiction from Ovid to the* Romance of the Rose. 1992

David Anderson. *Before the Knight's Tale: Imitation of Classical Epic in Boccaccio's* Teseida. 1988

Benjamin Arnold. *Count and Bishop in Medieval Germany: A Study of Regional Power, 1100–1350.* 1991

Mark C. Bartusis. *The Late Byzantine Army: Arms and Society, 1204–1453.* 1992

J. M. W. Bean. *From Lord to Patron: Lordship in Late Medieval England.* 1990

Uta-Renate Blumenthal. *The Investiture Controversy: Church and Monarchy from the Ninth to the Twelfth Century.* 1988

Daniel Bornstein, trans. *Dino Compagni's* Chronicle *of Florence.* 1986

Betsy Bowden. *Chaucer Aloud: The Varieties of Textual Interpretation.* 1987

James William Brodman. *Ransoming Captives in Crusader Spain: The Order of Merced on the Christian-Islamic Frontier.* 1986

Kevin Brownlee and Sylvia Huot, eds. *Rethinking the* Romance of the Rose: *Text, Image, Perception.* 1992

Otto Brunner (Howard Kaminsky and James Van Horn Melton, eds. and trans.). Land *and Lordship: Structures of Governance in Medieval Austria.* 1992

Robert I. Burns, S. J., ed. *Emperor of Culture: Alfonso X the Learned of Castile and His Thirteenth-Century Renaissance.* 1990

David Burr. *Olivi and Franciscan Poverty: The Origins of the* Usus Pauper *Controversy.* 1989

Thomas Cable. *The English Alliterative Tradition.* 1991

Anthony K. Cassell and Victoria Kirkham, eds. and trans. *Diana's Hunt/Caccia di Diana: Boccaccio's First Fiction.* 1991

Brigitte Cazelles. *The Lady as Saint: A Collection of French Hagiographic Romances of the Thirteenth Century.* 1991

Anne L. Clark. *Elisabeth of Schönau: A Twelfth-Century Visionary.* 1992

Willene B. Clark and Meradith T. McMunn, eds. *Beasts and Birds of the Middle Ages: The Bestiary and Its Legacy.* 1989

Richard C. Dales. *The Scientific Achievement of the Middle Ages.* 1973

Charles T. Davis. *Dante's Italy and Other Essays.* 1984

Katherine Fischer Drew, trans. *The Burgundian Code.* 1972

Katherine Fischer Drew, trans. *The Laws of the Salian Franks.* 1991

Katherine Fischer Drew, trans. *The Lombard Laws.* 1973

Nancy Edwards. *The Archaeology of Early Medieval Ireland.* 1990

Margaret J. Ehrhart. *The Judgment of the Trojan Prince Paris in Medieval Literature.* 1987

Richard K. Emmerson and Ronald B. Herzman. *The Apocalyptic Imagination in Medieval Literature.* 1992

Felipe Fernández-Armesto. *Before Columbus: Exploration and Colonization from the Mediterranean to the Atlantic, 1229–1492.* 1987

Robert D. Fulk. *A History of Old English Meter.* 1992

Patrick J. Geary. *Aristocracy in Provence: The Rhône Basin at the Dawn of the Carolingian Age.* 1985

Peter Heath. *Allegory and Philosophy in Avicenna (Ibn Sînâ), with a Translation of the Book of the Prophet Muḥammad's Ascent to Heaven.* 1992

J. N. Hillgarth, ed. *Christianity and Paganism, 350–750: The Conversion of Western Europe.* 1986

Richard C. Hoffmann. *Land, Liberties, and Lordship in a Late Medieval Countryside: Agrarian Structures and Change in the Duchy of Wrocław.* 1990

Robert Hollander. *Boccaccio's Last Fiction: Il Corbaccio.* 1988

Edward B. Irving, Jr. *Rereading* Beowulf. 1989

C. Stephen Jaeger. *The Origins of Courtliness: Civilizing Trends and the Formation of Courtly Ideals, 939–1210.* 1985

William Chester Jordan. *The French Monarchy and the Jews: From Philip Augustus to the Last Capetians.* 1989

William Chester Jordan. *From Servitude to Freedom: Manumission in the Sénonais in the Thirteenth Century.* 1986

Ellen E. Kittell. *From Ad Hoc to Routine: A Case Study in Medieval Bureaucracy.* 1991

Alan C. Kors and Edward Peters, eds. *Witchcraft in Europe, 1100–1700: A Documentary History.* 1972

Barbara M. Kreutz. *Before the Normans: Southern Italy in the Ninth and Tenth Centuries.* 1992

E. Ann Matter. *The Voice of My Beloved: The Song of Songs in Western Medieval Christianity.* 1990

María Rosa Menocal. *The Arabic Role in Medieval Literary History.* 1987

A. J. Minnis. *Medieval Theory of Authorship.* 1988

Lawrence Nees. *A Tainted Mantle: Hercules and the Classical Tradition at the Carolingian Court.* 1991

Lynn H. Nelson, trans. *The Chronicle of San Juan de la Peña: A Fourteenth-Century Official History of the Crown of Aragon.* 1991

Charlotte A. Newman. *The Anglo-Norman Nobility in the Reign of Henry I: The Second Generation.* 1988

Joseph F. O'Callaghan. *The Cortes of Castile-León, 1188–1350.* 1989

William D. Paden, ed. *The Voice of the Trobairitz: Perspectives on the Women Troubadours.* 1989

Edward Peters. *The Magician, the Witch, and the Law.* 1982

Edward Peters, ed. *Christian Society and the Crusades, 1198–1229*: Sources in Translation, including The Capture of Damietta by Oliver of Paderborn. 1971

Edward Peters, ed. *The First Crusade: The* Chronicle of Fulcher of Chartres *and Other Source Materials.* 1971

Edward Peters, ed. *Heresy and Authority in Medieval Europe.* 1980

James M. Powell. *Albertanus of Brescia: The Pursuit of Happiness in the Early Thirteenth Century.* 1992

James M. Powell. *Anatomy of a Crusade, 1213–1221.* 1986

Michael Resler, trans. Erec *by Hartmann von Aue.* 1987

Pierre Riché (Jo Ann McNamara, trans.). *Daily Life in the World of Charlemagne.* 1978

Jonathan Riley-Smith. *The First Crusade and the Idea of Crusading.* 1986

Joel T. Rosenthal. *Patriarchy and Families of Privilege in Fifteenth-Century England.* 1991

Steven D. Sargent, ed. and trans. *On the Threshold of Exact Science: Selected Writings of Anneliese Maier on Late Medieval Natural Philosophy.* 1982

Sarah Stanbury. *Seeing the* Gawain-Poet: *Description and the Act of Perception.* 1992

Thomas C. Stillinger. *The Song of Troilus: Lyric Authority in the Medieval Book.* 1992

Susan Mosher Stuard. *A State of Deference: Ragusa/Dubrovnik in the Medieval Centuries.* 1992

Susan Mosher Stuard, ed. *Women in Medieval History and Historiography.* 198

Susan Mosher Stuard, ed. *Women in Medieval Society.* 1976

Jonathan Sumption. *The Hundred Years War: Trial by Battle.* 1992

Ronald E. Surtz. *The Guitar of God: Gender, Power, and Authority in the Visionary World of Mother Juana de la Cruz (1481–1534).* 1990

Patricia Terry, trans. *Poems of the Elder Edda.* 1990

Frank Tobin. *Meister Eckhart: Thought and Language.* 1986

Ralph V. Turner. *Men Raised from the Dust: Administrative Service and Upward Mobility in Angevin England.* 1988

Harry Turtledove, trans. *The* Chronicle *of Theophanes: An English Translation of Anni Mundi 6095–6305 (A.D. 602–813).* 1982

Mary F. Wack. *Lovesickness in the Middle Ages: The* Viaticum *and Its Commentaries.* 1990

Benedicta Ward. *Miracles and the Medieval Mind: Theory, Record, and Event 1000–1215.* 1982

Suzanne Fonay Wemple. *Women in Frankish Society: Marriage and the Cloister 500–900.* 1981